Hospitality Networking

HOSPITALITY NETWORKING

Abhay Yadav

CENTRUM PRESS
NEW DELHI-110002 (INDIA)

CENTRUM PRESS
H.O.: 4360/4, Ansari Road, Daryaganj,
New Delhi-110002 (India)
Tel: 23278000, 23261597, 23255577, 23286875
B.O.: No. 1015, Ist Main Road, BSK IIIrd Stage,
IIIrd Phase, IIIrd Block, Bengaluru-560085 (INDIA)
Tel: 080-41723429
Email: centrumpress@gmail.com
Visit us at: www.centrumpress.com

Hospitality Networking

First Edition, 2013

ISBN 978-93-81460-16-0

PRINTED IN INDIA

Printed at Balaji Offset, Delhi.

Contents

Preface

Networking is one of the most effective and important ways to continually move your business forward. This is the perfect thing to network, entertain clients, reward colleagues, and share knowledge. Form alliances over dinner, meet key decision makers over a glass of champagne, or take away the necessary knowledge and new ideas to grow your business - all at Hospitality. Business networking is a socioeconomic activity by which groups of like-minded business people recognize, create, or act upon business opportunities. A business network is a type of social network whose reason for existing is business activity. There are several prominent business networking organizations that create models of networking activity that, when followed, allow the business person to build new business relationships and generate business opportunities at the same time. A professional network service is an implementation of information technology in support of business networking. Many business people contend business networking is a more cost-effective method of generating new business than advertising or public relations efforts. This is because business networking is a low-cost activity that involves more personal commitment than company money.

As an example, a business network may agree to meet weekly or monthly with the purpose of exchanging business leads and referrals with fellow members. To complement this activity, members often meet outside this circle, on their own time, and build their own one-to-one relationship with the fellow member.

Business networking can be conducted in a local business community, or on a larger scale via the Internet. Business networking websites have grown over recent years due to the Internet's ability to connect people from all over the world. Internet companies often set up business leads for sale to bigger corperations and companies looking for data sources. Business networking can have a meaning also in the ICT domain, i.e. the provision of operating support to companies and organizations, and related value chains and value networks. It refers to an activity coordination with a wider scope and a simpler implementation than pre-organized workflows or web-based impromptu searches for transaction counterparts (workflow is useful to coordinate activities, but it is complicated by the use of s.c. patterns to deviate the flow of work from a pure sequence, in order to compensate its intrinsic linearity; impromptu searches for transaction counterparts on the web are useful as well, but only for non-strategic supplies; both are complicated by a plethora of interfaces needed among different organizations and even between different IT applications within the same organization). A social network is a social structure made up of individuals (or organizations) called "nodes", which are tied (connected) by one or more specific types of interdependency, such as friendship, kinship, common interest, financial exchange, dislike, sexual relationships, or relationships of beliefs, knowledge or prestige.

Social network analysis views social relationships in terms of network theory consisting of *nodes* and *ties* (also called *edges, links,* or *connections*). Nodes are the individual actors within the networks, and ties are the relationships between the actors. The resulting graph-based structures are often very complex. There can be many kinds of ties between the nodes. Research in a number of academic fields has shown that social networks operate on many levels, from families up to the level of nations, and play a critical role in determining the way problems are solved, organizations are run, and the degree to which individuals succeed in achieving their goals. In its simplest form, a social network is a map of specified ties, such as friendship, between the nodes being studied. The nodes to which an individual is thus connected are the social contacts of that individual. The network can also be used to measure social capital – the value that an individual gets from the social network. These concepts are often displayed in a social network diagram, where nodes are the points and ties are the lines.

This book provides a systemic approach to understand this subject. The book will be very helpful for the researchers, veterinarians, students and persons involved in this subject.

—Author

1

Tourism and Travel Network

Nautical tourism is an increasingly popular way to combine love of sailing and boating with vacation and holiday activities. First defined as an industry segment in Europe and South America, it has since caught on in the United States and the Pacific Rim.

Not only is nautical tourism an enjoyable way to see unique parts of the world, it is also a very profitable industry. Many tourists who enjoy sailing combine water travel with other activities. Supplying the equipment and accessories for those activities has spawned businesses for those purposes. With many nautical enthusiasts living on board their vessels even in port, nautical tourists bring demand for a variety of goods and services. Marinas developed especially for nautical tourists have been built in Europe, South America and Australia.

Tourist services available at marinas catering to nautical tourists include:

- Leasing of berths for sailing vessels and nautical tourists who live on board.
- Leasing of sailing vessels for holiday and recreational use,
- Reception, safe-guarding and maintenance of sailing vessels.
- Provision of stock (water, fuel, supplies, spare parts, equipment and similar).
- Preparation and keeping sailing vessels in order.
- Providing information to nautical enthusiasts (weather forecasts, nautical guides etc.)

- Leasing of water scooters, jet skis, and other water equipment.

Nautical Tourism in Europe and Along the Mediterranean Coast

Among the more interesting locations frequented by nautical tourists, the Croatian coast offers services at 15 ports, touting it as "Mediterranean as it once was." Croatia's efforts have been so successful they have been offered to the tourism industry as a model for sustainable nautical tourism. Italy has gone to great lengths to attract boating tourists to its ports as well.

Nautical Tourism in the Pacific

Australia has invested $1.5 billion in facilities designed to attract nautical tourists and promote development of nautical tourism as a segment of the tourist trade.

Nautical Tourism in South America

A growing worldwide industry segment, nautical tourism has become popular in South America. The Brazilian Ministry of Tourism has a website devoted to the subject. Puerto Rico has seen its share of growth in nautical tourism as well. Not to be outdone, the Chilean Economic Development Agency has launched the Chilean Patagonia Nautical Tourism Program to develop and attract nautical tourists to the Chilean coast.

Nautical Tourism in the United States

Nautical tourism is big business, even in the United States. In the Southeast, the Tennessee-Tombigbee Waterway, a meandering river and canal system that traverses Alabama and Mississippi linking the Tennessee River with the Gulf of Mexico, has become a favourite boating trail for nautical tourists who want a diverse route with a scenic view. Originally conceived as an alternate shipping route for barges destined for the Midwest, the route proved too awkward for large tows. However, boating enthusiasts discovered it as a great way to see Middle-America. Stops along the way include Mobile, Alabama, Demopolis, Alabama, and Amory and Columbus in Mississippi. Travelling north from the Gulf, boaters can follow the Tennessee River its intersection with the Ohio and travel a circuitous route back to the Gulf by way of New Orleans.

Likewise, the Intracoastal Waterway system, which stretches from Texas to New Jersey, has long provided nautical tourists with a well-marked channel and an inside passage that allows boaters to travel from southern Texas up the eastern seaboard without having to venture onto the high seas. Using this route, boaters can stop at Galveston, Texas, any number of towns in southern Louisiana, including New Orleans. Farther west, Apalachicola, Florida provides a glimpse of Florida the way it used to be.

Pop-culture Tourism

Pop-culture tourism is the act of travelling to locations featured in literature, film, music, or any other form of popular entertainment.

Popular destinations have included:

- Los Angeles, California film studios.
- The Dyersville, Iowa cornfields featured in *Field of Dreams*
- New Zealand after *The Lord of the Rings* was filmed there
- Tom's Restaurant which is known to many as Monk's from *Seinfeld*
- Prince Edward Island, in which the Canadian novel *Anne of Green Gables* takes place, is a popular attraction for tourists, notably from Japan.
- South Korea because of the recent Hallyu phenomenon in East Asia.
- Japan for japanophiles or lovers of Japanese pop-culture.
- North Bend, Washington and in particular Twede's Cafe where much of the television show Twin Peaks was shot.
- Roslyn, Washington, which stood in for Cicely, Alaska in the television show Northern Exposure.
- Tunisia, location of the filming of the Star Wars movies.
- Pin Oak Court, Vermont South, Victoria, a suburban Melbourne shooting location for internationally popular soap opera *Neighbours*

- Santa Ynez Valley in Central California where much of Sideways took place.
- Burkittsville, Maryland, where tourists re-create the most gruesome scenes from The Blair Witch Project.
- Salzburg, Austria, where many scenes from the musical The Sound of Music were filmed.

Pop-culture tourism is in some respects akin to pilgrimage, with its modern equivalents of places of pilgrimage, such as Elvis Presley's Graceland and the grave of Jim Morrison in Pere Lachaise Cemetery.

Another pop-culture tourism destination is Vulcan, Alberta Canada. In the early 1990s this small rural community began to explore ways it could capitalize on the coincidence of the Town's name being the same as popular Star Trek Character, Mr. Spock's home planet: Vulcan, to develop its local tourism industry.

Poverty Tourism

Poverty tourism or poorism, also known as township tourism or slumming is a type of tourism, in which tourists travel to less developed places to observe people living in poverty. Poorism travel tours are popular in places like India, Ethiopia, and even places that have had natural disasters such as hurricanes and tsunamis. After Hurricane Katrina, Louisiana became a big poorism site.

Critics say poorism is likened to a kind of voyeurism, exploiting people less fortunate, snapping pictures and leaving nothing in return. Some poorism tours do use portions of the profits to help out however.

Slumming

Slumming (derived from *slum*) originally referred to a practice, fashionable among certain segments of the middle class in many Western countries, whereby one deliberately patronizes areas or establishments which are populated by, or intended for, people well below one's own socioeconomic level, motivated by curiosity or a desire for adventure. Most often these establishments take the form of bars or restaurants in low-income areas.

Recreational slumming was popular in Victorian London, where omnibus rides through Whitechapel were in vogue. Similarly, slumming tours were documented through the Five Points slums in Manhattan during the 1840s.

It's also associated with the middle 1980s, as an outgrowth of the yuppie subculture. The sense that upper-class establishments were phony, overpriced, and affected (ironically, the very criticisms levelled at yuppies themselves) made it fashionable among middle-class professionals to frequent "dives", due to their supposed authenticity and local colour. "Slumming" (also known as "class tourism") has come to refer to many activities that involve interaction with the less fortunate, especially when motivated by curiosity, adventure, laziness, boredom, and even outright greed and miserliness. The term, and to some extent, the practice, have consequently acquired an unpleasant connotation, having become associated with condescension, exploitation, affectation, and bourgeois insensitivity. Unlike bohemianism or voluntary simplicity, slumming rarely involves more than a temporary or superficial commitment on the part of its participants; it is by nature a touristic or voyeuristic activity.

In *Good Will Hunting*, for example, the main character uses "slumming" to describe sexual relationships between rich, well-educated girls and poorer boys, whom they might encounter around their universities.

South Africa

Township tourism is a term used to describe a form of tourism that emerged in post-apartheid South Africa and Namibia. South African settements are still visibly divided into wealthy, historically white suburbs and poor, historically black townships, because of the effects of apartheid and racial segregation. Before 1994 it was rare for tourists to visit townships. Increasingly the established South African tourism industry sees the townships as a resource for attracting tourism revenue. Smaller operations, including many emerging black tourism operators, see township tourism as a means of empowerment and of bolstering the self-esteem of people in these historically marginalised communities. Although township tours vary in form, they often differ from other tourism experiences in being interactive, socially minded, and potentially empowering for the communities involved. However they have also courted controversy, because of disputes about their safety, their voyeurism, and fears that they misrepresent South African culture(s).

Religious Tourism

Religious tourism, also commonly referred to as faith tourism, is a form of tourism, whereby people of faith travel individually or in groups for pilgrimage, missionary, or leisure (fellowship) purposes. North American religious tourists comprise an estimated $10 billion of this industry.

Tourism segments

Religious tourism comprises many facets of the travel industry including:

- Pilgrimages
- Missionary travel
- Leisure (fellowship) vacations
- Faith-based cruising
- Crusades, conventions and rallies
- Retreats
- Monastery visits and guest-stays
- Faith-based camps
- Religious tourist attractions.

Videos on Religious Tourism;

- Discover the World of Religious Tourism Video.

Hindu Religious Tourism Centres in India

The major Hindu religious tourism centres in India are:-

- Thirupathi temple, Andhra Pradesh.
- Akshar Dham, Gandhi Nagar, Gujarat.
- Amarnath Temple, Pahalgam, Jammu & Kashmir.
- Somnath Temple, Gujarat.
- Vaishnodevi Temple, Jammu, Jammu & Kashmir.
- Kailash Temple, Aurangabad, Maharashtra.

- Sun Temple, Konark, Orissa.
- Chidambaram Temple, Chidambaram, Tamil Nadu.
- Mahabalipuram Temple, Tamil Nadu.
- Rameswaram Temple, Tamil Nadu.
- Meenakshi Temple, Madurai, Tamil Nadu.
- Badarinath Temple, Uthranchal.
- Naina Devi Temple, Bilaspur, Himachalpradesh.
- Sabarimala Temple, Pathanamthitta, Kerala.
- Guruvayoor Temple, Guruvayoor, Trichur, Kerala
- Kodungallor Temple, Trichur, Kerala
- Chettikulangara Temple, Mavelikkara, Kerala.
- Padmanabhaswamy Temple, Trivandrum, Kerala.

Statistics

Although no definitive study has been completed on worldwide religious tourism, some segments of the industry have been measured:

- According to the World Tourism Organization, an estimated 300 to 330 million pilgrims visit the world's key religious sites every year.
- According to the U.S. Office of Travel and Tourism Industries, Americans travelling overseas for "religious or pilgrimage" purposes has increased from 491,000 travellers in 2002 to 633,000 travellers in 2005 (30% increase).
- According to the Religious Conference Management Association, in 2006 more than 14.7 million people attended religious meetings (RCMA members), an increase of more than 10 million from 1994 with 4.4 million attendees.
- The United Methodist Church experienced an increase of 455% in mission volunteers from 1992 with almost 20,000 volunteers compared to 110,000 volunteers in 2006.
- The Christian Camp and Conference Association states that more than eight million people are involved in CCCA member camps and conferences, including more than 120,000 churches.

- Religious attractions including Sight & Sound Theatre attracts 800,000 visitors a year while the Holy Land Experience and Focus on the Family Welcome Centre each receives about 250,000 guests annually. Religious tourism, also commonly referred to as *faith tourism,* is a form of tourism whereby people of faith travel individually or in groups for pilgrimage, missionary, or leisure (fellowship) purposes.
- 50,000 churches in the United States with religious travel programs
- One-quarter (25%) of travellers said they were currently interested in taking a spiritual vacation.

Space Tourism

Space tourism is the phenomenon of tourists paying for flights into space. As of 2009, orbital space tourism opportunities are limited and expensive, with only the Russian Space Agency providing transport. The price for a flight brokered by Space Adventures to the International Space Station aboard a Soyuz spacecraft is US$20–35 million. The space tourists usually sign contracts with third parties to conduct certain research while in orbit. This helps to minimize their own expenses.

Infrastructure for a suborbital space tourism industry is being developed through the construction of spaceports in numerous locations, including California, Oklahoma, New Mexico, Florida, Virginia, Alaska, Wisconsin, Esrange in Sweden as well as the United Arab Emirates. Some use the term "personal spaceflight" as in the case of the Personal Spaceflight Federation.

A number of startup companies have sprung up in recent years, hoping to create a space tourism industry. For a list of such companies, and the spacecraft they are currently building.

Russia announced on 3 March 2010 that they would be ending their space tourism program, at least for the next several years.

Early Dreams

After early successes in space, much of the public saw intensive space exploration as inevitable. Those aspirations are remembered in science fiction such as Arthur C. Clarke's *A Fall of Moondust* and also *2001: A Space Odyssey*, Roald Dahl's *Charlie and the Great Glass Elevator*, Joanna Russ's 1968 novel *Picnic on Paradise*, and Larry Niven's Known Space stories. Lucian in the second century AD in his book *True History* examines the idea of a crew of men whose ship travels to the Moon during a storm. Jules Verne also took up the theme of lunar visits in his books, *From the Earth to the Moon* and *Around the Moon*.

Robert A. Heinlein's short story *The Menace from Earth*, published in 1957, was one of the first to incorporate elements of a developed space tourism industry within its framework. During the 1960s and 1970s, it was common belief that space hotels would be launched by 2000. Many futurologists around the middle of the 20th century speculated that the average family of the early 21st century would be able to enjoy a holiday on the Moon. In the 1960s, Pan Am established a waiting list for future flights to the moon, issuing free "First Moon Flights Club" membership cards to those who requested them.

The end of the Space Race, however, signified by the Moon landing, decreased the emphasis placed on space exploration by national governments and therefore led to decreased demands for public funding of manned space flights.

Precursors

The Soviet space program was aggressive in broadening the pool of cosmonauts. The Soviet Intercosmos program also included cosmonauts selected from Warsaw Pact members (from Czechoslovakia, Poland, East Germany, Bulgaria, Hungary, Romania) and later from allies of the USSR (Cuba, Mongolia, Vietnam) and non-aligned countries (India, Syria, Afghanistan). Most of these cosmonauts received full training for their missions and were treated as equals, but especially after the Mir program began, were generally given shorter flights than Soviet cosmonauts. The European Space Agency took advantage of the program as well.

The U.S. space shuttle program included payload specialist positions which were usually filled by representatives of companies or institutions managing a specific payload on that mission. These payload specialists did not receive the same training as professional

NASA astronauts and were not employed by NASA. In 1983, Ulf Merbold from ESA and Byron Lichtenberg from MIT (engineer and Air Force fighter pilot) were the first Payload Specialists to fly on the shuttle, becoming the first non-NASA astronauts. In 1984, Charlie Walker became the first non-government astronaut to fly, with his flight paid for by his employer, McDonnell Douglas. NASA was also eager to prove its capability to Congressional sponsors. Senator Jake Garn was flown on the shuttle in 1985, followed by Representative Bill Nelson (now Senator) in 1986. As the shuttle program expanded, the Teacher in Space program was developed as a way to expand publicity and educational opportunities for NASA. Christa McAuliffe would have been the first Teacher in Space, but was killed in the Challenger disaster and the program was canceled. During the same period a Journalist in Space program was frequently discussed, with individuals such as Walter Cronkite and Miles O'Brien considered front-runners, but no formal program was ever developed. McAuliffe's backup in the Teacher in Space Program, Barbara Morgan, eventually got hired in 1998 as a professional astronaut and flew on STS-118 as a mission specialist where she spoke to many students as an educator during the trip.

With the realities of the post-Perestroika economy in Russia, its space industry was especially starved for cash. The Tokyo Broadcasting System (TBS) offered to pay for one of its reporters to fly on a mission. For $28 million, Toyohiro Akiyama was flown in 1990 to Mir with the eighth crew and returned a week later with the seventh crew. Akiyama gave a daily TV broadcast from orbit and also performed scientific experiments for Russian and Japanese companies. However, since the cost of the flight was paid by his employer, Akiyama could be considered a business traveler rather than a tourist.

In 1991, British chemist Helen Sharman was selected from a pool of 13,000 applicants to be the first Briton in space. The program was known as Project Juno and was a cooperative arrangement between the Soviet Union and a group of British companies. The Project Juno consortium failed to raise the funds required, and the program was almost cancelled. Reportedly Mikhail Gorbachev ordered it to proceed under Soviet expense in the interests of international relations, but in the absence of Western underwriting, less expensive experiments were substituted for those in the original plans. Sharman flew aboard Soyuz TM-12 to Mir and returned aboard Soyuz TM-11.

Orbital Space Tourism

At the end of the 1990s, MirCorp, a private venture by then in charge of the space station, began seeking potential space tourists to visit Mir in order to offset some of its maintenance costs. Dennis Tito, an American businessman and former JPL scientist, became their first candidate.

In conjunction with the Federal Space Agency of the Russian Federation and Rocket and Space Corporation (Energia), Space Adventures facilitated the flights for all of the world's first private space explorers. The first three participants paid in excess of $20 million (USD) each for their 10-day visit to the ISS.

On April 28, 2001, Dennis Tito became the first "fee-paying" space tourist when he visited the International Space Station (ISS) for seven days. He was followed in 2002 by South African computer millionaire Mark Shuttleworth. The third was Gregory Olsen in 2005, who was trained as a scientist and whose company produced specialist high-sensitivity cameras. Olsen planned to use his time on the ISS to conduct a number of experiments, in part to test his company's products. Olsen had planned an earlier flight, but had to cancel for health reasons.

After the Columbia disaster, space tourism on the Russian Soyuz program was temporarily put on hold, because Soyuz vehicles became the only available transport to the ISS. However, in 2006, space tourism was resumed. On September 18, 2006, Anousheh Ansari, an Iranian American, became the fourth space tourist (she prefers "private space explorer"). On April 7, 2007, Charles Simonyi, an American businessman of Hungarian descent, joined their ranks.

In 2003, NASA and the Russian Space Agency agreed to use the term 'Spaceflight Participant' to distinguish those space travellers from astronauts on missions coordinated by those two agencies. Tito, Shuttleworth, Olsen, Ansari, and Simonyi were designated as such during their respective space flights. NASA also lists Christa McAuliffe as a "Space Flight Participant" (although she did not pay a fee), apparently due to her non-technical duties aboard the STS-51-L flight.

Suborbital Flights

More affordable suborbital space tourism is viewed as a money-making proposition by several other companies, including Space Adventures, Virgin Galactic, Starchaser, Blue Origin, Armadillo Aerospace, XCOR Aerospace, Rocketplane Limited, the European "Project Enterprise", and others. Most are proposing vehicles that make suborbital flights peaking at an altitude of 100-160 kilometres. Passengers would experience three to six minutes of weightlessness, a view of a twinkle-free starfield, and a vista of the curved Earth below. Projected costs are expected to be about $200,000 per passenger.

As of November 2007 Virgin Galactic had pre-sold nearly 200 seats for their suborbital space tourism flights, according to the company's president.

The X Prize

On October 4, 2004, the SpaceShipOne, designed by Burt Rutan of Scaled Composites, won the $10,000,000 X Prize, which was designed to be won by the first private company who could reach and surpass an altitude of 62 miles (100 km) twice within two weeks. The altitude is beyond the Karman Line, the arbitrarily defined boundary of space. The first flight was flown by Michael Melvill on June 21, 2004 to a height of 62 miles, making him the first commercial astronaut. The prize-winning flight was flown by Brian Binnie, which reached a height of 69.6 miles, breaking the X-15 record.

Virgin Galactic

Virgin Galactic, one of the leading potential space tourism groups, is planning to begin passenger service aboard the VSS Enterprise, a Scaled Composites Space Ship Two type spacecraft. The initial seat price will be $200,000, but that price is expected to eventually fall to $20,000. To date, over two hundred people have made down payments on bookings. Headed by Sir Richard Branson's Virgin Group, Virgin Galactic hopes to be the first private space tourism company to regularly send civilians into space. A citizen astronaut will only require three days of training before spaceflight. Space Ship Two is a scaled up version of SpaceShipOne, the spacecraft which claimed the Ansari X Prize. Both spacecraft were designed by Burt Rutan's Scaled Composites. Launches will initially occur at the Mojave Spaceport in California, and will then be moved to Spaceport America in Upham, New Mexico. Tourists will also be flown from Kiruna, Sweden. The spacecraft will travel 360,000 feet (109.73 km/68.18 miles) high. This goes beyond the internationally defined boundary between Earth and space of 100 km. Spaceflights will last 2.5 hours, carry 6 passengers, and reach a speed of Mach 3. Space Ship Two will not require a space shuttle-like heat shield for atmospheric reentry as it will not experience the extreme aerodynamic heating experienced during reentry at orbital velocities (approximately Mach 22.5 at a typical shuttle altitude of 300 km, or 185 miles). The glider will employ a "feathering" technique to manage drag during the unpowered descent and landing. Space Ship Two will use a single hybrid rocket motor to launch from mid-air after detaching from a mother ship at 50,000 feet, instead of NASA's space shuttle's ground-based launch.

Project Enterprise

Project Enterprise was launched by the German TALIS Institute in 2004 and is the first project of its kind in Europe. The goal is to develop a rocket-propelled spaceplane by 2011 that will carry one pilot and up to five passengers into suborbital space. The plane will launch from the ground using rockets, and will return in an unpowered flight like Virgin Galactic's Space Ship Two. The prototypes and finished spaceplane will be launched from an airport near Cochstedt (Germany; Saxony-Anhalt).

Since 2004, the TALIS Institute has gained many industrial partners, including XtremeAir, who will manufacture the airframe, and Swiss Propulsion Laboratory SPL, who will deliver the propulsion components. XtremeAir is known for their acrobatic airplanes, and SPL has designed and tested liquid propellant rocket engines since 1998.

Current work is focusing on the first prototype, the "Black Sky": An existing acrobatic airplane that would be fitted with a single rocket engine and a new wing. The rocket engine is expected to deliver a thrust of 10 kN. The test program for this engine started in 2007 at SPL and is expected to fly by 2010.

Legality

United States: In December 2005, the U.S. Government released a set of proposed rules for space tourism. These included screening procedures and training for emergency situations, but not health requirements.

Under current US law, any company proposing to launch paying passengers from American soil on a suborbital rocket must receive a license from the Federal Aviation Administration's Office of Commercial Space Transportation (FAA/AST). The licensing process focuses on public safety and safety of property, and the details can be found in the Code of Federal Regulations. This is in accordance with the Commercial Space Launch Amendments Act passed by Congress in 2004.

Orbital Flights, Space Stations and Space Hotels

- EADS Astrium, a subsidiary of European aerospace giant EADS, announced its space tourism project on June 13, 2007.
- SpaceX is a private space company which is developing their own rocket family called *Falcon* and a capsule named Dragon, capable of sending up to 7 people to any space station, either ISS or a possible station by Bigelow Aerospace. Falcon 1 has already undertaken testflights and successfully completed its first commercial flight on July 14, 2009, deploying the Malaysian Razak SAT into orbit. Falcon 9 (which will be the rocket for the Dragon capsule) is currently in vertical position at Space Launch Complex 40 in Cape Canaveral, and will make its first testflight in late 2009. An initial prototype of the Dragon capsule is expected to be used on this test flight; SpaceX anticipates that Dragon could be qualified for human spaceflight within 3 years of the receipt of NASA CCDV funding.
- Space Adventures Ltd. have also announced that they are working on circumlunar missions to the moon, with the

price per passenger being $100,000,000. They are currently developing spaceports at the United Arab Emirates (Ras al-Khaimah) and in Singapore.

- Orbital space tourist flights are also being planned by Excalibur Almaz, using modernized *TKS* space capsules.

Several plans have been proposed for using a space station as a hotel. American motel tycoon Robert Bigelow has acquired the designs for inflatable space habitats from the Transhab program abandoned by NASA. His company, Bigelow Aerospace, has already launched two first inflatable habitat modules. The first, named Genesis I, was launched 12 July 2006. The second test module, Genesis II, was launched 28 June 2007. Both Genesis habitats remain in orbit as of mid-2009. As of 2006, Bigelow planned to officially launch the first commercial space station by 2012 (tagged *Nautilus*) which will have 330 cubic meters (almost as big as the ISS's 425 cubic meters of usable volume).

Bigelow Aerospace is currently offering the America's Space Prize, a $50 million prize to the first US company to create a reusable spacecraft capable of carrying passengers to a Nautilus space station.

Other companies have also expressed interest in constructing "space hotels". For example, Excalibur Almaz plans to modernize and launch its Soviet-era Almaz space stations, which will feature the largest windows ever on spacecraft. Virgin's Richard Branson has expressed his hope for the construction of a space hotel within his lifetime. He expects that beginning a space tourism program will cost $100 million. Hilton International announced the Space Islands Project, a plan to connect together used space shuttle fuel tanks, each the diameter of a Boeing 747 aircraft. A separate organization, Space Island Group announced their distinct Space Island Project (note the singular "Island"), and plans on having 20,000 people on their "space island" by 2020, with the number of people doubling for each decade. British Airways has expressed interest in the venture. If and when Space Hotels develop, it would initially cost a passenger $60,000, with prices lowering over time.

Fashion designer Eri Matsui has designed clothing, including a wedding gown, intended to look best in weightless environments.

Advocacy, Education, and Industry Organizations

Several organizations have been formed to promote the space tourism industry, including the Space Tourism Society, and others. More information about the future of Space Tourism can be found at Space Tourism Lecture, which is a free online Space Tourism Lecture handout collection. Since 2003 Dr. Robert A. Goehlich and Pierluigi Polignano teaches the world's first and only Space Tourism class at Keio University, Yokohama, Japan. UniGalactic Space Travel Magazine is a bi-monthly educational publication covering space tourism and space exploration developments in companies like SpaceX, Orbital Sciences, Virgin Galactic and organizations like NASA. The content of UniGalactic Space Travel Magazine can be found on UniGalactic web site.

Opinions of Commercial Space Tourism

A web-based survey suggested that over 70% of those surveyed wanted less than or equal to 2 weeks in space; in addition, 88% wanted to spacewalk (only 74% of these would do it for a 50% premium), and 21% wanted a hotel or space station.

The concept has met with some criticism from bureaucrats, notably Gunter Verheugen, vice-president of the European Commission, who said of the EADS Astrium Space Tourism Project "It's only for the super rich, which is against my social convictions".

Objections to "Space Tourist" Terminology

Dennis Tito, Mark Shuttleworth, Gregory Olsen, Anousheh Ansari and Richard Garriott have all expressed a preference to be called something other than "space tourist". In each case, they explained their preferences by pointing out that they carried out scientific experiments as part of their journey; Garriott additionally emphasized their training is identical to requirements of non-Russian Soyuz crew members, and that teachers and other non-professional astronauts chosen to fly with NASA are called astronauts. Garriott prefers "cosmonaut" or "astronaut", but will accept "private" in front of either. Tito has asked to be known as an "independent researcher". Shuttleworth proposed "pioneer of commercial space travel". Olsen preferred "private researcher." Ansari prefers the term "private space explorer". Alone among those who have paid to go to orbit so far, Charles Simonyi seems to have no concerns about calling it "space tourism", even in reference to his own experience. Asked in an interview "Do you foresee a day when space tourism is not just the province of billionaires - when it will be as affordable as plane travel?", he did not object to the implicit categorization of his own trip, but rather answered "Yes, the only question is when ...."

NASA and the Russian Federal Space Agency agreed to use the term "spaceflight participant" to distinguish those space travellers from astronauts on missions coordinated by those two agencies.

Although many space enthusiasts subscribe to the notion of space tourism as a potential burgeoning industry that could further the development and settlement of space, some of these same enthusiasts object to the use of the term "space tourist". Rick Tumlinson of the Space Frontier Foundation, for example, has said;

> *"I hate the word tourist, and I always will .... 'Tourist' is somebody in a flowered shirt with three cameras around his neck."*
>
> *Others with perhaps less enthusiasm for space development seem to agree. Alex Tabarrok has categorized it as a kind of "adventure travel". The mere fact of people paying for a travel experience does not, in his view, make that activity "tourism".*
>
> *"At best and for the foreseeable future space travel will remain akin to climbing Everest, dangerous and uncommon. Yes, we might see 100 flights a year but that's not space tourism - tourism is fat guys with cameras."*

War Tourism

War tourism is a term the media uses to describe the idea of recreational travel to war zones for purposes of sightseeing and superficial voyeurism. War tourist is also a pejorative term to describe thrill seeking in dangerous and forbidden places. There has been no proof of the concept in real life but the idea has gained currency in a number of media reports, none of which have actually interviewed or found a tourist who have visited active combat areas as a tourist. There have been a number of tourists caught up in war torn regions, many who visit active war zones like Israel, Lebanon, Myanmar, Algeria, Colombia and other regions at war. There are many freelance journalists who describe themselves humorously as "war tourists" (P.J. O'Rourke is the most famous) and mercenaries who have pretended to be tourists to avoid discovery as in Michael Hoare's attempt to take over the Seychelles disguised as "The Royal Order of Frothblowers".

During the 2006 Israel-Lebanon crisis, for example, Beirut was full of tourists who were forced to leave when fighting with Israel broke out. Tourists have also been targeted in Kenya, the Philippines and other regions due to their media value and damage to the country's tourist industry. It could be argued that continued tourism to these regions is war tourism, even though active combat is free from tourist access.

The initial myth of war tourism was actually started by a collection of stories by P.J. O'Rourke. His mocking and cynical view of journalism in conflict areas entitled 'Holidays in Hell: In Which Our Intrepid Reporter Travels to the World's Worst Places and Asks, "What's Funny About This" planted the idea that maybe journalists are after all tourists on an expense account.

The PBS TV show, Frontline, used the phrase war tourism to describe a practice in Iraq of US troops going on daylight patrols and returning in the evening to heavily defended large bases.

A book on this topic is Dark Tourism (Tourism, Leisure & Recreation) by Malcolm Foley and John Lennon. The authors explore the idea that people are attracted to regions and sites where "inhuman acts" have occurred. They claim that motivation is driven by media coverage and a desire to see for themselves, and that there is a symbiotic relationship between the attraction and the visitor, whether it be a death camp or site of a celebrity's death. Much of their focus in on ancient sites where "acts of inhumanity are celebrated as heritage sites in Britain (for example, the Tower of London, Edinburgh Castle), and the Berlin Wall" War tourism is also confused with "Battlefield tourism": going to places of historic importance or famous battle sites such as the German WW2 fortification, Ground Zero in New York, the Atlantic Wall or the Maginot Line in France.

Wildlife Tourism

Wildlife tourism can be an eco and animal friendly tourism, usually showing animals in their natural habitat. Wildlife tourism, in its simplest sense, is watching wild animals in their natural habitat. Wildlife tourism is an important part of the tourism industries in many countries including many African and South American countries, Australia, India, Canada, Indonesia, Malaysia and Maldives among many. It has experienced a dramatic and rapid growth in recent years world wide and is closely aligned to eco-tourism and sustainable-tourism.

Wildlife tourism is also a multi-million dollar industry offering customized tour packages and safaris.

Recent Developments

There has been an upmarket trend in the tourism over the last few decades, especially in Europe, where international travel for short breaks is common. Tourists have high levels of disposable income, considerable leisure time, are well educated, and have sophisticated tastes. There is now a demand for a better quality products, which has resulted in a fragmenting of the mass market for beach vacations; people want more specialised versions, quieter resorts, family-oriented holidays or niche market-targeted destination hotels.

The developments in technology and transport infrastructure, such as jumbo jets, low-cost airlines and more accessible airports have made many types of tourism more affordable. WHO estimates that up to 500,000 people are on planes at any time. There have also been changes in lifestyle, such as retiree-age people who sustain year round tourism. This is facilitated by internet sales of tourism products. Some sites have now started to offer dynamic packaging, in which an inclusive price is quoted for a tailor-made package requested by the customer upon impulse.

There have been a few setbacks in tourism, such as the September 11 attacks and terrorist threats to tourist destinations, such as in Bali and several European cities. Also, on December 26, 2004, a tsunami, caused by the 2004 Indian Ocean earthquake, hit the Asian countries on the Indian Ocean, including the Maldives. Thousands of lives were lost and many tourists died. This, together with the vast clean-up operation in place, has stopped or severely hampered tourism to the area. The terms *tourism* and *travel* are sometimes used interchangeably. In this context, travel has a similar definition to tourism, but implies a more purposeful journey. The terms *tourism* and *tourist* are sometimes used pejoratively, to imply a shallow interest in the cultures or locations visited by tourists.

Sustainable Tourism

"Sustainable tourism is envisaged as leading to management of all resources in such a way that economic, social and aesthetic needs can be fulfilled while maintaining cultural integrity, essential ecological processes, biological diversity and life support systems." Sustainable development implies "meeting the needs of the present without compromising the ability of future generations to meet their own needs" (World Commission on Environment and Development, 1987).

Recession Tourism

Recession tourism is a travel trend, which evolved by way of the world economic crisis. Identified by American entrepreneur Matt Landau (2007), recession tourism is defined by low-cost, high-value experiences taking place of once-popular generic retreats. Various recession tourism hotspots have seen business boom during the recession thanks to comparatively low costs of living and a slow world job market suggesting travellers are elongating trips where the dollar travels further.

Educational Tourism

Educational tourism developed, because of the growing popularity of teaching and learning of knowledge and the enhancing of technical competency outside of the classroom environment. In educational tourism, the main focus of the tour or leisure activity includes visiting another country to learn about the culture, such as in Student Exchange Programs and Study Tours, or to work and apply skills learned inside the classroom in a different environment, such as in the International Practicum Training Program.

Creative Tourism

Creative tourism has existed as a form of cultural tourism, since the early beginnings of tourism itself. Its European roots date back to the time of the Grand Tour, which saw the sons of aristocratic families travelling for the purpose of mostly interactive, educational experiences. More recently, creative tourism has been given its own name by Crispin Raymond and Greg Richards, who as members of the Association for Tourism and Leisure Education (ATLAS), have directed a number of projects for the European Commission, including cultural and crafts tourism, known as sustainable tourism. They have defined "creative tourism" as tourism related to the active participation of travellers in the culture of the host community, through interactive workshops and informal learning experiences.

Meanwhile, the concept of creative tourism has been picked up by high-profile organizations such as UNESCO, who through the Creative Cities Network, have endorsed creative tourism as an engaged, authentic experience that promotes an active understanding of the specific cultural features of a place.

More recently, creative tourism has gained popularity as a form of cultural tourism, drawing on active participation by travellers in the culture of the host communities they visit. Several countries offer examples of this type of tourism development, including the United Kingdom, the Bahamas, Jamaica, Spain, Italy and New Zealand.

Dark Tourism

One emerging area of special interest tourism has been identified by Lennon and Foley (2000) as "dark" tourism. This type of tourism involves visits to "dark" sites, such as battlegrounds, scenes of horrific crimes or acts of genocide, for example: concentration camps. Dark tourism poses severe ethical and moral dilemmas: should these sites be available for visitation and, if so, what should the nature of the publicity involved be. Dark tourism remains a small niche market, driven by varied motivations, such as mourning, remembrance, macabre curiosity or even entertainment. Its early origins are rooted in fairgrounds and medieval fairs.

Growth

The World Tourism Organization (UNWTO) forecasts that international tourism will continue growing at the average annual rate of 4 %. With the advent of e-commerce, tourism products have become one of the most traded items on the internet. Tourism products and services have been made available through intermediaries, although tourism providers (hotels, airlines, etc.) can sell their services directly. This has put pressure on intermediaries from both on-line and traditional shops.

It has been suggested there is a strong correlation between tourism expenditure per capita and the degree to which countries play in the global context. Not only as a result of the important economic contribution of the tourism industry, but also as an indicator of the degree of confidence with which global citizens leverage the resources of the globe for the benefit of their local economies. This is why any projections of growth in tourism may serve as an indication of the relative influence that each country will exercise in the future.

Space tourism is expected to "take off" in the first quarter of the 21st century, although compared with traditional destinations the number of tourists in orbit will remain low until technologies such as a space elevator make space travel cheap.

Technological improvement is likely to make possible air-ship hotels, based either on solar-powered airplanes or large dirigibles. Underwater hotels, such as Hydropolis, expected to open in Dubai in 2009, will be built. On the ocean, tourists will be welcomed by ever larger cruise ships and perhaps floating cities.

Latest Trends

As a result of the Late-2000s recession, international arrivals suffered a strong slowdown beginning in June 2008. Growth from 2007 to 2008 was only 3.7% during the first eight months of 2008. The Asian and Pacific markets were affected and Europe stagnated during the boreal summer months, while the Americas performed better, reducing their expansion rate but keeping a 6% growth from January to August 2008. Only the Middle East continued its rapid growth during the same period, reaching a 17% growth as compared to the same period in 2007. This slowdown on international tourism demand was also reflected in the air transport industry, with a negative growth in September 2008 and a 3.3% growth in passenger traffic through September. The hotel industry also reports a slowdown, as room occupancy continues to decline. As the global economic situation deteriorated dramatically during September and October as a result of the global financial crisis, growth of international tourism is expected to slow even further for the remaining of 2008, and this slowdown in demand growth is forecasted to continue into 2009 as recession has already hit most of the top spender countries, with long-haul travel expected to be the most affected by the economic crisis. This negative trend intensified as international tourist arrivals fell by 8% during the first four months of 2009, and the decline was exacerbated in some regions due to the outbreak of the influenza AH1N1 virus.

Types of Tourism in India

All types of tourism in India have registered phenomenal growth in the last decade ever since the Indian government decided to boost revenues from the tourism sector by projecting India as the ultimate tourist spot.

The reason why India has been doing well in all types of tourism in India is that India has always been known for its hospitality, uniqueness, and charm – attributes that have been attracting foreign travellers to India in hordes. The Indian government, in order to boost tourism of various kinds in India, has set up the Ministry of Tourism and Culture. This ministry recently launched a campaign called 'Incredible India!' in order to encourage different types of tourism in India.

The result was that in 2004, foreign tourists spent around US$ 15.4 billion during their trips to India. Being a country with tremendous diversity, India has a lot to offer in terms of tourism and related activities. The diversity that India is famous for, ensures that there is something to do for all tourists in India, no matter what their interests.

The different types of tourism in India are as follows:

Heritage Tourism

India has always been famous for its rich heritage and ancient culture. So the onset of heritage tourism in India was long anticipated. India's glorious past and cultural diversity make a potent blend which attracts millions of tourists each year to its heritage tourist attractions. The government of India and the Ministry of Tourism and Culture encourage heritage tourism in India by offering several benefits to the Indian states that are particularly famous for attracting tourists.

India's rich heritage is amply reflected in the various temples, palaces, monuments, and forts that can be found everywhere in the country. This has led to the increase in India's heritage tourism. The most popular heritage tourism destinations in India are:

- Taj Mahal in Agra
- Mandawa castle in Rajasthan
- Mahabalipuram in Tamil Nadu
- Madurai in Tamil Nadu
- Lucknow in Uttar Pradesh
- Delhi, the Indian capital.

Taj Mahal was built by a grief stricken Emperor Shahjahan as a memorial to his beloved wife Mumtaj Mahal. A world-renowned wonder, Taj Mahal Sits pretty on the northern side of this green paradise. It looks the same from all the four sides! The Quranic inscriptions on its four entrances are carved in such subtle increase in size that may appear to be of the same size from top to bottom! Shahjahan invited master craftsmen from as far as Italy and Persia to help design his ambitious tribute to love. The Taj Mahal is phenomenal not in the beauty alone that shines forth, but in the deep planning and design that went into its making, and the ethereal idea of immortalizing love. Delicate carvings in marble vie with gorgeous pietra dura for attention. Lapiz, Lazuli, Carnation, Mother of pearl, Agate and Emerald are inlayed in floral and geometrical patterns in the marble itself. This enchanting mausoleum, on the bank of river Yamuna started in 1631 it took 22 years to complete with the help of an estimated 20000 workers. The Mandawa castle in Rajasthan, built in 1775 reflects India's rich heritage and attracts thousands of tourists each year to Rajasthan which seems especially popular for its antique paintings, jade jewelry, palaces, and costumes. Mahabalipuram has sculptural and architectural sites which are considered the greatest in India. Mahabalipuram has cave temples that have been carved from granite blocks and belong to the 7th century. This is the primary reason why many heritage tourists in India visit this place. The tourism of heritage in India has also increased due to the interest of many foreigners in the temples of India. Madurai is known as the 'temple city' due to the presence of a large number of temples in the city. And for this reason, many tourists go and visit the place each year. The most important temple in Madurai is the Meenakshi temple. Heritage tourism India has also been popularized because a lot of tourists go to Delhi which is not only the capital of India but also has many heritage sites. The most famous heritage sites in Delhi are the Red fort, Jama Masjid, Humayun's tomb, and Tughlaqabad fort. Heritage tourism India has grown in recent years but there is scope for further development which can be attained only through combined efforts of the government of India and the tourism boards.

Ecotourism

Ecotourism India has developed recently, for the concept itself is a relatively new one. Ecotourism entails travelling to places that are renowned for their natural beauty and social culture, while making sure not to damage the ecological balance.

Ecotourism pertains to a conscious and responsible effort to preserve the diversity of a naturally endowed region and sustaining its beauty and local culture. Indians have been known since ages to worship and conserve nature. So the growth of ecotourism in India is but natural. Also the government of India has set up the Ministry of Tourism and Culture to promote ecotourism in India alongside other types of tourism.

Ecotourism in India has grown significantly in recent years in India since the country has a diverse geography which led to the development of many tourists destinations. These various destinations not only de-stress the tourists but also rejuvenate them. There are various ways in which tourists can enjoy nature in India. And this has given ecotourism in India a major boost.

Places such as Kerala, Lakshdweep Islands, the Himalayan region, north-east India, and Andaman and Nicobar Islands are some destinations in

India where tourists can participate in ecotourism-related activities. In Kerala, Thenmala is a planned ecotourism spot and is the first of its kind in India. Great care has gone into the care and preservation of Thenmala so that it caters to nature lovers and eco- tourists. Eco-tourists have been thronging India in large numbers for it has a rich source of flora and fauna. A great number of endangered and rare species are also to be found in the various national parks in India. The major national parks in India for ecotourism are:

- Corbett National Park in Uttar Pradesh
- Bandhavgarh National Park in Madhya Pradesh
- Kanha National Park in Madhya Pradesh
- Gir National Park and Sanctuary in Gujarat
- Ranthambore National Park in Rajasthan .

Ecotourism India has increased in the last few years. The government of India and Ministry of Tourism need to make concerted efforts to ensure that ecotourism in India is able to keep pace with ecotourism destinations across the world and making sustainable tourism a priority.

Adventure Tourism

Adventure tourism has recently grown in India. This involves exploration of remote areas and exotic locales and engaging in various activities. For adventure tourism in India, tourists prefer to go for trekking to places like Ladakh, Sikkim and Himalaya. Himachal Pradesh and Jammu and Kashmir are popular for the skiing facilities they offer. Whitewater rafting is also catching on in India and tourists flock to places such as Uttranchal, Assam, and Arunachal Pradesh for this adrenalin-packed activity.

Wildlife Tourism

India has a rich forest cover which has some beautiful and exotic species of wildlife – some of which that are even endangered and very rare. This has boosted wildlife tourism in India. The places where a foreign tourist can go for wildlife tourism in India are the Sariska Wildlife Sanctuary, Keoladeo Ghana National Park, and Corbett National Park.

Pilgrimage Tourism

India is probably the ultimate destination of all kinds of

pilgrims following any faith around the world. The great religions like Hinduism, Buddhism, Jainism, Islam, Christianity and Sikhism are the integral part of Indian culture and heritage whose values and faiths are mingled with the air, soil and the sky of India. You can feel the blissful serenity of the Indian atmosphere where Lord Buddha, Mahabir Jain, Shri Sathya Sai Baba and Guru Nanak once walked turning the Indian soil pious and blessed at the different circle of time wheel. There are numerous destinations in India which are considered sacred by people following different faith because of their religious importance. A visit to the Kedarnath or Badrinath will take you to the Himalayas which is believed to be the abode of 330 million gods and goddesses and you can feel the immense divinity in the air itself. It is widely believed that after breathing in the holy atmosphere of Varanasi or Haridwar or taking a dip into the sacred Pushkar Lake or river Ganges washes away the sins and helps one to attain nirvana (salvation). The divine Buddha pilgrimages, Bodhgaya and Sarnath are the destinations of thousands of Buddhist pilgrims every year coming from each and every corner of the earth.

Famous Pilgrimage

- Ajmer
- Pushkar
- Haridwar
- Amarnath
- Badrinath
- Gangotri
- Kedarnath
- Yamunotri
- Chardham Yatra
- Rishikesh
- Manikaran
- Paonta Sahib
- Rewalsar
- Omkareshwar

- Ajmer Sharief
- Rameswaram
- Mathura Vrindavan
- Puri
- Guruvayur
- Shirdi Saibaba
- Amarnath Cave
- Vaishno Devi
- Jagannath Temple
- Konark Sun Temple
- Tirupati Temple.

Pilgrimage Places

- Himachal Pradesh
- Rajasthan
- Uttranchal
- Kerala
- Maharashtra
- Tamil Nadu
- Jammu And Kashmir
- Madhya Pradesh
- Madhya Pradesh
- Karnataka
- Andhra Pradesh
- Temples
- Mosques
- Gurudwaras
- Churches.

Famous Tourist Destinations

The World Tourism rankings are compiled by the World Tourism Organization (UNWTO) as part of their World Tourism Barometer publication.

International Tourist Arrivals by Country of Destination 2008

The top international destinations in 2008 are:

Rank	*Country*	*International tourist arrivals*
1	France	79.3 million
2	United States	58.0 million
3	Spain	57.3 million
4	China	53.0 million
5	Italy	42.7 million
6	United Kingdom	30.1 million
7	Ukraine	25.4 million
8	Turkey	25.0 million
9	Germany	24.9 million
10	Mexico	22.6 million

10 Unique Tourist Destinations in the World

Let's tour the world and see these unique places.

Let's begin our travel in the third largest continent – North America.

Dinosaur Provincial Park: Canada

The first destination in our list is Dinosaur Provincial Park. This unique tourist destination which is a UNESCO World Heritage Site is located in Alberta, Canada.

The park is famous for being one of the greatest dinosaur fossil beds in the world, attracting more than 350,000 tourists annually. Thirty-nine dinosaur species have been discovered at the park and more than 500 specimens have been removed and exhibited in museums across the globe.

From North America, let's slide down to South America – the land of the Incas, who were regarded as "Romans of Americas" because of their ability to conquer.

Salar De Uyuni, Salt Flat: Bolivia

Second on the list is the Salar de Uyuni. This is the world's largest salt flat at 10,582 km^2 or 4,085 square miles. It is located in the southwest of Bolivia, near the crest of the Andes, 3,650 meters high. The major minerals found in the salar are halite and gypsum.

Due to its large size, smooth surface, high surface reflectivity when covered with shallow water, and minimal elevation deviation, Salar de Uyuni makes an ideal target for the testing and calibration of remote sensing instruments on orbiting satellites used to study the Earth.

Salar de Uyuni is estimated to contain 10 billion tons of salt, of which less than 25,000 tons is extracted annually. Every November, Salar de Uyuni is also the breeding grounds for three species of South American flamingoes: the Chilean, James's and Andean flamingoes.

From South America let's proceed to Asia, the continent with the largest population.

Chocolate Hills: Bohol, Philippines

Chocolate Hills is the most famous tourist attraction in Bohol. This popular tourist spot is currently ranked number 6 in the list of New Seven Wonders of the world. Chocolate Hills consist of around 1,268 perfectly cone-shaped haycock hills with heights ranging from 40 to 120 meters. The Chocolate Hills is a wonder of nature The Hills are considered as a Philippine National Geological Monument. During the summer, the dome-shaped, grass-covered limestone hills dry up and turn brown transforming the areas into rows and rows of chocolate "kisses," hence the name. There is no natural formation like these in the world. From a distance, they look like half a ball grown out of the ground. The molehill-shaped and almost uniformly sized hills dot the landscape with green and brown.

Fansipan Mountain: Vietnam

For mountain climbers, Fansipan Mountain is one of the best mountains to climb. This tourist spot is currently ranked number 12 in the list of the New Seven Wonders of the world. Fansipan Mountain is located 9 km south-west of Sapa Townlet in the Hoang Lien Mountain Range. Fansipan is branded "the Roof of Indochina" with a towering height of 3,143 m. Fansipan had been proposed to be one of the very few eco-tourist spots of Vietnam, with about 2,024 floral varieties and 327 faunal species.

The peak of Fansipan is accessible all year round. The best time to make the ascent is from mid-October to mid-November, and again in March, when the flowers all flourish and the climbers may behold the carpets of brilliant blossoms, violets and orchids, rhododendrons and aglaias. Fansipan Mountain also contains rice terraces like the famous Banawe Rice Terraces in the Philippines.

Mount Mayon: Albay, Philippines

The majestic Mount Mayon, which is considered as the world's near perfect cone-shaped volcano, is one of the candidates of the New 7 Wonders of Nature and is currently ranked number 9 in the list. This scenic volcano is located south of Manila, in the province of Albay, Philippines. Mayon Volcano is the Philippines' most active volcano (47 eruptions since 1616) and is considered to be the world's most perfectly formed volcano for its symmetrical cone.

Pamukkale Springs: Turkey

Do you want to experience a new kind of bathing? Well, then try taking a bath in a hot springs at Pamukkale. Pamukkale which means "cotton castle" in Turkish, are located in south-western Turkey. It is a natural site and a famous tourist attraction. This unique hot spring is 2,700 meters long and 160 meters high and can be seen from a great distance. About 250 litres of hot water that contains large amount of hydrogen carbonate and calcium rises from the spring every second. This natural phenomenon leaves thick white layers of limestone and travertine cascading down the mountain slope, which resemble a frozen waterfall.

The Burren: Ireland

This place is truly a unique place to see. It is a place where there are no trees to hang a man. A place where there is not enough water to drown him. And if you finally succeeded in killing him, it's too rocky to bury him. This place occupies an area of approximately 300 sq. kilometers.

Burren's landscape is special. The limestone is split and weathered. Everywhere are traces of Megalithic Tombs (like this famous Poulnabrone), ring forts, souterrains, cairns, holy wells and stone rows. There are relics of human habitation dating back almost 6000 years. In this area alone there are more than 60 wedge tombs and the densest concentration in Ireland.

The Burren is situated south of Galway in County Clare, Ireland. Burren means "stony places." The vast amount of stone works on the imagination of people. Not only 3000 years BC, but even today stones are piled up into nice shapes, maybe even with some (unknown) purpose.

There are also different rock formations in this place. This area is also rich in historical ecclesiastical sites.

Camargue Marsh: France

The Camargue is home to more than 400 species of birds, the brine ponds providing one of the few European habitats for the greater flamingo.

The marshes are also a prime habitat for many species of insects, notably (and notoriously) some of the most ferocious mosquitoes to be found anywhere in France. It is also famous for bulls and the Camargue horse.

From Europe, let's go down to the hottest continent in the world – Africa.

Djoudj Sanctuary: Senegal

The Djoudj National Bird Sanctuary is a UNESCO World Heritage Site. It lies on the southeast bank of the River Senegal in Senegal, north east of St-Louis. It provides a range of wetland habitats which prove very popular with migrating birds. Situated in the Senegal River delta, the Djoudj Sanctuary is a wetland of 16,000 ha, comprising a large lake surrounded by streams, ponds and backwaters.

It forms a living but fragile sanctuary for some 1.5 million birds, such as the white pelican, the purple heron, the African spoonbill, the great egret and the cormorant. There are about 400 species of birds and a wide range of wildlife that inhabit the park.

Mariana Trench: Pacific Ocean

This is the right place for those who are fond of underwater or deep-sea adventure – the Mariana Trench. It is good place to see some of the most unique deep-sea creatures too, like the amphipod above.

Marianas Trench is the deepest part of the world's oceans, and the deepest location on the surface of the Earth's crust. It has a maximum depth of about 11 km (6.8 mi), and is located in the western North Pacific Ocean, to the east and south of the Mariana Islands, near Guam.

Tourism in Indian Sub-continent

The vast and varied region that we call Southeast Asia offers something for everyone. Hot sun and warm water, dense jungle, frigid mountaintops, crowded cities, steamy markets and a wealth of outdoor pursuits, from scuba diving to bungee jumping to off-road dirt biking. Existing under a diverse cultural, historical and linguistic framework that remains as varied and complex as ever, along with plenty of tourist-friendly infrastructure, you'll remember your trip from the moment you first step into the humid air to your last bowl of spicy street-noodles.

Thailand is without a doubt the transport hub of the region, as well as the most popular country in terms of tourist numbers. Extensive and cheap road, rail and air travel networks ensure easy access to Vietnam, Malaysia and Singapore, which follow closely in terms of popularity; all three offer pristine natural beauty of all forms - from bamboo forests to endless rice paddies - and huge, bustling cities to shop, sleep, eat and play in (indeed, Singapore is one huge city in and of itself).

Indonesia and the Philippines cover vast areas of ocean with thousands of islands, some as big as a small country, some as small as a city block.

Both offer rugged and nearly untouched marine and forest parks - dive with endangered green sea turtles near the Philippine island of Palawan or climb into the clouds on Indonesia's volcanic Dieng Plateau. The less-populated but still culturally rich Laos and Myanmar offer stunning ruins, ancient but active customs, and a glimpse into what their richer and more populous neighbours were like before the endless incursion of Coca-Cola, 7-Eleven and the internet.

Some Highlights

Asian Metropolises

Large, sprawling and endlessly fascinating, the streets of Bangkok, Jakarta, Hanoi, Phnom Penh, Manila and Kuala Lumpur each offer enough variety and spectacle to satiate any thirst - as long as you don't mind the hustle and bustle.

Beaches

From the pristine water around Malaysia's east-coast islands to the party beaches of Krabi in Thailand, every country in the region can offer several beach-bum paradise locales where you can tan during the day and dance into the night.

Ruins

Some of the most fantastic archaeological ruins on the globe lay here; from the majestic Angkor Wat in Cambodia, to the sprawling Bagan plain in Myanmar, to the ancient and mysterious Hindu temples in My Son, Vietnam. Countless others masterpieces of history are dotted around the region.

Ho Chi Minh Trail

During the Vietnam War, this nature-trail from hell helped the Viet Cong move supplies, troops and weapons around while fighting the war that could not be won. Most of it snakes through Vietnam, but it also runs through parts of Laos and Cambodia.

Cameron Highlands

A lush, elevated plain of rolling hills and tea plantations, Malaysia's answer to a Canadian prairie is a popular way to escape the coastal heat.

Mt. Kinabalu

See nearly the entire Malaysian province of Sabah from as high as you can go, at the top of this massive but surprisingly easy to climb mountain that dominates the north-eastern tip of Borneo.

Ha Long Bay

A postcard photographer's dream, this bay on Vietnam's north-eastern tip is possibly the most visited natural attraction the country has, with craggy limestone spires jutting out of the blue waters of the South China Sea.

The Killing Fields

A sobering reminder of one of Asia's darkest moments, this sorrowful but historically important site is one of the locations used by Cambodia's Khmer Rouge to detain, torture and ultimately kill over 1 million Cambodians in the late 1970's.

Sri Lanka

Sri Lanka is one of the most visited tourists destinations in the world. Surrounded by water all around, Sri Lanka is situated in the midst of Arabian Sea. The most remarkable features of Sri Lanka is the beauty of its exotic beaches. The island country's rich cultural heritage and majestic landscape makes it an amazing tourists destinations. The world famous Maria band of Sri Lanka will surely get your booty pooping to its beats.

Bangladesh

Bangladesh is blessed with unique beauty from nature. Explore the various archaeological, historical and cultural sites of Bangladesh which will contribute towards an unparalleled travel experience to this part of the world. The main attractions of for tourists includes the famous Bangladeshi cuisine, beautifully hand crafted items, many serpentine rivers and green hills of Bangladesh. Get face to face with the famous Royal Bengal Tiger in this part of the world.

Bhutan

Bhutan can be termed as a cultural destination. Endowed with rich cultural heritage of Buddhism, Bhutan has different shades of this religion in many different aspects. Besides this, numerous places of spiritual atraction are admired by tourists across the world. The neatly carved wooden houses and superior quality crafts of Bhutan makes it a preferred location for tourists around the globe.

Maldives

Tourism forms the backbone of Maldives. The island country enjoys tropical climate with plenty of sunshine throughout the year. The palm fringed islands, pretty beaches, clear waters and beautiful flora and fauna of Maldives will provide you the most admired hospitality and accommodation for a memorable travelling experience. With the latest threat of its submergence in water, Maldives is a must tour destination.

Pakistan

Pakistan has numerous places of tourists interests. The Karakoram highway, Hunza valley, Khyber pass and the ancient civilization ruins - Mohen Jo Daro and Harappa are on the top chart and comes under the most visited attractions in Pakistan. Pakistan is blessed with a variety of natures work in the form of excellent mix of dry mountains, sea, deserts, waterfalls, forests and ice covered mountains.

Nepal

Nepal is the land of adventure. Home to 8 out of the 10 highest peaks in the world, Nepal is an ideal place for adventurous sports such as trekking, climbing etc. The world highest peak Mt. Everest stands tall in the crown of Nepal and attracts a lot of tourists from across the world. Shopping in Nepal will drive you crazy. Pokhara, Chitwan National Park, Nepal Ganj, Nagarkot and Annapurna are some of the most visited destinations in Nepal.

2

Quality in Hospitality Industry

Mobile Catering

A mobile caterer serves food directly from a vehicle or cart that is designed for the purpose. Mobile catering is common at outdoor events (such as concerts), workplaces, and downtown business districts.

Event Catering

Event ranges from box-lunch drop-off to full-service catering. Caterers and their staff are part of the food service industry.

When most people refer to a "caterer", they are referring to an event caterer who serves food with waiting staff at dining tables or sets up a self-serve buffet. The food may be prepared on site, i.e., made completely at the event, or the caterer may choose to bring prepared food and put the finishing touches on once it arrives.

The event caterer staff are not responsible for preparing the food but often help set up the dining area. This service is typically provided at banquets, conventions, and weddings. Any event where all who attend are provided with food and drinks or sometimes only hors d'oeuvres is often called a *catered event*.

Many events require working with an entire theme or color scheme. A catering company or specialist is expected to know how to prepare food and to make it attractive. As such, certain catering companies have moved toward a full-service business model commonly associated with event planners. They take charge of not only food preparation but also decorations, such as table settings and lighting.

The trend is towards satisfying all the clients senses with food as a focal point. With the correct atmosphere, professional event caterers with experience can make an event special and memorable.

Beautifully prepared food alone can appeal to the senses of taste, smell, and sight-perhaps even touch, but the decorations and ambiance can play a significant part in a successfully catered event. Catering is often sold on a per-person basis, meaning that there is a flat price for each additional person. However, things like lighting and fire permits are not scaled with the guest count, so per-person pricing is not always appropriate. It is necessary to keep the cost of the food and supplies below a price margin in order to make a profit on the catering.

As many others in the food service industry, caterers and their staff work long hours. It is not uncommon for them to work on holidays or 7 days a week during holiday event seasons.

A comprehensive, formal full-service catering proposal is likely to include the following elements:

Time-line matters: rental arrival time, staff arrival time, bar open time, meal serve time, bar close time, rental pickup, out-of-venue time. Each of these factors affects the catering price.

For example, a rental quote for an "anytime" weekday delivery is usually much more economical than an "exact-time" delivery.

- General menu considerations: Clients may have specific dietary or religious needs to consider. these include Halal, Kosher, Vegetarian, Vegan and food allergy requests. Increasingly, clients are interested in food sustainability and food safety.
- Hors d'oeuvres: it should be clear if these are passed or stationary. Most caterers agree that three or four passed items are appropriate for the one-hour period prior to a meal.
- Meal Rentals: May include tables, chairs, dance floor, plants, tabletop (china, flatware, glassware, linens, chargers), bar glassware, serving equipment, salt/peppers, etc. It should be clear whether table and chair setup and

take-down is included. Most rental companies do not automatically include setup and take-down in the rental charges.

- Labour: Verbiage varies from caterer to caterer, but generally speaking, an event will have a Lead/Captain/ Event Manager, a Chef, perhaps a Sous Chef or Kitchen Assistant, Wait staff and Bartenders. The labour on a plated dinner is generally much higher than the labour on a buffet, because a plated dinner involves double the china, and usually a minimum of three served courses, plus served coffee. Simply put, there's a lot more to do. To do it properly requires roughly 10 to 50% more staff. On a large event, this can be substantial, especially if overtime or doubletime applies.
- Service Charge: Sales Tax, Some quotes will include lighting, fire permits, draping, florals, valet and coat check. Many venues discreetly get a "cut" of the catering bill. Caterers are contractually committed to not disclose this fee specifically in their contracts with the clients. Therefore, catering will sometimes cost substantially more at one venue versus another.Also, caterers must compete with illegal operators. A legitimate caterer will have a business license and a health permit both showing the address of the place from which they do business.

Catering Officers on Ships

Merchant ships often carry Catering Officers-especially ferries, cruise liners and large cargo ships. In fact, the term "catering" was in use in the world of the merchant marine long before it became established as a land-bound business. The "Careers Scotland" website gives the following definition of a Catering Officer's duties:

Merchant Navy catering officers oversee the purchase, preparation and serving of food and drink to crew members and passengers. They are also responsible for accommodation services, including the provision of linen, bedding and laundry. They may be in overall charge of administration, organising record keeping, wage payment, and the interpretation of customs and immigration records that apply while the ship is in port. On larger ships, responsibilities may be shared with the purser, who looks after passengers' comfort and facilities such as banking and shopping, while the catering officer concentrates on organising stores, overseeing the preparation of menus and meals and generally managing dining rooms and services. On a cruise liner, catering officers may be known as 'hotel services managers'. Merchant Navy officers sometimes work in difficult and uncomfortable conditions. They spend long periods of time away from family and friends.

Airline Meal

An airline meal or in-flight meal is a meal served to passengers on board a commercial airliner. These meals are prepared by airline catering services. The first kitchens preparing meals in-flight were established by United Airlines in 1936.

These meals vary widely in quality and quantity across different airline companies and classes of travel. They range from a simple beverage in short-haul economy class to a seven-course gourmet meal in long-haul first class.

Contents

The type of food varies depending upon the airline company and class of travel. Meals may be served as "one tray" or in multiple courses with no tray and with a tablecloth, metal cutlery, and glassware (generally in first and business classes). The airline dinner typically includes meat (most commonly chicken or beef) or fish, a salad or vegetable, a small bread roll, and a dessert. Caterers usually produce alternative meals for passengers with restrictive diets. These must usually be ordered in advance, sometimes when buying the ticket. Some of the more common examples include:

- Cultural diets, such as French, Italian, Chinese, Japanese or Indian style.
- Infant and baby meals. Some airlines also offer children's meals, containing foods that picky children will enjoy such as baked beans, mini-hamburgers and hot dogs.
- Medical diets, including low/high fiber, low fat/cholesterol, diabetic, peanut free, non-lactose, low salt/sodium, low-purine, low-calorie, low-protein, bland (non-spicy) and

gluten-free meals.

- Religious diets, including Kosher, Halal and Hindu, Buddhist and Jain vegetarian (sometimes termed Asian vegetarian) meals.
- Vegetarian and vegan meals. Some airlines do not offer a specific meal for vegetarians; instead, they are given a vegan meal.

Cutlery

Before the September 11th attacks in 2001, first class passengers were often provided with full sets of metal cutlery. Afterward, common household items were evaluated more closely for their potential use as weapons on aircraft, and both first class and coach class passengers were restricted to plastic utensils (also known as "Sporks"). This restriction has since been relaxed in many countries.

Other Non-food Items

Condiments (typically salt, pepper, and sugar) are supplied in small sachets. For cleanliness most meals come with a napkin and a moist towelette. First and business class passengers are often provided with hot towels, proper salt and pepper shakers, free movies, drawing for various electronics not limited to laptop computers and various other forms of electronics.

Breakfast

During morning flights a cooked breakfast or smaller continental-style may be served. On long haul flights and (short/ medium haul flights within Asia) breakfast normally includes an entrée of pancakes or eggs, traditional fried breakfast foods such as sausages and grilled tomatoes, and often muffins or pastry, fruits and breakfast cereal on the side. On shorter flights a continental-style breakfast, generally including a miniature box of breakfast cereal, fruits and either a muffin, pastry, or bagel. Coffee and tea are offered as well, and sometimes hot chocolate.

Quality

Food on board the flight ranges in price from free (many airlines, especially those in Asia and all airlines on long-distance flights) to as much as ten dollars (Midwest Airlines). Quality may also fluctuate due to shifts in the economics of the airline industry, with private jet passengers receiving the equivalent of five-star food service.

On the longest flights in first class and business class, most Asian and European airlines serve multicourse gourmet meals, while airlines based in the US tend to serve large, hearty, meals including a salad, steak or chicken, potatoes, and ice cream.

Some long-haul flights in first class (from mostly Asian carriers) offer such delicacies as caviar, champagne, and sorbet. The cost and availability of meals on US airlines has changed considerably in recent years, as financial pressures have inspired some airlines to either begin charging for meals or abandon them altogether in favour of small snacks (Southwest Airlines).

Eliminating free pretzels saved Northwest $2 million annually. The carrier lost nearly $3.3 billion since 2001. Air China has reported that each domestic flight's meal requires RMB50 (US$7.3) while international flights require RMB70 (US$10). However. Air China is also minimizing costs by loading only 95% of all meals to reduce leftovers and storing non-perishable foods for emergencies.

Taste

Meals must generally be frozen and heated on the ground before takeoff, rather than prepared fresh. Guillaume de Syon, a history professor at Albright College who wrote about the history of airline meals, said that the higher altitudes alter the taste of the food and the function of the taste buds; according to de Syon the food may taste "dry and flavourless" as a result of the pressurization and passengers, feeling thirsty due to pressurization, many drink alcohol when they ought to drink water.

History

In 1958 Pan Am and several European airlines went into a legal dispute over whether certain airline food sandwiches counted as a meal.

Food Safety

Food safety is paramount in the airline catering industry. A case of mass food poisoning amongst the passengers on an airliner could have disastrous consequences. For example, on February 20, 1992, shrimp tainted with cholera was served on Aerolineas Argentinas Flight 386. An elderly passenger died and other passengers fell ill.

Technical Crew Meals

Food safety with technical crew meals (pilots and flight engineers) is sometimes even stricter than for passengers. Many foodstuffs are banned completely from crew meals, including all egg products and often any dairy that has not been ultra-heat treated. The meals supplied on some airlines are labeled with the position of the crew member for whom they are intended, and no technical crew member eats any of the same products as his or her colleague. This ensures that each pilot eats a different meal to minimize the risk of all pilots on board being ill. This situation was a key part of the plot of the movie "Airplane!"

Catering and Customer

Effective customer relations is one of those hidden cogs that can help keep a catering business turning smoothly. From marketing of catering services to event planning to post-party follow-up, an open pipeline of communications and an underlying commitment to customer service are the foundation of some of the most successful catering operations.

At Harvard Univ., where catering underwent a complete overhaul five years ago, the motto—and operational creed—of the upscale Crimson Catering division is "Excellence Measured By Your Satisfaction."

Harvard Express, the lower-ticket, self-service arm, is no less committed to customer service. It promises nothing less than "A Simple Guarantee: 100% Satisfaction."

The strategy appears to be working—the two catering operations generate combined sales of approximately $1.3 million, 75% of it from Crimson Catering.

The top challenge: "Our biggest challenge is maximizing business from existing customers," says Elaine Smart, asst. dir. for catering and residential dining services, who was brought in five years ago to create a new identity for the Harvard catering business.

"We strive for the highest possible degree of customer satisfaction, rather than trying to build the number of customers."

All marketing materials, for both divisions, have been carefully designed to be as user-friendly as possible, she points out. Crimson Catering menus and brochures are updated four times a year to keep fatigue from setting in among regular clientele. "We consider our menu to be our best marketing piece. Each is individually and professionally designed, in full colour with seasonal themes. They're very nicely done, so they won't get lost on people's desks."

Thank-yous count: To ensure client retention, Smart or one of her staff contacts each customer personally after every event to thank them for their business. Customers receive handwritten thank-you notes with a personalized gift such as a logoed coffee mug and a tin of homemade brownies and cookies.

Included is an easy-to-use Function Evaluation Form, a tri-fold, postage-paid self-mailer soliciting feedback on everything from the pre-function planning experience to the presentation of food and linen. Negative evaluations warrant a phone call to discuss what went wrong and what correctional steps might be made in the future.

"Harvard may be big, but it's a closed environment," explains Smart. "Because we don't have exclusivity on-campus, we're up against everyone in the city. We believe that our customers are entitled to the best. And in order to get the business, we have to be the best."

As image-builder: For Scott County Food Service Catering, in Georgetown, KY, catering is only as good as the image of the foodservice department in the local community—an image fed Eleanor Hall works hard at constantly.

"Initially, administration did not want us catering, so we had to work hard to gain their trust," notes Hall, who now counts sales of $15,000-$20,000 a year from catering.

Employees involved in catering throughout the 10-school district are cross-trained in presentation and prep and encouraged to apply new standards of quality to school lunch. When the district first got involved in catering she also gave classes on garnishing and sent someone from each school to a cake-decorating class to help develop their talent. "I encourage people to garnish school lunch, because I want the quality of school foodservice to be as good as the catering," explains Hall. "We have a lot of talent here and I want to keep developing it. We did a reception for the Chamber of Commerce where everybody gave it their all, and the guests were very surprised that school foodservice could do the things we do. This is a good way for people in town to see what we're capable of." 25 meeting areas: Technology helps catering manager Joseph Swinski stay in touch with customers at GTech Corp. in West Greenwich, RI. With 25 different conference and meeting areas and sales of more than $200,000 a year—approximately one-quarter of it involving visiting high-level dignitaries being courted for orders of lottery systems and supplies—the company needs efficient, cost-effective catering that is also highly flexible. For convenient ordering of day-to-day catering functions, Swinski created standard self-service menus and pricing, and an easy-to-use Function Request Form which is available on the in-house e-mail system.

An administrative assistant can simply pull up the menus and forms, fill them out and send them in, receiving same-day confirmation and the assurance that catering is one less thing to worry about in the course of a busy workday. The Request Form is linked to a program that calculates prices, schedules the room, and integrates with ordering functions, as well.

This system allows Swinski and his staff to concentrate more time and energy on the high-profile, custom-designed work. (In a typical week, GTech hosts as many as half-a-dozen groups from around the world who are coming to view the systems—and purchase them.) The company has taken the unusual step of creating a marketing position to coordinate every aspect of the multiple-day visitor events, from booking hotels to planning the agenda. Anna Ragosta acts as the ultimate "client," making the complex, often sensitive planning process easier and more comfortable for the host team.

Organizational Forms in the International Hotels

Organizational Form Variation in the Hotel Industry There are three organizational modes under which a given hotel can operate.

These differ along two dimensions. First, they vary in the level of the central firm's equity involvement; and second, they vary in the extent to which the firm retains operational control. The three organizational forms are:

Firm owned and operated Here, the hierarchical firm is the equity owner and full residual claimant. Hotel managers are employees of the hotel company. Management contracts In this case, the hotel is owned by an outside group of investors, who have hired the firm to run the hotel under its brand. The contracts are fairly long term, lasting up to and sometimes beyond 10 years. Employees of the hotel firm administer the unit as though it were owned and operated, but the firm is recompensed via management fees. These are generally a percentage of gross revenues, sometimes supplemented by guaranteed annual minimum or lump-sum payments. Franchised In this case, the hotel is owned and run by a separate entity, which pays fees to the firm in exchange for the rights to use the brand for some period of time. The contract also specifies that the franchisees must adhere to certain guidelines set by the company to ensure that it meets certain quality thresholds. Like the management contracts, franchising arrangements tend to be long-term.

These different forms give hotel firms flexibility in how they respond to incentive issues and the regulatory environment, making the industry a particularly suitable context to consider how firm boundaries are affected by institutions.

Institutions and Equity

Like the telecommunications, manufacturing and energy industries that have been the mainstay of the literature on institutions' economic impact (e.g. Henisz & Zelner (2001); Smarzynska & Wei (2002); Gutierrez (2003)), the hotel industry is characterized by large, up-front capital investments.

In the case of large resorts, these up-front costs may routinely be as much as $100 million (Contractor & Kundu (1998a)). Super-premium facilities can cost even more. For example, the recently constructed Wynn Las Vegas is reported to have cost $2.7 billion. Furthermore, hotel firms are also susceptible to government intervention and hold-up problems after construction. For example, a hotel's operating expenses can be modified by governmental manipulation of the costs of obtaining operating licenses, or meeting sanitary and safety standards.

These issues, combined with the relative lack of alternative uses for its assets, make the hotel industry vulnerable to ex-post policy changes. While cases of outright asset expropriation are uncommon, the international business press is full of stories about sudden changes in the regulation of hotels. For example, in June 2006, the United Arab Emirates' Economic Department decreed that all hotels and hotel apartments required licenses to "serve alcohol, and open bars, nightclubs and restaurants which show artistic programmes." Such changes in regulation can have profound impacts on the profitability of operating hotels in affected markets. Indeed, major hotel chain operators like Accor and Marriott explicitly talk about political risk, economic uncertainty, and/or the impact of regulatory changes in their discussion of strategy and financial outlook in their annual reports.

Institutions and the Incentive to Maintain Control

The strength of a brand, and thus the benefit of being associated with a well-known brand, critically depends on the capacity of the brand owner to deliver what customers expect. This in turn crucially depends on the behavior and hard work of local managers and their ability and willingness to abide by firm policies. In the context of an industry such as lodging, and others where firms operate chains of outlets, the physical distance between headquarters and local operations makes it difficult to observe the behavior of employee managers.

The agency theoretic solution to this problem is that the firm should devise a high-powered incentive contract for its local managers. This, in fact, is what franchising achieves: by making the local operator a residual claimant, the firm obtains higher effort from its managers, and thus greater output locally. This solution is expected to be especially valuable when local effort has a large impact on output, and when it is particularly difficult to observe the provision of such effort.

While franchising an outlet, or hotel, addresses the "incentive to shirk" problem, it creates another type of incentive problem, however. As residual claimants, franchisees bear the burden of maintaining quality and abiding with company policies valued by customers, but because they operate under a common brand, they share the benefits of these behaviours with other franchisees.

Lafontaine & Raynaud (2002)). As noted by Brickley & Dark (1987) and Brickley (1999), freeriding on the brand is especially likely to be a problem in non-repeat industries such as lodging, where customers cannot discipline local operators because they rarely frequent the same outlet.

Lafontaine & Raynaud (2002) argue that franchisors address this problem of franchisee freeriding by including a number of clauses in their contracts that impose constraints on the behavior of franchisees, such as, for example, specific operations procedures, input sourcing requirements, minimum advertising requirements. Whether or not the franchisee abides by these rules is observable to the franchisor, at least in more transparent contexts, and the franchisee who is found in violation of such rules can be terminated on this basis. Combined with franchisee rents from local operations, these rules and the opportunity to terminate non-complying franchisees yield a selfenforcement mechanism. In other words, the franchisee who wishes to continue to earn the rents associated with being part of the franchise chooses to abide by the requirements in the contract and does not free-ride. Lafontaine & Raynaud (2002) argue that such a mechanism complements the residual claims in franchise contracts as they address the free-riding problem generated by franchisee ownership of local outlets.

While the self-enforcing aspect of franchise contracts can be relied upon to address free-riding, it relies critically on the capacity of the franchisor to observe certain aspects of local operations and interpret them correctly. It also requires that the terms of the contract be enforceable, and that non-complying franchisees can be terminated. In more volatile environments, however, these conditions may not be satisfied.

One well-known example of a franchisee in a repeat industry who chose to ignore company standards and policies in an international context was Raymond Dayan, the owner of the exclusive territorial rights for Paris, France for McDonald's. By 1982, Dayan had 12 restaurants in operation in Paris, but:

McDonald's in Paris was considered a "QSC [Quality, Service, Cleanliness] wasteland" by everyone else in the system. The company's strict specifications on food products had been blatantly ignored. Hamburgers were prepared without all of the standard ingredients. Food was held so long and served so cold that McDonald's managers inspecting the stores found it difficult to eat Veteran managers insist that they have never seen McDonald's units maintained in a filthier state: cooking oils were rancid and black, layers of grease covered the floors and walls, litter was strewn about the store, and grease dripped from the vents into cups hung from the ceiling. In fact, the stores were so unclean that McDonald's franchisees elsewhere around the world began hearing complaints about them from their own local customers who had seen Dayan's units while visiting Paris.

When McDonald's tried to terminate Dayan's license, Dayan sued in Illinois court, arguing that McDonald's was just trying to take back from him what turned out to be a very profitable market. The judge in this case ruled in McDonald's favor, and McDonald's was able to terminate Dayan's license. In other cases and other contexts, however, local courts have been the locus of the suits, and they have favoured the local franchisee to the detriment of the franchisor or the chain. Where free-riding is expected to be particularly problematic, for example when the brand is very valuable, or when outlets are very large and thus more likely to generate more externalities, or in markets where enforcement is difficult, the cost of franchisee free-riding is high. In those cases, firms may opt for a contract that does not generate local incentives to free-ride, namely a contract that does not make the manager's welfare dependent on the profits of the local unit. Consistent with this argument, Lafontaine & Shaw (1999), for example, find evidence that franchisors with more valuable brands, and those whose outlets are larger, indeed operate more of their outlets corporately.

A number of discrete choice variables are used to capture different aspects of the Company's choice of organizational form for a given outlet. The first takes the value of 1 if an outlet is franchised or under a management contract and thus indicates whether the Company has chosen an equity involvement. The second takes the value of 1 if the hotel is company-owned or operated under a management contract, indicating whether or not the Company manages the unit itself. A third variable is coded as 0 if a given hotel is company owned and operated, 1 if operated under a management contract, and 2 if franchised.

The impacts of the market development variables represent something of a puzzle. Market size (proxied using the log of population and the log of per capita GDP) increases the likelihood that the company takes an equity stake in the business, which was not a prediction that emerged from our model. These two variables also increased the probability that the Company controls an outlet using its own employees as predicted, though this effect is never statistically significant. These results suggest that there may be rents to owning a hotel in larger markets that the Company cannot gain access to except by owning the outlet.

Finally, the results for hotel size and monitoring cost variables on the probability that the Company uses employee managers are generally consistent with our model's predictions. As hypothesized, larger outlets are more likely to be operated with employee managers as are hotels in culturally similar countries. Physical distance has a negative but insignificant impact. Interestingly, the Company's experience in the host country has a negative and significant impact on the likelihood that the Company's employees manage a given hotel. This may suggest that the Company needs time to find franchisees it trusts not to degrade the value of its brands, or that increased experience in a country make it easier for the Company to obtain and interpret information about local operations, making franchising more feasible.

Globalization in the Hotel and Catering Sector

The influence of global processes on the development of economy is reflected in the intensity and directions of tourist flows, and, therefore, in the development strategies of tourist companies. The fast progress in information technology, economic growth of developing countries and political changes in many countries of the world, traffic development etc. have been the main factors for accelerating the growth of global tourist market. Due to the process of globalization and offensive strategies in the last few decades, multinational companies are able to penetrate and expand their business activity more easily on the once inaccessible markets. During this period, no other social and economic phenomenon has had such an impressive development as international tourism. There have been significant quantitative, quality, structural, economic, geographical, sociological and other changes in the sphere of demand as well as that of offer. Therefore, nowadays there is almost no country in the world that is not involved in different aspects of tourist flow and business trips to a higher or lower extent.

These trends have been manifested in the hotel industry, as an economic activity and material basis for tourism. According to them, world's tourist flows have been influencing the intensity of growth and the structure of accommodation capacities, the level of hotel concentration, or dispersion in space. In that sense, monitoring the quantitative dimension of hotel industry development includes the analysis of spatial and structural expansion of hotel capacities, as the basis for understanding the development and modern tendencies in the world's hotel industry.

Basic indicators of hotel industry development in the world framework can be seen through the dynamics of the growth of accommodation capacities, territorial distribution of accommodation facilities, new organizational forms of business, improvement of material basis by applying technical and technological innovations, diversification processes, that is, establishing a significant number of types on one hand, and product standardization processes in the function of obtaining a recognizable market identity, on the other hand.

The Concept and Development of Hotel Chains

The traditional form of hotel industry consisting of small hotels individually owned is changing every day and is starting to resemble the form of other industries where large companies increase their share on the market. These companies in the accommodation industry are most often called hotel chains. "A hotel chain implies establishing a business system from a number of objects under the same name, which function in the narrower and wider business environment'.

The nucleus of every hotel is related to stepping out of the business framework of a single object, that is, to the purpose of establishing the technical, technological and organizational business concept which is checked and affirmed and the style of business which is recognizable, by implementing the existing facilities into the system or by constructing new ones on chosen locations. In the initial phase of development, it is a smaller number of accommodation capacities and the narrower zone of influence. The further development of a hotel chain implies the increase in capacities as well as territorial expansion by taking into account the basic principles and following global trends in tourism on the world market.

Since the 1950s, the expansion of the demand for hotel service in the world has been directly influenced by the increase in traveling, that is, the increase in tourist, as well as business and other trips variously motivated. The development of hotel chains has also been influenced by traveling within the borders of countries, which has also had the tendency towards increasing. However, during the 20th century, the development of business regarding hotel chains was not continuous. Therefore, according to the means and characteristics of market dealings in the development of international hotel chains, two periods can be detected.

The first period lasted until the 1970s and was characterized by intensive traffic development, above all air and road traffic, the appearance of new tourist destinations and the expansion of tourism in general. During this period, there was an occurrence of gradual internationalization of dealings in hotel business. The carriers of the growth and development were primarily hotel companies in the USA. During this period, some of the most famous hotel chains in the world, such as InterContinental, Hilton, Holiday Inns etc. were established.

The second period was marked by the increase in the number of international hotel chains and their capacities abroad, greater versatility in business dealings, gradual abandoning of the concept of one (unique) brand and introducing new, multiple (multiplied) brands. By introducing more brands, multinational hotel companies differentiated their services according to the needs of a greater number of segments, above all tourist and business trips. Adapting to the above mentioned changes is evident both in the policy of distribution and of location: apart from resort centres, the main orientation is towards large cities as business centres and towards international communication, particularly airports and highways.

An important feature of this period is the appearance of new ways of providing the growth and development of international hotel chains, as well as significant engaging of capital and companies from other branches of economy into hotel business. Unlike other companies involved in hotel business, hotel chains have defined standards in all business areas, their own philosophy and marketing strategy, a unique booking system, human resource education etc., all of which make them not only recognizable on the market but also the main carriers of tourism development in the future. The pronounced domination of hotel chains from the USA is gradually reducing and the share of British, French, Japanese and German, and in the last few years Chinese companies, is increasing.

The Capacities of International Hotel Chains

According to the estimation of the World Tourism Organization, the overall accommodation capacities are over 20 million rooms. International Hotel and Restaurant Association (IHRA) keeps records of over 300 hotel chains different in size, ownership structure, types of business connections, the quality of hotel capacities, business concepts, prices etc. According to the information for 2008, 300 ranked hotel chains in 54.400 hotels had over 7.2 million rooms at their disposal.

In other words, business systems that operated as hotel chains comprised one third of the world's accommodation capacities. Ten leading hotel companies in 2008 managed over 4.1 million rooms, which comprised 56.6% of ranked hotel chains capacities. The top five leading hotel companies alone had 2.8 million rooms, or 38% of the complete recorded offer of hotel chains. This shows a high degree of the so-called corporation concentration. If considered according to the company's origin country, an absolute domination of the USA and European countries is evident, with over 90% of the world's offer of hotel chains.

For the last twenty years, a more intensive increase in Asia, the Pacific, Africa etc. is noted in terms of the growth dynamics of capacities and their spatial distribution. The carriers of the capacities increase in these regions, apart from companies from the USA and Europe, are national hotel chains from China, Japan, Singapore, UAE, JAR, Egypt, etc. The leading Asian and the thirteenth hotel chain in the world for its accommodation capacities is Jin Jiang from Shanghai, which had about 80 thousand rooms at its disposal. The increase in accommodation capacities in other parts of the world leads to the mitigation of unevenness in the offer of hotel capacities.

Factors in Forming Hotel Chains

Numerous factors have influenced the formation of international, specialized hotel chains, that is, their beginnings and development. There are various connections and relations among these factors; therefore it is very difficult to determine which were dominant in forming a particular hotel chain. They can be divided into two main groups: external and internal factors.

External factors include general circumstances that served the establishment and expansion of international hotel chains. External factors which have influenced the occurrence of this type of hotel enterprises are: a) the expansion in the demand for hotel services in the world (driving factors of tourist traveling and business trips) and b) the need to accelerate the economic growth of certain regions in the world.

Strong economic growth, enabled by exceptional technological improvements and the increase of work productivity under changed market conditions, with simultaneous significant political and social changes in the world, have had significant influence on the fact that in the last few decades the most important driving factors of tourist travel have been revealed.

The most important factors of the increase in the size of tourist travel are: the level of urbanization and industrialization, the standard of living, the quality of work and living environment, available free time, advertising, traffic development, prices etc. Significant political and social changes, as well as the world market liberalization, have brought about the large increase in business trips. It is estimated that this segment of traveling comprises around 25% of overall realized catering consumption in the world. In the USA, in the overall structure of hotel guests, the share of passing business travellers is dominant with 29% as well as participants in conferences and meetings with 25%.

The need to accelerate the economic growth of certain regions of the world is considered to be the main factor in the appearance of some of the most famous international hotel chains. A typical example is InterContinental Hotels Group (IHG). This hotel chain was founded by the airline company Pan American World Airways (Pan Am) in 1946, for the purpose of improving tourism and increasing accommodation capacities in Latin America. The first hotel was bought in 1949 in Brazil. According to the information for 2008, 4.186 hotels were part of the IHG hotel chain.

Hilton Hotels Corporation is the second most famous American chain whose international expansion is explained by the need for economic growth of less developed areas. Namely, Conrad Hilton, the founder of the corporation, provided a contract in 1948 re garding the management of the first large hotel in Puerto Rico, which was built by the Commonwealth as a part of the economic growth program. The success of the Hilton's hotel was the basis for the tourist "boom" of Puerto Rico, and, consequently, the improvement of the economic situation in the Carrribean. According to the information for 2008, Hilton Corporation is ranked as the fourth international hotel chain in the world regarding the number of rooms, which, in 2008, managed 3.265 accommodation facilities in 78 countries on the world.

Distinction should be made between this kind of forming of famous hotel chains and engaging many others in numerous underdeveloped areas, which are attractive and perspective for tourism and business, for the purpose of spreading the already existing international activities, using the advantage, expanding their share of the market etc. It is necessary to distinguish between the phase of forming and later developmental stages of international hotel chains.

Internal factors are closely connected with external factors, and are thus necessary to be viewed through their interdependence. Internal factors are: certain brand and quality guarantee as well as greater efficiency in business (diversification of offer). Each hotel chain is trying to offer services which are different form other chains' services in certain segments, but which present significant experience for the client, that is, present a level of satisfaction that the consumer experiences while staying at a particular hotel.

Therefore, those hotel chains that offer to their consumers a certain brand and guaranteed quality will have the competitive advantage. Their brand (or brands) is recognizable among customers by its quality, price, means of providing service and other features of the particular chain. Service quality is an extremely important factor, through which it becomes internationally recognized (Best Western, Hilton, Holiday Inn, Hyatt and other corporations). That is why one of the important elements of market performance are promo slogans, for example, the Hilton hotel chain has a slogan "When an American does business, the way of the American's business ends in the Hilton", the Marriott hotel chain "When Marriott does it, it does it right" etc.

International business provides greater efficiency. Through diversification of their offer, hotel chains reduce the risk of business through product variety and geographical diffusion. It enlarges the range of their complete offer and encourages the creation of new units abroad. The combination of expansion and diversification as the direction of growth has enabled the world's most famous hotel chains to enter international hotel business, that is, to grow from national into international companies; thus, for instance, Holiday Inn started its business with motels, and Marriott as a restaurant etc.

According to all this, the advantage of hotel chains is in their size, that is, more rational and efficient business dealings, or saving due to economies of scale. One should bear in mind that efficient business can be done by individual hotels with large capacity, but the complete profitability is accomplished by large hotel groups. The more efficient business dealings of hotel chains are reflected in: saving in finance and marketing, saving when purchasing various products and services, saving related to management, technical saving as well as that related to risk diversification. Apart from that, large hotel chains manage accommodation capacities of different ranges, and are able to offer a product with a different price range: a complete service in a luxury hotel, luxurious suites for everybody, mid-range hotels for a wider circle of consumers, moderate prices with limited service, resort hotels, economic motels etc.. On the other hand, hotel chains, as any other large company, have problems in communication, supervision and expenses.

The Process of Territorial Expansion of Hotel Chains

The development of international tourism in the last few decades has brought significant changes in business orientation of hotel chains, out of which the process of territorial expansion has a special role. The quantitative growth of hotel chains inevitably leads to their territorial expansion towards certain macro tourist regions of the world and permanent increase in accommodation capacities. The process of geographical expansion of hotel chains appears as a concrete manifestation of the growth strategy. The development and business behavior of companies in the modern world economy can be manifested through four orientations: ethnocentric, polycentric, regiocentric and geocentric.

In the first, ethnocentric phase, a company is by its vision and orientation focused on the domestic market. In its business dealings, the company relies on the national market and its resources, as well as national culture in thinking, deciding and taking action. This orientation is a characteristic of smaller hotel companies which observe internationalization from the point of the possibility of implementing their ethnocentric business orientation abroad. That is why such companies choose markets that are geographically and ethnographically close, for example, Canada for companies from the USA.

The polycentric business orientation represents the beginning of geographic diversification and internationalization of business, by creating branches and representative offices in another country. Stepping onto the international market changes the business philosophy and leads to adjusting the business to the economic conditions of new countries, while the culture in behavior and decision-making is domestic. The strategy of these companies is "to adjust all branches to the economic conditions of those countries in which they do business, and through their growth relatively independent parts-divisions are created." Regiocentric orientation in business implies higher ambitions in terms of territorial growth, but within the region. Business activities of a company are directed to consumers and resources of one or more areas and their integration into the local economy. Besides that, the culture in business behavior is regional, consumers in those areas are target groups, people from the region are used in business dealings, and financial sources are redistributed within the area of business. Hotel chains that operate on the territory of Europe within tourist macro regions can serve as an example.

Geocentric orientation in hotel chain business looks at the world as a potential market. With this business orientation, national, regional and intercontinental barriers are surpassed and a business strategy is created with the aim of competitiveness on the global market. The majority of hotel chains that are nowadays multinational –global passed through the above-mentioned three phases on their way of development. Each hotel enterprise is potentially oriented towards international business.

One of key indicators of geocentric and global orientation of international hotel chains is seen in their territorial prevalence in the world. Territorial prevalence is expressed through the number of countries in which international hotel enterprises are present with accommodation facilities with their name. Therefore, along with accommodation capacity, territorial prevalence is also an important indicator of the growth strategy in international hotel business.

The biggest international hotel chain, according to the number of rooms and guests, IHG (InterContinental Hotels Group), is present with its hotel capacities in 100 countries of the world. Within this hotel giant, which in 4.400 hotels has over 180 million tourist days, seven world brands operate, the most famous being Holiday Inn Hotels & Resorts and Holiday Inn Express. Therefore, hotel brands – chains which symbolize hotel business in the USA, operate today within the English company with its headquarters in Windsor. Although InterContinental Hotels Group is formally a European company, its largest hotel branch is made of typically American hotels. This indicates its global orientation in business and permanent territorial expansion towards new markets with different levels of hotel development. For the USA market, due to certain tax releases, there is a characteristic increase in the shares of catering companies by companies primarily dealing with real estate. Among such companies is Starwood Hotel & Resort Worldwide, which became the corporation of global importance after purchasing Sheraton Westin hotel chain. In 2008 this company had accommodation facilities in 97 countries.

French Accor is present in 95 countries, thus confirming its international business orientation, and also Best Western International in 80 countries, as well as hotel chains Hilton Hotels Corp. and Carslon Hotels Worldwide operating in 78 and 74 countries respectively. The second place on the list of leading hotel corporations, Wyndham Hotel Group (previously Cendant Corporation), was formed as a global service with diversified business activities in 1977. This hotel chain appeared with its accommodation capacities outside the North American continent in 1999. Although Wyndham corporation has over 7.000 hotels and accommodation capacities in 66 countries of the world, its business orientation is still directed towards the USA market. The example of Wyndham shows that size does not necessarily imply international orientation. This corporation, for example, had only 100 hotels outside North America in 1998. However, the process of its internationalization has intensified by signing business arrangements with foreign partners, primarily from Eastern and Central Europe, so that today this company is leading in the number of hotels around the world.

Some big companies accelerate their territorial expansion towards new markets using the strategy "centre and cog", developed by airline companies. Namely, in order to compete with independent hotels, hotel chains first build luxurious brand hotels in big cities, and then spread towards surrounding smaller towns with secondary brands. The best example of this strategy is the American hotel chain Marriott International, which is expanding on the Russian market through Moscow and St. Petersburg, as primary and strategic centres, and the towns of Nizhniy Novgorod, Samara, Kazan and Yekaterinburg as secondary markets.On the global level, hotel chains more often achieve better results than independent hotels. However, on some markets, such as Hong Kong, Singapore, Sao Paolo, Sydney, Budapest, Amsterdam etc., independent hotels are more booked. The ever discriminating demand, when high quality in the domain of basic service is understood, forces hotel chains to find new ways of animating their clients. One of the ways of improving accommodation capacities is building the so-called theme hotels, which represent an independent tourist attraction with its architecture, decor and atmosphere.

"Imitating the already affirmed tourist attractions is used as the most powerful means of achieving this aim, through historical eclecticism in architecture, appropriate interior design and decor." The most spectacular example is Las Vegas, where there are many mega hotels with casinos exploiting various themes (Egypt, Paris, New York, Rome, Venice): Venetion/Palazzo with 7.128 rooms, MGM Grand with 5.044 rooms, Luxsor with 4.048 rooms etc. The leading hotel chain regarding the number of theme mega hotels is MGM Mirage with around 50.000 rooms in 17 objects (Las Vegas, Makao, Rino etc.).

Types of Hotel Chains in the World

As a consequence of harsh competition and for the purpose of obtaining the best possible position on the international market, the process of enlarging international hotel chains and forming new companies including renowned hotel chains is present. The aim of forming new hotel companies is providing necessary financial resources for maintaining and improving their business standards. Hotel chains as a part of such companies continue their activities using their recognizable trademarks, but they also carry the trademark of the new founded company, for which it represents certain publicity on the global level. Apart from that, there is differentiating between hotel chains on the market (from budget to luxurious) in the sense of business orientation, according to various segments and target groups of clients. According to the methodology of the international magazine "Hotels", there are three types of hotel chains: corporate chains, management companies and voluntary chain associations.

Corporate chains are recognized by their brand or hotel brands, or a well-known trademark. The biggest corporate chains develop many brands-trademarks, which in the best way show the service type and quality. Business activities on the national and international scales are done in different ways, therefore, franchising contracts, management contracts, various sale norms while including companies from other branches of economy and other means are used. Accommodation capacities of leading hotel chains in the world are enormous: accommodation capacities of IHG (InterConinental Hotels Group) in 2008 were over 585.000 rooms in over 4.100 hotels, Wyndham Hotel Group 550.000 rooms in over 7.000 hotels etc.

Management companies are companies (operators) that manage various hotel brands of corporate chains or their parts, their own brands, as well as independent hotels (hotels outside the chains), which do not have their own brand. In hotel business, a management contract represents a way of business cooperation based on providing special, professional services by specialized companies. There can be different types of contracts between hotel chains-hotel owners and management companies:

- Joint investments contract (when the management company – operator is an equal partner in the joint ownership over a hotel, and, thus in profit);
- Lease contract (when the management company temporarily, or for a certain period of time rents an object and pays a certain amount of money for that);
- Management contract (when the management company can, but does not have to be an investor, but manages a hotel for agreed compensation);
- Franchise contract (when the management company takes the franchise from the franchise receiver).

Management companies are much smaller in size and capacity than corporate chains. Accommodation capacities with a smaller number of rooms dominate their structure, so the differences in the average size of objects are significantly smaller than with corporate chains.

The largest number of management companies manages objects of famous hotel chains in the USA, such as: Holiday Inns, Sheraton, Best Western etc. In the USA, big corporate chains have in their structure management companies who control different hotels.

For example, corporate chain Marriott International, apart from the hotels in its ownership, on various grounds also manages around 900 hotels which are not in its ownership. The biggest management companies that do not own hotels are: Extended Stay Hotels (manages around 700 hotels), Interstate Hotels&Resorts (manages around 230 hotels) etc. Unlike corporate chains, management companies are less oriented towards the international hotel business.

A special form of activities in hotel business is franchising. The franchising system in national and international framework is used by the largest corporate chains. To hotel enterprises (or entrepreneurs) which receive a franchise, this system provides work technology according to the standards of the franchiser, thus achieving appropriate service quality and control; using the brand name of the franchiser, which makes him recognizable on the market, enables various kinds of help with bookings, sales, promotion, human resource training etc. However, the biggest advantage of the franchise receiver lies in the fact that, by entering the business system of a large hotel chain, it avoids the risks and problems of providing the market for their services.

The advantage of a hotel company that gives a franchise is the fact that it provides a significant number of selling points in their own and other countries without large investments. The company spreads on the market with minimum financial risk. Leading corporate hotel chains are the biggest givers. The best examples are corporate chains: Wyndham Hotel Group (out of 7.043 hotels, 7.016 are franchised), Choice Hotels International (all the hotels are franchised), InterContinental Hotels Group (86% are franchised) etc. Voluntary chains (associations) base their activities on providing service of global marketing and reservations to independent hotels and corporate chains, particularly those of national character. These voluntary chains are also called consortiums. Consortiums are voluntary associations of a group of independent hotels, national and international chains, whose main aim is to animate the demand and enlarge their offer on the international market.

The origin of voluntary chains is related to internationalization and globalization of hotel business. Hotel enterprises join voluntary chains when they are not able to follow the expansion in business activities both in the material sense and in human resources. Activities of voluntary chains are related to: sales and reservations, advertising and other promotional activities, cooperation with airline companies, providing other services etc. In 2008, 25 biggest voluntary chains covered sales, promotion and other activities in 26.000 hotels and around 2.9 million rooms. The number of rooms was expanded by 5% in comparison to 2007. The biggest voluntary chain in the world is British Utell, an affiliate of the company Pegasus from the USA. According to the information for 2008, this chain served 11.900 hotels with around 1.380.000 rooms. The chain, in comparison to 2007, increased its services by another 400 hotels.

According to the information for 2008, the largest number of voluntary chains was based in Europe. Unlike big voluntary chains, which are mainly related to the European market, management companies are more numerous on the USA market.

Conclusion

Economic globalization, readily available markets, traffic development and advancements in information and other technologies have all caused an increase in the number of tourist, business and other kinds of trips, thus deeply influencing the transformation of hotel business. One of the most important transformations and one of the most important characteristics of business dealings in hotel enterprises is included in business integrations and connections as well as territorial expansion. High concentration of accommodation capacities in certain parts of the world (the USA, the Mediterranean, the Alps etc.) forces hotel chains to find new destinations for their enlargement and territorial expansion. That is why the end of the 20th and the beginning of the 21st century have been marked with changes in spatial distribution and more intense increase in accommodation capacities in the areas of former socialist countries, Asia, the Pacific and Africa.

Internationalization provides hotel chains the improvement of their position on the global market. In order to obtain better positions on the international market, huge financial transactions have appeared recently, leading to changes in the ownership structure and the formation of new companies, both on the national as well as international (global) level. In this way, financial resources are obtained, as well as increased influence on the market, maintenance and innovations in business standards. Besides carrying the trademark of a newly founded company, hotel chains continue doing their business under their own recognizable trademark-brand. The branded name of a hotel chain has numerous advantages, such as greater marketing power, ensured product quality originating from established standards, help in management, easier approach to financial institutions etc. However, the mass usage of hotels by clients with different buying powers will maintain a wide range of objects as well as prices.

Importance and Usage of Dress Code

Clothing is an aspect of human physical appearance, and like other aspects of human physical appearance it has social significance. All societies have dress codes, most of which are unwritten but understood by most members of the society. The dress code has built in rules or signals indicating the message being given by a person's clothing and how it is worn. This message may include indications of the person's social class, income, occupation, ethnic and religious affiliation, attitude, marital status, sexual availability and sexual orientation. Clothes convey other social messages including the stating or claiming personal or cultural identity, the establishing, maintaining, or defying social group norms, and appreciating comfort and functionality.

For example, wearing expensive clothes can communicate wealth, the image of wealth, or cheaper access to quality clothing. All factors apply inversely to the wearing of inexpensive clothing and similar goods. The observer sees the resultant, expensive clothes, but may incorrectly perceive the extent to which these factors apply to the person observed. (cf. conspicuous consumption). Clothing can convey a social message, even if none is intended.

If the receiver's code of interpretation differs from the sender's code of communication, misinterpretation follows. In every culture, current fashion governs the manner of consciously constructing, assembling, and wearing clothing to convey a social message. The rate of change of fashion varies, and so modifies the style in wearing clothes and its accessories within months or days, especially in small social groups or in communications media-influenced modern societies. More extensive changes, requiring more time, money, and effort to effect, may span generations. When fashion changes, the messages communicated by clothing change.

History

Europe

In the Middle Ages the European nobility used a dress code to differentiate themselves from the other classes.

The Americas

The indigenous peoples of the Pacific Northwest Coast had a complex social structure, including slaves, commoners, and nobles, and dress codes to indicate these social distinctions. John R. Jewitt, an Englishman who wrote a memoir about his years as a captive of the Nuu-chah-nulth people in 1802-1805, describes how, after some time living there, Maquina and the chiefs decided that he must now be "considered one of them, and conform to their customs".

Jewitt resented the imposition of this dress code, finding the loose untailored garments very cold, and attributed to them a subsequent illness of which he almost died. He was not allowed to cut his hair, and had to paint his face and body as a Nootka would.

Signifier

Gender: Various traditions suggests that certain items of clothing intrinsically suit different gender roles. In particular, the wearing of skirts and trousers has given rise to common phrases expressing implied restrictions in use and disapproval of offending behavior. For example, ancient Greeks often considered the wearing of trousers by Persian men as a sign of effeminacy.

Social Status

In many societies, people of high rank reserve special items of clothing or decoration for themselves as symbols of their social status. In ancient times, only Roman senators could wear garments dyed with Tyrian purple; only high-ranking Hawaiian chiefs could wear feather cloaks and palaoa or carved whale teeth. In China before the establishment of the republic, only the emperor could wear yellow.

Occupation

Military, police, and firefighters usually wear uniforms, as do workers in many industries. School children often wear school uniforms, while college and university students sometimes wear academic dress. Members of religious orders may wear uniforms known as habits. Sometimes a single item of clothing or a single accessory can declare one's occupation or rank within a profession.

Ethnic and Political Affiliation

In many regions of the world, national costumes and styles in clothing and ornament declare membership in a certain village, caste, religion, etc. A Scotsman declares his clan with his tartan. A French peasant woman identified her village with her cap or coif.

Clothes can also proclaim dissent from cultural norms and mainstream beliefs, as well as personal independence. In 19th-century Europe, artists and writers lived *la vie de Boheme* and dressed to shock: George Sand in men's clothing, female emancipationists in bloomers, male artists in velvet waistcoats and gaudy neckcloths. Bohemians, beatniks, hippies, Goths, Punks and Skinheads have continued the (countercultural) tradition in the 20th-century West.

Religious Affiliation

A Sikh or Muslim man may display his religious affiliation by wearing a turban and other traditional clothing. Many Muslim women wear head or body covering that proclaims their status as respectable women and as considered a means for covering the Awrah. A Jewish man may indicate his observance of Judaism by wearing a yarmulke.

Marital Status

Traditionally, Hindu women wear *sindoor*, a red powder, in the parting of their hair to indicate their married status; if widowed, they abandon *sindoor* and jewellery and wear simple white clothing.

However this is not true of all Hindu women; in the modern world this is not a norm and women without sindoor may not necessarily be unmarried.

In many Orthodox Jewish circles, married women wear head coverings such as a hat, snood, or wig. Additionally, after their marriage Jewish men of Ashkenazi descent begin to wear a Tallit during prayer. Men and women of the Western world may wear wedding rings to indicate their married status, and women may also wear engagement rings when they are engaged.

Laws and Social Norms

In New Guinea and Vanuatu there are areas where it is customary for the men to wear nothing but penis sheaths in public-this is uncommon in more developed areas. Women wear string skirts. In remote areas of Bali, women may go topless. In India, Hindu contemporary daily dress like saris tend to often show bare stomachs, but the feeling of culture and tradition covers such exposure.

In the United States, a few businesses or restaurants display dress code signs requiring shoes and shirts, claiming to be there on account of a health code, although no such health codes exist,. these signs have remained popular since businesses looked for ways to reduce the number of hippies in their facilities. Also, it is common belief that there are laws against driving barefoot, however, no such laws exist. It is quite uncommon for people to be nude in public in the United States, however, there are a few private beaches and resorts that cater to such a population.

Private Dress Codes

Dress codes may be enforced by private entities, usually imposing a particular requirement for entry into a private space. "Dress code" may also refer to a social norm.

- By religious law or tradition
- For employees, pupils/students, etc.-sometimes a uniform; sometimes depending on the day, see Casual Friday;
- For customers, e.g. for a disco, nightclub, casino, shop or restaurant

- In special parties; sometimes a specific costume is requested
- Fetish clubs often require patrons to dress in fetish clothing
- As social rules in general.

Schools worldwide also have dress code. Dress code prevents people from wearing clothing deemed inappropriate by social custom.

Dress codes function on certain social occasions and for certain jobs. A school or a military institution may require specified uniforms; if it allows the wearing of plain clothes it may place restrictions on their use. A bouncer of a disco or nightclub may judge visitors' clothing and refuse entrance to those not clad according to specified or intuited requirements.

Some dress codes specify that tattoos have to be covered.

A "formal" or white tie dress code typically means tail-coats for men and full-length evening dresses for women. "Semi-formal" has a much less precise definition but typically means an evening jacket and tie for men (known as black tie) and a dress for women. "Business casual" typically means not wearing jeans or track suits, but wearing instead collared shirts, and more *country* trousers (not black, but more *relaxed,* including things such as corduroy). "Casual" typically just means clothing for the torso, legs and shoes. "Wedding Casual" defines yet another mode of dress, where guests dress respectfully, but not necessarily fancily. Basically, no jeans and T-shirts.

Transparent or semi-transparent clothing can play with the boundaries of dress-codes regarding modesty. Dress codes usually set forth a lower bound on body covering. However, sometimes it can specify the opposite, for example, in UK gay jargon, *dress code,* means people who dress in a militaristic manner. *Dress code* nights in nightclubs, and elsewhere, are deemed to specifically target people who have militaristic fetishes (e.g. leather/skinhead men).

Work Place

White collar work place clothing has changed through the years. In a corporate office, appropriate clothes are clean, formal clothes such as a shirt, necktie, and suit, or other similar outfits. Previous business dress code eras (the 1950s in the U.S.) featured standardised business clothes that strongly differentiated what was acceptable and unacceptable for men and women to wear while working. Today, the two styles have merged; women's work clothes expanded to include the suit (and its variants) in addition to the usual dresses, skirts, and blouses; men's clothes have expanded to include garments and bright colours.

Casual wear entered corporate culture with the advent of the Silicon Valley, California, technology company featuring informal work clothes on the job. Additionally, some companies set aside days — generally Fridays ("dress-down Friday", "casual Friday")— when workers may wear informal clothes. The clothing a company requires its worker to wear on the job varies with the occupation and profession.

Some businesses observe that anti-discrimination law restricts their determining what is appropriate and inappropriate workplace clothing. Yet, in fact, most businesses have much authority in determining and establishing what work place clothes they can require of their workers. Generally, a carefully drafted dress code applied consistently does not violate anti-discrimination laws.

Business Casual

Business casual dress, also "smart casual", is a popular work place dress code that emerged in white-collar workplaces in Western countries in the 1990s, especially in the United States and Canada. Many information technology businesses in Silicon Valley were early adopters of this dress code. In contrast to formal business wear such as suits and neckties (the international standard business attire), the business casual dress code has no generally-accepted definition; its interpretation differs widely among organizations and is often a cause of sartorial confusion among workers. The job search engine Monster.com offers this definition: *In general, business casual means dressing professionally, looking relaxed, yet neat and pulled together*. A more pragmatic definition is that business casual dress is the mid ground between formal business clothes and street clothes. Examples of clothing combinations considered appropriate for work by businesses that consider themselves as using the business-casual dress code are:

- for men: a shirt with a collar (tennis shirt) and cotton trousers, "khakis": in American English
- for women: a tennis shirt and trousers Generally, neckties are excluded from business casual dress, unless worn in untraditional ways. The acceptability of blue jeans and denim cloth clothing varies – some businesses disallow them as sloppy, not casual, yet tolerate men wearing blue jeans with a sports coat. Long sleeve shirts are also deemed appropriate. however this MUST be worn with a tie.

A survey was conducted to investigate the nature and use of employee dress codes of organizations that market professional services. The study sample consisted of personnel administrators employed in selected service organizations that are members of the American Society of Personnel Administrators; the total sample included 1000 administrators. The analysis of responses revealed that dress is important in marketing services and that compliance to a dress code is a criterion for employee performance evaluation. While most administrators agreed that dress is a significant factor in their companies' success, few organizations had formal written dress codes; dress codes are most often communicated orally. Traditions in the professions, the expectations of customers, Chief Executive Officers of the organizations, and past experiences were the factors that dominate the development of dress codes. On the question of dress code requirements for male vs. female employees, the study revealed that more service organizations specify dress for males than for females. For traditional business attire, comparing the dress codes of the different service organizations revealed several significant relationships.

In recent years much emphasis has been placed on the importance of dress and appearance for professional success. Often organizations make an effort to manage dress and appearance so as to communicate to the client/customer in the most effective manner. Such controls have traditionally been manifested in policies called "dress codes." The responsibility for the administration of dress codes has conventionally been treated as a personal function.

"Proper" business dress has long been a part of the norms of professional services practitioners such as bankers, accountants, stock brokers and management consultants. However, it is interesting to note that in the marketing literature there is little attention devoted to dress as it relates to the marketing of professional services. This is particularly interesting when one considers the growth of professional service industries as a part of the U.S. economy and the broadscale increases in attention focused on services marketing by practitioners and academicians.

The marketing literature does, however, address the issue of personal appearance as it relates to the personal sales interview. It is well documented from a behavioural standpoint that dress has a significant impact upon perception and image formation as a part of the interpersonal communication process. Peak (1986) discovered that when personality traits are correlated with clothing styles, persons who wear conservative clothing are perceived as being more intelligent, mature, generous, sincere, trustful, understanding and dependable than those wearing more "daring" styles. According to Premeaux and Mondy (1987), dress establishes a level of respect and authority. This is often necessary to get the work done. In a study on occupation and grooming (Littrell and Verger, 1986) it was found that less positive characteristics are attributed to those who were groomed "poorly" than to those well groomed.

There is an essential difference between the professional salesperson and the professional service practitioner which underlies the justification of this study. Sales personnel are designated as the "front-line" customer contact persons for an organization which markets goods. Management, as well as salespersons themselves, are not only aware of the role of personal appearance and dress in interpersonal communication, but have employed the resources necessary to incorporate dress codes into promotion and marketing strategies. On the other hand, it is argued that professional service practitioners see themselves as "doers" rather than, sellers" (Bloom, 1984). Therefore, it is felt by some that these employees do not focus the necessary attention on those behavioural factors important in selling or marketing as would designated marketing personnel (Bloom, 1984). As Denny (1981) states:

One of the fundamental misconceptions many accountants have about marketing is that...someone else can bring in the new clients and then they can take over and do the work. Unfortunately they are wrong...It takes an accountant to sell accounting services.

The literature dealing with services marketing]ends support to the premise that the dress behavior of employees could be a salient attribute of the buyer when involved in the purchase process of a professional service. Two commonly cited characteristics of services, intangibility and inseparability, give credence to this postulate, as discussed below (Zeithaml, 1985).

Because services are intangible in nature, perceptual and communication problems exist during the exchange process which make the true quality of the service difficult to evaluate and distinguish (Nickels, 1984). Pricing and valuation problems result, leading the buyer to feel uncertainty (Lovelock, 1981). With complex technical services such as legal, financial or consulting research, the problem is magnified because of the lack of knowledge of the buyer (Bloom, 1984). It can be argued that because the buyer cannot see (touch, smell or feel) the true quality of the service for evaluation that he might use surrogate criteria such as the behavior of the practitioner, the physical appearance of the facility or other tangible cues. Dress behavior, then, can become a tangible evaluative criteria for the buyer, regardless of the relationship dress has to the skills of the practitioner or quality of the service performed.

Another theoretical argument offered which distinguishes services from goods is that of inseparability. Often production and consumption of services cannot be separated temporally or spatially (Chase, 1978). Consequently, personal contact exists between the producer and consumer, allowing the buyer to have the perceptual exposure necessary to observe behavioural and physical characteristics of the seller.

The premise set forth as the rationale for this study is that through their behavior, each practitioner in a service organization which has customer/client contact plays a role in marketing that organization's service. Since dress is an important aspect of that behavior which plays a role in the communication process during this interaction, dress behavior can be a salient factor in the exchange process. If this premise is accepted, and dress is perceived to be important in marketing of professional services, then the question of management or control of employee dress arises. One would assume that organizations would make an effort to manage appearance so as to communicate to the client/customer in the most effective manner.

Results

The personnel administrators responding to the questionnaire clearly indicated that appearance of professional employees was a significant factor when a potential client or customer evaluated their company's services.

Of the 304 responding personnel administrators, 73% indicated that a dress code, either formally or informally communicated, had been established for their service organizations. Among those respondents whose organizations employed any type of dress code, 67% noted that individual employee compliance to the code was a criterion for employee performance evaluation. Eighty-five percent of the respondents indicated that compliance to a dress code was either absolutely necessary or very important when employers underwent performance evaluation.

3

Jumpstarting Hospitality Industry

It should be pointed out that the indicators presented here must be treated with caution as national accounting systems do not include accounting procedures which deal adequately with this sector; estimates of the contribution of the tourist sector to macroeconomic aggregates may be the result of different methods of calculation. Comparisons may therefore, in some cases, be subject to discussion. Further, with respect to employment, it may be that the survey itself may have given rise to confusion and it may not be at all possible to compare the responses.

Contribution to Gross Domestic Product

Twelve countries provided information on this question. In five countries this sector accounted for less than 10% of gross domestic product; in four others it contributed more than 10% but less than 15%; in the others, tourism was the source of more than 50% of gross domestic product.

Although one would expect that the contribution of tourism to gross domestic product would be in inverse proportion to the size of the particular country-given the more diversified economies o f the larger countries of the region and the greater dependence on tourism in many of the smaller islands-this variable shows no clear pattern of behaviour, corresponding to types of States or territories, which would allow relative levels of contribution to gross domestic product to be linked to particular groups of States or territories. Thus for the larger countries-Colombia, Mexico and Venezuela-the contribution of tourism to gross domestic product was 1.5%, 3% and 13.1% respectively. Guyana, also a large country though less developed, reported 15%. Participating countries which could be classified as medium-sized-Costa Rica and the Dominican Republic-reported contributions from tourism activities of 7.5% and 11.5% respectively. The Eastern Caribbean islands recorded contributions ranging from 4.6% in St. Vincent and the Grenadines to 60% in Antigua and Barbuda, with 5% in Martinique, 12% in Barbados, 50% in the Turks and Caicos Islands and 55% in the Bahamas.

The percentage contribution of tourism to gross domestic product in each country may be seen as indicative of the importance of this sector in relation to other sectors of the national economy; very high contributions may be a sign of heavy economic dependence on tourism.

In Antigua and Barbuda, the Bahamas and the Turks and Caicos Islands tourism bears an enormous burden. In Barbados, the Dominican Republic and Venezuela, where input is greater than 10%, tourism is a fairly important sector. It is relatively important in Costa Rica where it accounts for 7.5% of gross domestic product. For the economies of Martinique, St. Vincent and the Grenadines, Mexico and Colombia, by contrast, this sector is less important-judging from this variable-as it accounts for no more than 5% of gross domestic product.

This indicator does not however reveal the relative importance of tourism activity from an international point of view. Among the States and territories of the Wider Caribbean Region, Mexico, where the tourist sector accounts for only 3% of gross domestic product, is the most important tourist destination, after the United States; Antigua and Barbuda and the Turks and Caicos Islands on the other hand, although generating more than 50% of gross domestic product through tourism activity, are of little importance in terms of their share of the international tourism market. To arrive at a better appreciation of each State or territory's position in the context of regional or international tourism, one must determine the absolute contribution of the sector to gross domestic product in each country.

Contribution to Employment

Only seven cases responded to this question according to the terms specified in the survey-percentage contribution to employment. Three of them-the Bahamas, Barbados and the Turks and Caicos Islands-reported that tourism contributed more than 20% to employment. For St. Vincent and the Grenadines, Martinique and Costa Rica the contribution of the tourist sector was 10%, 4.2% and 2.5% respectively.

In Colombia and the Dominican Republic 130,000 and 50,000 jobs respectively, were directly created by tourism.

Apart from an apparent qualitative correspondence with the responses concerning contribution to gross domestic product, there was no information pointing to objective conclusions.

Contribution to Foreign Exchange Earnings

Eight of the States and territories responding to the questionnaire did not deal with this question, these were Antigua and Barbuda, Belize, Guyana, Martinique, Mexico, Surinam, Turks and Caicos Islands and Venezuela. The figures given by those States and territories which did respond confirmed the importance of the sector to foreign exchange earnings. Figures given for foreign exchange earnings ranged from 25% for Costa Rica to 75% for the Bahamas with St. Vincent and the Grenadines reporting 35%, the Dominican Republic 45% and Barbados 60%.

Finally, Colombia and the Dominican Republic recorded annual foreign exchange earnings from tourism of 440 million and 1200 million American dollars respectively.

Hotel Capacity and Number of Visitors

Information was requested on the number of rooms, occupancy levels, annual number of visitors and number of all-inclusive resorts. The relative importance of tourism for the States and territories which participated, as tourist destinations, in the survey.

Number of Rooms and Occupancy Levels

Responses fell into clear categories. At the highest level was Mexico with 150,000 rooms, followed, though not closely, by Colombia with a little over 43,000 rooms; next in line were

Venezuela and the Dominican Republic with between 25,000 and 30,000 rooms, the Bahamas and Costa Rica with about 13,000 rooms each, Barbados and Martinique between 6,000 and 7,000, Belize almost 3,000 and Guyana, St. Vincent and the Grenadines and Turks and Caicos with a little over one thousand rooms each. Antigua and Surinam provided no information on this topic.

Hotel occupancy levels ranged between 40% and 69%. Guyana with 40% occupancy was well below the other participating cases. Barbados, Costa Rica and Turks and Caicos reported 50% occupancy; the Bahamas, Colombia, Martinique and Mexico fell between 54% and 56%, while Venezuela and the Dominican Republic recorded 68% and 69% respectively. The other cases provided no information on occupancy levels. Higher occupancy levels may be seen as indicative of traveller preference, attributable no doubt to lower hotel rates and possibly cheaper tourist packages. If this is so then occupancy levels may be considered an indicator of competitiveness on the tourism market.

All-Inclusive Resorts

The purpose behind the survey item-number of all-inclusive resorts-was to elicit information about a specific category of tourism generally considered to be the exact opposite of ecological tourism. However, as the responses to the specific survey question, of which there were eight, seemed to give different interpretations, they were of no assistance.

The informants in three cases-Barbados, Colombia and St. Vincent and the Grenadines-reported that there were no all-inclusive type hotels. Costa Rica has 192 tourist centres of which 10% were classifiable as all-inclusive. Mexico has 43 such resorts, Guyana 10, Antigua and Barbuda 6, the Bahamas 7 and Turks and Caicos only one.

Visitor Arrivals

The following figures for annual visitor arrivals were extracted from the responses received (figures are rounded):

* Antigua and Barbuda 194,000 86,000*
* Bahamas 3,600,000 1,600,000*
* Barbados 394,000 105,000*

* Belize 215,000 116,000*
* Colombia 856,000
* Costa Rica 580,000 377,000*
* Martinique 751,000 409,000*
* Dominican Republic 1,100,000
* St. Vincent & Grenadines 155,000 97,000*
* Turks & Caicos 56,000
* Venezuela 598,000 244,000*

It must be borne in mind that the relationship between the annual number of visitors and the number of rooms may vary. No pattern could be observed on which to base any type of analysis.

Ecotourism

This section of the survey is aimed at establishing whether or not ecotourism is practiced in the country or territory in question, what definition is given to this concept, whether there exist similar tourism activities identified by another name and what restrictions could have halted initiatives towards developing this type of activity in cases where it could have taken place. Concepts and definitions are present.

Almost all the responses received offered concepts and definitions. Generally speaking, the answers revealed that ecotourism and ecological tourism are synonyms. Only in the case of Costa Rica is there a distinction-ecotourism is seen as the commercialization of the concept of ecological tourism. In its response, the Dominican Republic makes a few minor distinctions between ecotourism, alternative tourism, ecological tourism and adventure tourism.

The definitions offered include various elements: among those worthy of mention are the following. Ecotourism is defined generally as an activity centered on the observation and the enjoyment of nature. Others see it as linked exclusively to national parks and other types of protected areas where there is still an untouched environment. It is defined as an "educational-recreational activity that is organized, controlled and small-scale", as an activity to be accompanied by an "environmental interpretation and/or education programme." Other responses expand the concept even further and incorporate into it elements such as "research into and preservation of the country's natural wealth". In addition, in defining the activity, the expressions "any cultural manifestation" and "understanding the cultural history", are also used. In some responses, emphasis is placed on the economic benefits to local populations, thereby providing greater incentives for preserving protected areas and other forms of natural manifestations and cultural expressions. Finally, some responses included sporting activities such as deep-sea diving and other water sports as well as golf and horseback riding.

The definitions proposed contain many common elements despite greater or lesser emphasis on certain aspects, many of which are already included in more generic definitions adopted by different organizations. Nevertheless, as far as definitions are concerned, there appears to be no major discrepancies between those proposed in the responses to the survey. However, in practice, the perception of ecotourism may vary significantly from one country or territory to another.

However, the question of factors likely to have hindered the development of "ecotourism" activities was not discussed in any of the responses received although in all cases, activities of this nature were being carried out. In one case, it was pointed out that conditions were not yet appropriate for ecotourism while, in another, all the factors highlighted in the questionnaire had been present at one time or another. These factors include the absence of adequate conditions, a lack of interest on the part of relevant sectors, lack of qualified personnel, insufficient knowledge of the area, lack of understanding of the benefits to be derived from this activity and finally the reduced number of areas with natural beauty which lend themselves to ecotourism and other types of tourism.

Protected Areas

Protected Terrestrial Areas

The total number of existing and planned protected areas, as well as their respective size. This information was given in the answers to the above-mentioned survey. The fourteen countries which responded to the survey dealt with this question, albeit somewhat superficially with regard to planned areas. In two cases-Barbados and St. Vincent and the Grenadines-it was reported that there were no land-based protected areas even though some had been proposed and, while in four other cases, there were no definite plans to create new ones.

Certain conclusions on ecotourism and its future may be drawn from information presented earlier, on its own, or in conjunction with information gathered from the survey. It should be stated, in absolute terms, that if the concept of ecotourism is restricted to activities such as excursions, sightseeing or other activities carried out in naturally protected areas, the greatest potential for the development of ecotourism would have to be in those countries with larger areas under protection. It has been shown that the countries with larger protected areas practice ecotourism on a larger scale: 21 areas of approximately 34,000 km^2 in Colombia, 6 areas of about 33,000 km2 in Mexico and 38 areas of more than 73,000 km2 in Venezuela. Belize, with 31 protected areas, reports that ecotourism is practiced in all of them. However, neither the size of the protected areas nor the proportion of these areas devoted to ecotourism implies better use of ecotourism, or greater development of this activity. In fact, in Costa Rica, one of the countries where nature-oriented tourism is most developed, ecotourism is practiced in 1,200 km2 in 13 of the 27 terrestrial protected areas mentioned in the survey, which covers a total area of nearly 12,000 km^2.

The main attraction, common to all the States and territories which responded to the survey, and present in the areas where ecotourism is practiced, is nature. However, there are other important attractions in the protected areas open to ecotourism such as cultural, historical, anthropological, archaeological, geological and scientific attractions. In one case, beaches were indicated as an important attraction.

Coastal Protected Areas

The data obtained from the survey on coastal protected areas is present. It should be pointed out that, in some cases, the protected areas defined as land-based include some coastal areas. In three cases-those of Barbados, Martinique and St. Vincent and the

Grenadines-there are no coastal protected areas; all other States and territories claim to have such areas, some of which are devoted to ecotourism. The largest areas were reported in Mexico and Venezuela-each having nearly 30,000 km^2-followed by Costa Rica with 5,600 km^2 and the Bahamas with nearly 2,900 km^2. The other States and territories have protected coastal areas of between 700 and 1,800 km^2. Only Barbados and Surinam are considering the creation of new coastal protected areas.

Nature is also the most important attraction in coastal protected areas. The responses are however more specific, especially in terms of the natural attractions which represent a great diversity of ecosystems, fauna and coastal formations. With regard to fauna, avifauna and marine fauna are most prominent, with certain species in abundance, mangroves, coral reefs, beaches, special landscapes and formations; archaeological, anthropological and cultural attractions.

With the exception of the cases of Mexico and Venezuela outlined earlier, the areas in question are small. It is hoped that with the evolution of a Protocol on specially protected areas and wildlife, signed in 1992 by all the States and territories of the Wider Caribbean, will lead to a significant growth in the total size of protected coastal areas.

Marine Protected Areas

Marine protected areas cover an even smaller surface area than coastal protected areas. It is possible that the boundaries between the one and the other is not quite clear; in any event, the distinction between the three types of protected areas that have been discussed is not formally established in any of the cases studied.

Venezuela reported the greatest expanse of marine protected areas with approximately 4,400 km^2; this is followed by Costa Rica with 3,100 km^2, Mexico with 2,300 km^2 and Colombia with a little under 700 km^2. At the other extreme, the Turks and Caicos Islands with 31, Antigua and Barbuda with 25, and Belize with 2 km^2, respectively.

The attractions mentioned are virtually the same as those specified for the coastal zones, except that there is great emphasis on sporting activities such as deep-sea diving and recreational fishing. Also highlighted were the whales in Colombia, and the marine prairies of Venezuela.

Non-protected Areas

There were very few responses to this question. One observation which could probably be generalized and applied to most of the countries and territories of the Wider Caribbean is that made by Belize which states that ecotourism-related activities take place in almost the entire country and that it would be very difficult to identify all the non-protected areas where this type of activity is carried out.

Frequency of Visitors and Areas most Visited

It was only necessary to answer this section of the survey if the section relating to protected and non-protected areas was not completed; the question was not always correctly interpreted.

Seven countries and territories provided no information on the frequency of visitors. Of those that did, only Costa Rica and the Dominican Republic provided some figures.

Costa Rica stated that 280 thousand local tourists and 318 thousand foreign tourists visited protected areas during 1992. The Dominican Republic estimated that some 389 thousand visits were made to areas of special interest such as islands with undeveloped beaches, cays and zones of high biodiversity and outstanding geological formations.

The other cases gave qualitative information on the frequency of visits. In Antigua and Barbuda, the areas most frequently visited were Devil's Bridge and some reefs. Guyana has a number of areas as designated tourist zones which are included in the packages offered to visitors and these are, consequently, the most frequently visited. Martinique points out that the attraction to which most visitors go is the ruins of St. Pierre, a city destroyed in 1902 by a volcanic eruption; the ruins were declared a part of the heritage of mankind. St. Vincent and the Grenadines noted that the areas most frequently visited were those most easily accessible (the Botanical Garden) or most promoted (waterfalls) or exceptionally appealing for excursions (cays). Surinam indicated that the areas most visited were those with natural attractions, indigenous to the country. On the other hand, Venezuela reported that the most frequently visited areas were those developed for ecotourism, the main attraction of which was wildlife, especially avifauna.

Institutions, Standards and Planning

The answers relating to these matters in the survey. None of the States and territories responding to the survey indicated economic policies affecting tourism or related activities, except for Guyana and St. Vincent and the Grenadines where reference was made to the existence of fiscal incentives for the expansion of tourism infrastructure, and Martinique where the economic policies of France apply to the territory.

Organizations Involved in Ecotourism

Generally speaking, the questions were aimed at identifying those organizations responsible for or with interest in the tourism sector and in environmental protection. It may be said that these organizations, in addition to being actively involved in the study, promotion and organization of ecotourism, have a "potential" vocation towards this activity which, sooner or later, will cause them to become more involved.

Nevertheless, a number of organizations are already developing activities relating to certain types of ecotourism. They are basically organizations responsible for administering protected areas and have an almost direct link to large contingents of tourists interested in visiting them and to various national non-governmental organizations and travel agencies.

Costa Rica has declared that there are several tourist agencies offering ecological tourism packages. Its National Parks Service is very involved in promoting ecotourism in some protected areas. In Mexico, several non-governmental organizations, as well as a governmental organization, the National Tourism Foundation, (FONATUR) are promoting ecotourism. In the Dominican Republic, the National Parks Administration created a Department of Ecotourism and there was at least one tourism agency specializing in ecotourism. In St. Vincent and the Grenadines, an advisory group on Ecotourism was established while in Suriname a company was formed to develop the tourist areas (METS) and it is believed that they are taking ecotourism aspects into consideration. In the

Turks and Caicos Islands, there are some non-governmental organizations involved in ecotourism while in Venezuela, several of these organizations as well as government agencies in the tourism sector have begun to develop ecotourism.

Criteria for Regulating Tourism and the Environment

Colombia, Costa Rica, Martinique (French standards), Mexico and Venezuela are the countries which possess the most developed legislative framework in the area of environmental protection. In the other States and territories responding to the survey, there are different legal bodies dealing with the question of the environment: it was difficult to determine the scope of these bodies from the answers to the survey.

In none of these responses were criteria aimed at regulating tourism activities mentioned. The Dominican Republic was the only country to make reference to a management plan developed in 1990 but never implemented. Furthermore, it is the only country which did not mention the existence of any legal instrument that addresses the protection of the environment. Colombia indicated a draft study of policies and guidelines for the development of ecotourism.

Planning

With the exception of Belize, Barbados, Martinique and St. Vincent and the Grenadines, the countries and territories reported the existence of various types of initiatives for integrating environmental protection, tourism and ecotourism into development plans.

The following are the most significant aspects relating to planning. Worthy of mention are those countries where ecotourism is an important element in the creation and management of protected areas (Colombia), in regional management plans (Costa Rica), in environmental management plans for coastal areas appropriate for tourism (Mexico), in the incorporation of environmental protection into plans for tourism development, management, plans for parks, among other initiatives (Dominican Republic), into management plans for physical, insular and tourism development (Turks and Caicos) and in the Sustainable

Development Plan for Tourism and Recreation in the Amazon (Venezuela).

The responses also contained references to plans for developing areas where ecotourism would be an important element. The following initiatives are worthy of mention: the development of a Marine Reserve for Birds and a Wildlife Sanctuary in Antigua and Barbuda; the national evolutionary conservation strategy of Barbados; the identification and study in Colombia of protected areas where ecotourism could be vital for regional development; a plan for the Guanacaste conservation zone in Costa Rica; designation of areas with conditions appropriate for ecotourism within the context of the Mexican government's environmental management plans; the development of certain areas in the Dominican Republic where private-sector ecotourism would be the main focus; studies on cays in St. Vincent and the Grenadines; the identification of certain protected areas for ecotourism (Suriname) and; plans for an integrally-planned environmental tourism centre in Venezuela.

Current Status of Ecotourism

The responses to the survey questions relating to priority requirements for the development or sustainability of ecotourism, to local facilities and/or experience in the area of training for ecotourism and to the achievements or shortcomings of ecotourism.

Priority Requirements

The survey identifies nine factors likely to contribute to the development or sustainability of ecotourism as well as the need to establish an order of priority among them. Those factors likely to be given the highest priority (Nos. 1, 2 and 3 in the hierarchy were selected and are present. The following are the factors that were given the highest priority by the countries and territories which responded to the survey. The number of times that the factor was selected is also indicated:

* Infrastructure 7
* Qualified personnel 6
* Institutions 5
* Hotel facilities 4

* Legislation 4
* Incentives 3
* Transport/communication 3
* Information 2

It may be observed that the factors "infrastructure", "qualified personnel" and "institutional structure" were most frequently chosen as priority factors for the development or sustainability of ecotourism. These were followed by the factors "hotel facilities" and "legislation", which were given equal weight; then by "incentives" and "transport and communication". Finally, the factor "information" was mentioned in only two cases.

Local Facilities and Experience in Each Country for Training in Ecotourism

Countries and territories were asked whether or not they possessed adequate infrastructure or experience to train persons in ecotourism, whether they foresaw future demand in this area and if they were planning to carry out training programmes in ecotourism. Five countries did not respond to this survey item; of those that did, the responses were varied. Antigua and Barbuda, Bahamas, Colombia, Mexico and St. Vincent and the Grenadines reported that they possessed neither the necessary facilities nor local experience locally to train their staff in ecotourism. Costa Rica and Venezuela, on the other hand, have the necessary experience and local facilities to provide training in ecotourism. All seven agreed, however, that there was a growing demand for training. Turks and Caicos did not respond either to the question regarding facilities and experience for training nor to possible future demand for training. In the case of the Bahamas, Colombia, Costa Rica, Mexico and Venezuela, there are plans for training in ecotourism. There are no such plans in Antigua and Barbuda or in St. Vincent and the Grenadines. Turks and Caicos recognizes that training is a necessity and that this need could be satisfied through in-house seminars.

Achievements and Failures of Ecotourism

No responses were received from Antigua and Barbuda, Bahamas, Belize, Guyana, Martinique or Surinam. Those countries that did respond to this question, however, generally did not refer to geography.

In three cases, Barbados, Colombia and Mexico, success was linked to fairly specific aspects, the most important of which is conservation. It was pointed out that ecotourism has given greater value to conservation activities has won greater respect for the natural and cultural environment, and has increased public awareness. The countries also indicated that ecotourism has encouraged activities aimed at protecting certain species. On the other hand, among the successes attributed to ecotourism are the diversification of the tourism industry, the popularization of conservationist values, economic benefits to local communities and certain programmes for assisting indigenous communities.

Costa Rica considers that the achievements that may be attributed to ecotourism are not yet evident in that country. Turks and Caicos, which considers its tourism to be 100% ecotourism, warns of the risks associated with that activity. St. Vincent and the Grenadines, as well as Venezuela, list among achievements, acceptance of or interest in this activity.

With regard to the failures associated with ecotourism, responses to the survey were quite varied. Barbados, as well as Turks and Caicos, pointed to the risk of degradation caused by visitor overload. Colombia has indicated out that these failures are linked to poor management of tourism on the part of institutions and a lack of adequate planning. Costa Rica and Mexico have reported no failures linked to this activity. St. Vincent and the Grenadines has cited instances in which the activity led to the displacement of a local community. Venezuela declared that its failures were linked to lack of resources available to the organization responsible for the management of national parks.

The Challenges to Sustainability in Island Tourism

Islands are special places with a natural attraction for tourists and a special challenge to sustainability. The thousands of islands on the face of the earth include some of the finest and most sought after destinations, such as the Balearic Islands, the Hawaiian Islands, the Galapagos Islands, the Canary Islands, the French Polynesian Islands, and the Caribbean islands. The mystique associated with islands is dependent on a blend of different lifestyles, indigenous cultures, unique land formations, flora and fauna, and ocean and coastal resources. To keep that mystique alive and thriving, islands must implement sustainable tourism policies in all areas including environmental, economic and socio-cultural. This paper will examine the unique challenges that islands face as they attempt to build sustainability into their tourism development policies. It will also propose policies to assist in attaining and maintaining quality island tourism.

Types of Island Tourism Destinations

Islands vary in many ways, and understanding the various types clarifies for the decision-makers the policies that need to be used. One classification is islands' climate which can be cold, temperate or tropical. Even though tropical islands (Caribbean, Hawaii, French Polynesia) tend to have most allure for tourists, cold and temperate islands also have environmental or cultural features and lifestyles that attract tourism– for example the Shetland islands off the coast of Scotland. Baum 1997 describes the general attractivity of North Atlantic islands, including their remoteness, their small size, the slower pace of life, the chance to go back-in-time, the wilderness environment, the water-focused society and the sense of difference yet fam. Very cold islands such as Iceland and Greenland offer unique landscapes and flora and fauna and are alternate destinations often attracting scientists, photographers and other specialized travellers. Another island classification is the proximity to the related mainland and also its size. Islands that are more remote and distant face more challenging accessibility and transportation issues due to their isolation. Visitors will tend to stay longer in islands that are remote and larger, whereas those close to the mainland and smaller may experience more excursionist tourism. For example, Cousin Island in the Seychelles, hosts only day visitors that leave the island at the end of each day. The island's choice to host excursionists versus stay-over visitors requires a careful evaluation of the strengths and weaknesses of each type of tourism.

A third classification is whether an island is a single island or part of an archipelago. Multi-destination travel in island chains may be an added attraction for tourists, whereas the peace, or 'sun, sand, sea' experience of a single island vacation may be the choice for others. Cooperative marketing and complementary product development is important for archipelago islands. This will create a diverse touristic experience giving archipelagos an advantage over single islands, particularly if they are small.

A fourth classification is the governance of the island destination. Some islands have autonomous governments and others are part of the mainland government system. Those with autonomy have more control over the direction of sustainable development of the island.

They are also more likely to reap the maximum economic benefits from tourism, without any revenue being leaked to the mainland through taxes and other means. Islands under the jurisdiction of the mainland need to ensure adequate representation in the government decision-making.

Fifth, some island destinations have growing resident populations (which may be due in part to tourism) and other with weak economies are experiencing declining populations. In the latter case, there is a special need to ensure economic viability to prevent the out-migration of residents – especially young ones who look for opportunities elsewhere. Some islands, of course, have no human population and are simply nature-reserves, and others are privately owned with their own policies.

The last classification relates to the homogeneity of the population and the socio-cultural sustainability of island destinations. Islands with homogeneous, indigenous populations are particularly vulnerable to tourism development since they have different cultures with different values than the source markets. The close interaction that islands create between hosts and guests must be managed. Islands with more heterogeneous populations may be more resilient to socio-cultural impacts.

It is clear from the categories above that islands differ in many ways from the mainland and from each other. Each island has its uniqueness and that uniqueness needs to be nurtured and strengthened through sustainable tourism policies. The next section will examine the specific issues and problems that islands face in sustainable tourism development.

Sustainability Issues Facing Island Destinations

Many researchers have studied tourism in an island context. Some of these studies relate to specific islands (Malta, Briguglio and Briguglio, 2002, Seychelles, Shah 2002, French Polynesia, Salvat and Pailhe 2002, Boracay Island, Philippines, Trousdale, 1999, Canary Islands, Gil, 2003, Hawaiian Islands, Sheldon et al. 2005) and others address island tourism in a general, conceptual manner. All islands must address issues of economic impact, environmental consequences and those relating to the social, cultural and political fabric of the island all of which are affected by the density of tourism on the island. High tourist and resident densities in islands such as Malta are the source of many sustainability problems and carrying capacity needs to be considered.

Measures of tourism density are important for policy makers to assess possible growth scenarios. One measure of tourism density or saturation, which considers all three areas of impact is the Tourism Penetration Index (TPI). TPI includes three variables: 1) visitor spending per capita of population (economic measure), 2) average daily visitors per 1000 population (social measure), and 3) hotel rooms per square kilometre of land (environmental measure) (McElroy and Albuquerque, 1998). McElroy and Albuquerque used this to cluster Caribbean islands into different clusters depending on whether their TPI is low, intermediate or high value. McElroy notes that for islands with low TPI's the most important challenges are establishing profitability and international recognition, for those with intermediate TPI controlling growth is the most important, and for those islands with the highest TPI the greatest challenge is to sustain vacation quality. The next sections will address the economic, environmental and socio-cultural challenges faced by islands in their quest to sustainability.

Economic Issues

A challenge to the economic health of an island is the often limited economic resource base. Islands may have few resources or viable industries other than tourism to provide revenue and employment for the local population. The value of agricultural and mining commodities on the international markets is declining and fishing is less reliable as fish populations are being depleted, and global warming is changing the nature of coastlines and fish movements. Tourism can be an economic catalyst for small island development. In fact, Croes (2004) suggests tourism as a tool for small islands to enlarge their economies and overcome the disadvantages of smallness. The extra market demand produces economies of scale and increases efficiency and decreases costs of production. Tourism also increases competition, encourages new start-up businesses, democratizes market structure, and deters rent-seeking behaviours and corruption. He also argues that this competition can provide greater consumer choice, trade openness and increase the quality of life for residents.

Despite this, the revenue form tourism must remain in the island economy as much as possible. Policies of import substitution to ensure minimum economic leakages, and 'buy local' policies to maximize linkages are essential. Taxation policies, entrepreneurial subsidies, and investment incentives are all useful to strengthen the economy. If development strategies are such that the incoming wealth is leaving the island economy, tourism needs to be re-designed. Islands under the governance of the mainland need to ensure a fair share of tax revenue due. Islands under their own governance will gain most economically.

Seasonality in island tourism is another challenge to the economic sustainability of the island and the well-being of the island people. Fluctuations in visitor arrivals must be understood and mitigated through product and market diversification so that employment stabilizes and tourism infrastructures and superstructures are well utilized. Escalating land prices represent another economic concern in islands forcing local residents out of the housing market. This promotes out migration, leading to a possible dissolution of the culture, and second home ownership by foreigners. These trends if unmitigated can generate a serious chain of problems for the island economy.

Environmental Issues

Environmental issues of sustainability on islands are multi-faceted, since islands have diverse land formations, coastal areas, and wildlife species. Tourism often contributes to the environmental degradation in small, island states which are host to fragile ecosystems rich in biodiversity. The isolation of the island environment created the biodiversity, and by opening to tourism, some of that sheltered biodiversity is endangered. Islands' prime tourist environmental resource is often the coastal regions (beaches, sand dunes, coral reefs) that are easily damaged, heavily used, and requiring of careful visitor management. The large amount of waste (solid and liquid) created by tourism is a problem since space for its disposal on islands is limited.

Socio-Cultural Issues

Islands face complex socio-cultural issues, particularly those with indigenous populations. Tourism on islands, particularly small ones, brings hosts and guests into closer contact than on mainland destinations, creating a more vulnerable situation for social disruption. Crime, commoditization of culture, and loss of traditional lifestyles, moral standards and family life impact islands more than mainland destinations. Studies of resident sentiment and response to tourism in the islands of Malta and Hawaii (2003, Sheldon et al 2005) show the importance of this component. Community integration is key to successful and sustainable tourism development, meaning that all islanders affected by tourism must be involved in the planning process. Stakeholders on islands are not only in closer proximity but also have long histories of conflict making it even more important to involve them in the decision-making process.

Approaches to Overcome the Challenges to Island Tourism

The experience of many island destinations over the years has provided a rich source of policies that can assist with sustainability on all levels. The next section presents examples of some of these policies.

Long-term, Stakeholder-involved Planning

Long term planning, developed with comprehensive community and stakeholder input is becoming and important foundation for tourism on islands. Plans also need to be values-based plans and reflect the indigenous culture and traditions. Long range planning must consider the balance of supply and demand of tourism, both quantitatively and qualitatively. A study of tourism in the Canary Islands showed that when these two growth patterns were out of balance the industry is not healthy. Once the plans have been put in place, methodologies to measure and monitor impacts of tourism are essential. This requires the assignment of government agencies to the task of ongoing monitoring of effects.

The need for stakeholder-driven planning and indicator development is essential. In Hawaii for example, a process that covered almost two years brought together stakeholders to define their vision, goals and indicators for sustainable tourism. Community involvement to guide tourism planning, development, management, research and evaluation of community-based tourism projects has been implemented in Taquile Island in Peru. On this island, decision-making powers, local control and ownership, and type of employment patterns were measure of community involvement in the planning process.

Empowerment of the Island Community and Culture

Empowerment of the island community and culture is a necessary part of planning. Frameworks to protect and conserve the social and cultural structure are important also. A building of cultural pride through story-telling and memory of traditions, and a sense of identity are paramount.

This may involve the re-enlivenment of festivals, arts, language, folk lore and policies to encouraging local people to engage in entrepreneurial activities. Efforts towards sustainable tourism in French Polynesian islands found the meaningful integration of culture into the tourist experience difficult to accomplish. Achieving a balance of respect for the culture and providing tourists with the opportunity to learn about and appreciate the culture is the core of the challenge

Tourist and resident education are a critical part of island sustainability. To empower the residents education and training programs are needed for meaningful careers in the industry. This may involve distance education since islands do not always have comprehensive tertiary education programs in tourism. Residents also need to learn about the impact tourism is having on their community, through the sharing of statistics and facts. The receptivity and openness to change and innovation is also needed. Education for tourists is also important. They need to learn about the unique cultural and environmental features of the island and appropriate behaviours.

Environmental Management

Given the challenges to the island's ecosystems, environmental management is crucial for island sustainability. The paucity of land causes land usage issues, and the trade-off of land for tourism versus agriculture and other industries, or preservation and conservation needs to be addressed. The environmental resources are a main visitor attraction and tourist interfaces with those resources need to be planned and cared for. Conlin, 2002 in a study of Tasmania tourism, gives nine different types of parks or reserves that can be created (national park, state reserve, nature reserve, game reserve, conservation area, nature recreational area, regional reserve, historic site and private sanctuary). This may include designation of zones that are off-limits to tourists, and those that are only visitable with guides and interpreters. Islands with unique wildlife must also take steps to sustain those populations.

Tourism can actually assist as an anti-poaching mechanism and an engine for conservation management when residents realize the economic value of the wildlife as in the Seychelles. Policies to keep the land and ocean unpolluted are also necessary. Waste management and recycling programs are essential, particularly on small islands. Also the use, through incentive programs if necessary, for alternative fuel sources will make the destination more sustainable. The shortage of land for landfills may need waste to be sent to the mainland for some islands. Recycling programs for all types of waste are essential, and the use of alternative energy sources (wind, solar, geothermal) is an important consideration since tourists use much higher per capita user of energy than locals and rarely can islands survive on fossil fuels. Water shortages also are common on islands, limiting the amount of tourism development. Environmental management includes recovery from natural disasters to which islands are so vulnerable. Disasters such as tidal waves, volcanic eruptions, cyclones, drought and rise in sea level are all natural hazards that islands face. Funds for conservation and disaster management are needed and can be gained through taxation, visitor fees or other mechanisms.

Visitor Management

Visitor impact is so much greater on islands, requiring tools of visitor management to ensure island sustainability. Control of numbers of tourist arrivals is possible through the methods of transportation. Once the tourists arrive on the island they need information and guidance on possible attractions, tours and events. One method of visitor management is the zoning of land for different uses, and the creation of national parks and conservation areas to conserve historic sites, biological and geological diversity, preserve water quality, and to encourage education. The management of visitors on coral reefs is another issue of environmental management faced by many islands such as Hawaii and the French Polynesian islands.

Clear signage, information and interpretive information assist the tourists in finding and understanding the attractions. Guides, rangers, wardens and other staff can guide tourists through delicate environments. The recognition that visitors seek education and knowledge of species and land formations requires good interpretative systems. The private sector such as tour operators need guidelines for places that are off-limits or have restricted access. The Galapagos archipelago with its unique biodiversity had to use visitor management techniques due to the large volume of visitors (including scientists, writers, photographers) wanting to see the nature reserves. They attempted to control tour operators by asking them to adhere to cruise itineraries fixed by the national parks however that has not been totally successful. Standards and certification for employee performance particularly in the tour-guiding arena will help with the interpretation and sustainability of the island.

Knowledge and Information Systems

Knowledge and information systems can help islands market their tourism product and also manage their tourist resources. Web-based marketing by the public sector and by private suppliers helps islands locate and target the market segments they want, and reduces the reliance on tour operators. Destination management systems with comprehensive product databases and other information to assist and educate the potential tourist are an important competitive tools in the matching of tourist and island experience. Because islands are smaller, it may be easier to install location specific technologies and databases and data communication systems. These could include mobile visitor information systems, geographic information systems (GIS) mapping systems, global positioning systems (GPS), and intelligent transportation systems. GIS system scombine data and spatial information to help planners conduct spatial analysis of touristic areas. They have been used for example in the Cayman Islands to assess the impact of tourism on fragile reefs and in China for disaster monitoring using remote sensing data. Location specific information can be displayed on hand-held devices to assist travellers in their knowledge of the destination and its attractions. They also can keep visitors on appropriate routes through warning messages, and can direct visitors' attention to an item or species of interest.

The placement of GPS devices on wildlife may increase visitors' chances of viewing the species. The use of GPS devices on tourists can help to rescue them from dangerous situations in the ocean, the mountains or other wilderness areas. Information technology can support the planning and stakeholder involvement processes on islands. For example, expert systems which simulate the knowledge-base of an expert can be used to facilitate decision making for sustainable tourism. Groupware can be applied to build stakeholder consensus, and the Internet is a valuable resource to gain community input from residents in remote communities.

Accessibility and Transportation

Accessibility and transportation to island communities is an important area of policy for islands. Different transportation modes both to the island and on the island are usually necessary, and can be used as a control mechanism for how many tourists visit the island. The security, safety and costs of such transportation are also important considerations. The balance of public and private transport use by tourists is a policy variable. Once tourists use their own transportation (hire car, motorbicycle), the control of their activities on the island is drastically reduced. Some islands prohibit motorized vehicles in certain areas, others suggest the use of electrical vehicles that are quieter and less pollutive. Air transportation to islands is most common, however it leaves islands vulnerable to stoppage of flights due to strikes, terrorism etc., and vulnerable to high fares if there is little competition on the route. It also requires the use of land for airports. The low-cost carriers that serve many European island destinations today is fuelling growth in second homes since owners can travel very cheaply to their island property. With out this cheap form of transportation, the development of a second home tourism market is in jeopardy.

The ocean is a natural option for transportation – both functional and recreational. Yachts, boats and ferries of different types are useful to transport the visitors from island to island. In the Hawaiian Islands a high-speed ferry between the islands is being added to provide additional capacity to the inter-island flights. Large cruise ships, and their interest in island ports-of-call, make expansion of island tourism a distinct possibility. The large 2,500 berth cruise ships are potential sources of extra visitors, however they bring with them needs and impacts that may not always be in the best interests of the sustainability of the island. Accessibility to the island also includes data, voice and fax communications and credit card use. These are necessary for a destination to function well.

Marketing and Market Diversification

Marketing and market diversification is important for islands. Markets may be domestic or international, but the match between island facilities and resources and the tourist is the most important consideration. Domestic markets are likely to create less socio-cultural disturbance and may therefore be preferred. When defining market segments, islands often try to identify niches to generate the highest expenditure for the island, as was done in the Canary Islands. Hawaii's Strategic Plan 2005-2010 has a similar focus on the quality visitor and focuses on expenditures and length of stay in its marketing plans. Product innovation to match those segments and the extension of the life cycle for island tourism products are important components of island tourism marketing. The development of niche markets based on the islands resources is an important market strategy. For example in Tasmania, Australia, they focused on agricultural based tourist activities such as farm-stays, agricultural museums, wineries, and other activities based on crops such as lavender and raspberries (Conlin, 2002). Some islands with very popular and delicate attractions may choose to practice de-marketing of sites that are over visited. The type of infrastructure and superstructure that the island invests in will also determine the type of tourists that come. For example, the building of only luxury hotels in French Polynesia attracted only high-income visitors. Many islands are famous for the "sun, sand and sea" image and may want to diversify their product to attract a different type of tourist, for 'sun, sea and sand' can be found in many islands.

Summary

This paper has identified some of the challenges facing islands in sustaining their tourism industry. It has also recommended some policies and approaches to assist in this area. Each island is unique and has unique attributes. The challenge to sustainable management is to keep those unique elements that are part of the mystique that attracts tourists. Shifts toward homogeneity of tourism experiences without giving the visitor an experience of 'sense of place' will not be sustainable in the long run either for the host community or for the tourism markets.

Understanding Tourist Beaches as Eco-social Landscapes

Now coral reefs are not merely pretty,...of much greater consequence is their vital importance of protecting our shores, this may not be generally realised. We had a nice example of this in Barbados recently when a certain hotel, in order to improve its beach facilities, bulldozed a certain piece of inshore reef to make a "white hole" for bathing. Although the area removed was perhaps only 20 x 30 yards, the consequent change in wave action resulted not only in the removal of the sandy beach previously existing but also the knocking down of the sea wall of the hotel itself. So here we have a very close ecological connection between tourism and the natural environment.

While tourism development can have significant affects on environments, much of the critical scholarship on tourism and its affects on local places has focused upon social impacts. Scholars such as sociologists Chris Rojek and John Urry (1997) have approached tourism as a specifically cultural process, while others, such as anthropologist Ian Munt (1994a; 1994b) have written ethnographies of "the toured". The political economy of wealth flows from developing world destinations to developed world capital and its local effects was insightfully described by Stephen Britton. While such work is vital to understanding tourism development as a social practice, the human-environment tradition in geography mandates a synthesis of social *and ecological* processes as they interact in place and across space.

The importance of environments to tourism has been acknowledged in the tourism literature. As noted by researchers working in the tropical Pacific, and in the Caribbean, the environmental effects of tourism can be especially significant on small islands. Though Edington and Edington recognized the need for better understandings of ecological processes that closely interact with tourism in 1986, Hall and Page have recently lamented the continuing poverty of such understandings.

Antigua, a small island in the West Indies provides a good illustration of how tourism might affect environments and environments affect tourism, and how we might understand and manage those interactions more effectively for all concerned. With nearly one-half million visitors spending approximately $250 million each year, tourism is vital to Antigua's formal economy. The industry employs over half of the Antiguan labour force, generates a per capita GDP of US$7,500, and is responsible for sixty percent of the island's gross domestic product issues directly from the (ABDT 1996; ABMF 1996; EU-ACP 1996; Courier 1997, 36; Gortier 1997, 32). Antiguan tourism is focused upon its beaches to an extreme degree. Over 95 percent of all hotel rooms are in beach resorts. Antigua has little night life, few heritage tourism sites, and minimal shopping venues outside its duty-free mall at the base of a relatively new cruise ship quay. Antigua is know for and promoted as a place for quiet and/or romantic beach vacations. Peter Ramrattan, the head of Antigua's Hotel and Tourism Association characterized the island's tourist clientele as the "newly wed and the nearly dead" (1997). Though now adding "The heart of the Caribbean" to the Antiguan brand, the slogan "365 powdery white sand beaches... one for every day of the year" has been used for decades (AHTA 1996, 31).

The social construction of beaches as tourism places has been well explored generally in Corbin (1994), Lencek and Bosker (1998), and Shields (1990). The relationship between Antigua's coastal environment and the governance of tourism development has been complex and highly problematic. I have described these conflictual social processes specific to Antigua's beaches elsewhere and refer the reader to discussions for further background. While those social processes are central to the dialectic amongst Antiguan coasts and their users, the physical condition of the coast has recently become equally worthy of consideration. In 1996, it became clear that Antigua's beaches were eroding (AHTA 1997, 3; CCA 1991; COSALC 1996; UPR 1994); the environmental basis of Antigua's national tourism economy was disappearing into the Caribbean.

As in many developing world economies, tourism development in Antigua is a project dominated by the national government and foreign investors. In Antigua the government is also charged with, and is the only agent capable of caring for common lands and resources such as its beaches. Also typical of landscapes caught up in the extensification and intensification of economic activity (i.e. development), the Antiguan government has not responded effectively to environmental degradation and so beach erosion now threatens the well being of Antigua and its people.

The goal of this paper is *not* to analyze the problem of beach erosion; we have outlined the socio-ecology of erosion carefully elsewhere. Rather, my interest here is to elaborate a conceptual framework that tourism planners could use generally in their address of human-environment relations. This is not a wholly original project. Concern over environmental degradation at the behest of economic development has spawned many venerable projects aimed at preserving or conserving valued environments. In order to learn from what has gone before, we review three different attempts at developing tools for planning development that have been especially relevant in tourism management in the developing world: these are sustainable development, indicators of environmental health, and what Harris and Nelson refer to as "whole economy analysis" (1993). In that discussion we identify some of the aims and strengths of each, and some of the problematic assumptions that weaken their ability to integrate environmental with social processes.

Antigua serves as a robust illustration for such a review. In the third section I develop a tourism planning paradigm that encompasses formal, informal, and ecological economies, as well as the interaction between those economies. In the fourth section I apply that planning framework to Antigua's situation today and use it to make concrete recommendations that might more effectively address their beach erosion problem.

Alternative Paradigms for Managing Tourism Environments

There are several alternative paradigms tourism planners may turn to as they seek to mediate the environmental impacts of tourism development. Sustainable development, environmental indicators, and "whole economies" have all been recommended. While each of these planning frameworks seek to integrate economy with ecology, each have inherent problems in their application to tourism-environment relations generally and in Antigua in particular. These problems are important because they suggest areas that any new paradigm must improve upon.

Sustainable Development

Sustainable development, first formalized by the Brundtland Commission in *Our Common Future* (1987) describes one of the most institutionalized and far ranging attempts to mitigate the ill effects of economic development upon environments. Sustainable development arose from the conservation movement's encounter with free market economics. Because mainstream economics recognizes only matters valued in markets, it does not encompass many concerns dear to conservationists and a host of others. Matters valued outside of markets, whether it be child-caring in and for a household, human appreciation of natural beauty, water filtered and made more useful by a wetland, or nitrogen fixed in soil by clover: all are considered external to economy. The Brundtland Commission prescribed the internalization of economic externalities. Though appealing, the prescription is problematic, as it would require nothing less than "a restructuring of national politics, economic, bureaucracy, ... and a new system of international trade and finance".

Adams observes that the concepts of sustainable development *have been* helpful in "laying out principles for peasant agriculture, or expounding the benefits of appropriate technology and the importance of indigenous value systems and technical knowledge" (ibid, 57). For tourism development, sustainability has been useful for ecotourism and forms that Poon has categorized as "new tourism" (1993). Such tourism uses "wilderness" or "authentic" cultural landscapes as their primary product. However, because its scope and scale is necessarily small, "new tourism" cannot serve as a development pole for a national economy. It is mass tourism that has served as a growth pole for the national economies of many small island states, and it is mass tourism that must concern the planners in places like Antigua where the tourism industry has already matured. Preservationism is equally problematic. In Antigua not only is there little beach wilderness left to preserve, but where they persist they often do not conform to tourism ideals of a beach paradise and must be significantly changed, sand and palms imported, wetlands drained, gardens and accommodations built.

Environmental Indicators and Planning for Sustainability

Some have suggested that the solution to environmental impacts lies in better monitoring through environmental indicators. As Hughes observes, the idiom of sustainable development has turned to the certainty promised by scientific quantification in understanding environmental relations; yet indicators are often poor windows into complex biospheric processes (2002, 458). Many political ecologists have problematized one-dimensional indicators. In a critique of using "indicators" to manage reef health in tourism areas, Butler notes that visitor declines are among the most common indicators of non-sustainability, and that in "many cases such indicators come too late for satisfactory remedial action, even if that had been possible" (1993, 39). As Hall and Page assert, index driven technical fixes often maintain the appearance of normalcy while environmental degradation continues (1999, 52). The number of tourist visits, for example, may be poor indicator of environmental sustainability. In Antigua, technical fixes such as beach nourishment address the symptom of beach erosion, but not the cause.

Tourists see no problem, but more careful surveys indicate that beaches are eroding and that the coralgal community that both provides sediment inputs and moderates wave energies is in decline. Simultaneously, those very fixes are further degrading the coralgal communities that once produced beach berms so valued in the tourism industry. Antigua's case demonstrates the inefficacy of environmental indicators. Though beach erosion and coral decline have been documented, those indicators have not successfully directed scientific management in an address of the underlying problems. To address the problem in a sustainable way, one must also understand why the coralgal community is dying, one must understand holistically why the reefs are dying, and what ill affect tourism has on the production of the beaches it values so much.

Whole Economies?

Where sustainable development fails by dichotomizing humans from nature, relying upon rational management, technical fixes, and insufficient environmental indicators, the authors of "whole economy" frameworks attempt to bridge the divide between the "conditions of production" (nature and not-for-market human production) and production for exchange. The efficacy of the paradigm is illustrated by Harris and Nelson (1993) who apply a "whole economy" approach specifically to planning for tourism development in Pangandaran, Indonesia.

The authors describe an "ABC Resource Survey Method" which encompasses abiotic elements (A); biotic elements (B); and cultural elements (C). Though the method sounds hopefully holistic, the A and B portion of their "whole economy" unfortunately are treated as inert spatial "resources" to be mapped and valued for their appeal to human "appreciation for nature" (ibid, 184). Unlike traditional economics, such substantivist economic frameworks do seek to encompass *all* human production—from businesses, governments, collectives, voluntary activities, mutual aid, and households. However, whole economies are anthropocentric, and do not include *non-human* production. Thus, the human-nature dichotomy, with its attendant problems for understanding human-environment relations remains.

Problems with Management

These alternative techno and econo-centric paradigms share a fundamental and problematic model of environments as mechanistic and passive. No dialectic between human and other biospheric systems is allowed or imagined possible. However, environments are not immune to human use. They respond and change to human activity as they do to all disturbances. In Antigua, developers have treated beaches as passive or dead objects which are motivated by physical forces. Beach erosion, therefore, has been categorized as an engineering problem whose solution lays in moving sand from artificial jetties, reef bottoms, and Antigua's sister island, Barbuda, and deposited in front of resorts. However, in the long term, this techno-centric management has only exacerbated the problem of beach erosion. In order to understand beach erosion it is important to understand beaches. Briefly, throughout the insular tropics, most beach sand is biogenic, i.e. it is produced by living organisms. Such beaches are primarily composed of the accumulated bodies of calcium carbonate fixing corals and micro-algae (hereafter referred to as *coralgal* communities), and free floating foraminifera living in the reef environment. Wave action breaks those calciferous bodies and moves them across the sea floor, often depositing them on shore where they form beach berms. In addition to supplying sand to beaches, these living communities create sea floor roughness that works to moderate erosive wave energies. Coralgal communities thus produce and maintain beaches.

Dredging sand from off-shore reefs for beach nourishment is problematic to this process on several counts. Dredging physically destroys portions of these living sand sources. In addition, dredging mobilizes fine sediments that can require years to sequester. Those fine sediments hurt coralgal communities in several ways. They cause turbidity that decreases photosynthesis and growth both among the tiny palm tree shaped Halimeda alga and the zooanthellae alga that live symbiotically in coral polyps. When the fine sediments do settle, they can mantle micro-alga and corals, neither of which have the ability to uncover themselves. Finally, when fine sands are deposited upon beaches they are easily re-mobilized by wave action and move back over the coralgal community. Nourishment can increase turbidity and degrade coralgal communities for years.

Beaches are the by-product of a living community, a community that, like all life, is directed toward, and interested in its own perpetuation. When its life-activity is disrupted, its vitality diminishes. Beaches and the living non-human communities that produce them cannot be treated as passive physical elements. They can be managed, but they must be managed in a way that recognizes their self-interestedness in their own persistence.

New Conceptual Tools

Planning for sustainable development could be made more effective by changing two conceptual fields, both of which arise from assumptions that humans and non-humans are essentially different.

As Costanza, Wainger, and Bockstael (1995) observe, research into *systems* tends to dichotomize our worlds into economic or ecological models. Ecological models tend to include humans only as exogenous disturbances and economic models rend to reduce ecology to a set of constraints. In that rubric, "the studies are completed using different terms and units of measurement, and the studies neglect to account for the interaction between the processes and populations" (ibid, 45). A category is needed that is capable of encompassing all production, all value. Wealth, broadly conceived as all matters valued by living beings can provide such a category. I refer to work by Pierre Bourdieu to formalize wealth as a category that is both useful in making sustainable planning policy and encompasses formal, informal, and non-human production.

Secondly, ecological systems are not well described as passive or as mechanically manageable. Through a more careful examination of beach erosion in Antigua the value of conceptualizing non-human communities as active and self-interested can be made apparent. Towards that end, I refer to evolutionary biologist Mae-Won Ho's (1993) development of "coherence" as a pragmatic way to understand biospheric dialectics.

Wealth

To re-conceptualize wealth in a way that seeks similarities between humans and other life, it is helpful to categorize wealth by what it does, rather than what it is. Such a categorization leads to two propositions: first, broadly defined, wealth is anything that has value to some valuing entity; and second, wealth is inessential matter its value is relative and its form is changed by living beings into other forms. Though one cannot ask non-humans what they value, valuing can be observed empirically by watching for choice. Coral polyps, for example, differentially anchor to surfaces that are more sunny than those that are less so. In that practice they demonstrate choice, and therefore valuing. Corals value sunlight because the *zooanthellae* algae that live behind a thin transparent membrane covering the hard calciferous surface of the polyps' shell produce carbohydrates through photosynthesis. Corals depend upon those carbohydrates as a necessary source of food. In their life-activity, the *zooanthellae* transform sunlight, water, and nutrients (some of which are the by-product of the corals' life-activity) into food. Corals with their *zooanthellae* symbiants, and micro-alga like *Halimeda,* transform matters they value, sunlight, water, dissolved nutrients, into matters that they value even more, carbohydrates and other metabolites. Reflecting human exceptionalist assumptions of his time, Marx defines this activity as the labour process: "purposeful activity aimed at the production of use-values. It is an appropriation of what exists in nature for the requirements of man" (1976, 290). If one is willing to grant non-humans the ability to value their own production, the word "man" could accurately be replaced with "life" with interesting implications for Marxist theory.

In 1847, James Joule did characterize this transformative process. He observed that in life-activity, as something is quantitatively consumed, it is simultaneously qualitatively transformed. As life is distinct in its self-organization, life is also marked by its intentional transformation of energy into matter and information, into energy and matter, and matter into energy and information. All fit into the category of wealth, which is understood functionally as matters useful to life in its drive to extend itself in time and space.

Bourdieu formalized this same transformative process in human/social activity. In his research into social exchange and its interaction with *knowledge,* Bourdieu endeavored "to grasp capital and profit in all their forms and to establish the laws whereby the different types of capital (or power, which amounts to the same thing) change one into the other" (1986, 243). Bourdieu demonstrated that people "trans-substantiate," i.e. transform or exchange, one capital into or for another (ibid). Our categories of power, knowledge and money are explicitly *inessential* in that they have no intrinsic, immutable, or universal quality. Bourdieu explained that through our life-activity people produce and transform wealths as needed (Bourdieu 1984, 1986; also Shilling 1993, 127). We accumulate knowledge, associations, power, and money which help us to be appropriate and effective in various situations. He asserted that we then invest available wealths of one sort into other forms of wealth as needed. Raymond Williams (1980) has forcefully argued that the by-products of life activity also have agency in the biosphere and may act to degrade or destroy wealths. After Gallagher (1989) I adopt the term "illth" to refer to matters which destroy or diminish various forms of wealth.

Coherence as a New Spatial Metaphor

As "embodied selves," we are complex wealth transforming and wealth managing mechanisms. Through and in our physical being, we organize stores and flows of power, knowledge, and money. We transform one into the other as needed according to our abilities. In this life activity we are very much like a plant transforming sunlight, nutrients into material wealth in accordance with genetic and environmental information. Humans do what life does. All life organizes flows and accumulates stores of wealth. Through their activity living beings transforms each of these inessential categories of wealth into the other.

This basic process of wealth acquisition, transformation and use-value production suggests a spatiality that does not conform to dominant spatial metaphors people use to understand living beings or their life activity. Though not the sort of thing most people think about in their daily lives, a debate regarding the nature of our existence—are we object as Parmenides argued, or in accord with Heraclitus are we process, or as Nagarjuna suggests, are we neither or both—extends at least to the fourth century BCE. Though proponents argue for mutual exclusivity, both seem to be true at once. One's hand is clearly a solid object in space capable of moving other objects. Yet, its substance is in flux. Very few of the atoms that originally constituted one's hand are still there. New material is constantly flowing into place as the old leaves. Forty years ago, biologist Clifford Grobstein observed this quality of life as an explicitly spatial phenomenon.

Despite this *constant turnover of energy and materials,* there is a net increase in the mass of the complexes at higher levels of structure. Even more remarkable than this is that *continuity of properties* is preserved in the large molecule complexes.

Life is characterized by consistent form, constituted by flows, organized into ever greater complexity. 28 Social scientist Michel Foucault describes the spatiality of entities in a similar fashion, suggesting that "the living being wraps itself in its own existence ... and constitutes itself as a new space" (1970, 278). The space life creates of itself is an "interior one of anatomical coherences and physiological compatibilities, and the exterior one of the elements in which it resides and of which it forms its own body" (ibid, 274). Life is marked by its ability and insistence upon organizing flows of matter and energy into coherent forms in accord with information stored within individuals and taken from their environments. Coherence is a helpful concept in grasping processes that are at once transient and permanent.

Scientists of non-human life have also found coherence useful in describing life. Though he did not specifically use the term "coherence" in his characterization of life, Grobstein wrote that life is "characterized by replication, metabolic turnover, and exquisite regulation of energy flow constitutes a spreading centre of order in a less ordered universe" (1964, 1). In her analysis of life as an energetic/spatial process, evolutionary biologist Mae-Won Ho asserts that living beings are "organized heterogeneities, or dynamic structures on all scales" (Ho 1993, 21), and that "*An individual is simply a field of coherent activity*" (ibid, 178).

A contemporary of Foucault, French social philosopher Henri Lefebvre also noted this tension between continuity of form and fluidity of environmental wealths and illths: The living organism may be defined as an apparatus which, by a variety of means, captures energies active in its vicinity. It absorbs heat, performs respiration, nourishes itself, and so on. ... Around the living organism, both those energies which it captures and those which threaten it are *mobile:* they are 'currents' or 'flows.' By contrast, in order to capture available energies the organism must have at its disposal apparatuses which are *stable* (1991, 176).

We create security in stabilizing those flows, our access to them, and their access to us. Life is unique in this, it is distinguished by it. *Unlike* an inanimate dynamic form such as a standing wave, living beings are not constituted solely by external forces; they act to bring those flows to and through themselves. Life reaches out into the world. Serres (1982) suggested that we think of organisms as seeking homeorrhesis (constant flow), rather than by homeostasis (constant state).

Applying New Tools to Planning

This ontological metaphor of coherence translates directly into planning for sustainable development. People concerned with the sustainable use and development of tropical island beaches, for example, are obliged to follow the flows that create and maintain those highly valued sandy strands to reefs and coralgal communities. More importantly, in order to attain sustainable use of beaches and coasts, one should ask what inputs do coralgal communities value and which abhor, which flows are wealthy and which are damaging.

While resilient to indigenous disturbances, such as hurricanes, coralgal communities can be seriously damaged by flows of terrestrial sediments and nutrients. Both flows interfere with coralgal photosynthesis—the conversion of sunlight into food and biomass. Sediment flows can mantle small and immobile corals and micro-alga. Excessive nutrients allow large leafy macro-alga to grow rapidly and shade the coralgal community from the sun.

Because Antiguan reefs are in decline, it is reasonable to search for flows that are wealthy, but are now missing, and/or for flows that are damaging and have become more present. Field work and historic environmental information indicate that tourism related "development" on Antigua's coasts has produced both, less wealth and more illth. Resort development in Antigua has followed the path of least resistance, first developing the already picture perfect pocket beaches on the remote Atlantic coast. Once the few pocket beaches on the Atlantic coast were occupied, developers began to build on the more populated Caribbean coast. Though Antigua's Caribbean coast beaches are generally long and conform well to "tropical beach" archetypes (white sand beaches fronted by warm, gentle seas and backed by swaying palms), beyond their fringing palms, they are also typically backed by basin mangroves – a landscape feature inconsistent with tourist expectations. Through sand mining, the blockage of tidal channels, and intentional filling and or dredging, these mangroves have been widely degraded if not destroyed. Maps 1 and 2 illustrate the extent of damage. As a result the flows between coralgal communities have been disrupted, altered, and/or terminated.

Previously, mangal communities mediated and transformed these reef damaging flows of sediment and nutrients into wealths, flows that reef communities find useful (Alevizon 1994). Several mangrove species have dense concentrations of aventicious (above ground) root stalks that effectively slow water flow, trapping sediment born in run-off. Salt ponds also work to sequester and transform the nutrients carried in surface run-off. Through various processes the soils are able to absorb significant amounts of nutrients such as phosphorous, nitrogen, organic carbons, and metals commonly present in sewage and waste water. Through their life activity, mangroves also sequester and transform nutrient flows into *biomass*, stems and leaves. The leaves that drop from the mangroves anchor a food chain which sustains the larval fish of numerous species. Many of these fish move to reefs as they mature. There, they graze upon macro-alga which would otherwise shade the coralgal community. Tourism related alterations along the coasts of Antigua have undermined the living communities and wealth exchanges that produced and maintained Antigua's beaches.

The primary question for those interested in truly sustainable development of tropical sun, sand, and sea tourism then becomes "how can human projects co-exist with the non-human projects whose products and by-products are also valued by humans?" At minimum, non-human communities are important from the perspective of human self-interest. A less ego or anthropocentric perspective might acknowledge that non-human beings are self-interested and value their production and lives as they work continuously and with purpose to maintain themselves and those with whom they are in mutualistic inter-relationships. Such an acknowledgement further implies that non-human beings are morally considerable, and that humans interested in "sustaining" their socio-economies might adopt the culture of co-evolution which for millennia has guided life toward long-term richness and security rather than short-term monetization and resulting impoverishment. It is vital that planners have a framework that helps them understand the inter-play of wealth and illth among all living communities involved in eco-social projects.

Despite the economic benefits of tourism, Antiguans have grown increasingly resistant to continued resort development. They understand that approximately 90 percent of all resort rooms are owned by non-Antiguans, and that profits made on the island therefore flow to distant continents as Antiguan environments are impoverished. The wealth that is produced by Antiguans and on Antigua belongs there. And many Antiguans are unwilling to submit to the exploitation implicit in the taking of the wealth that they produce—for the benefit of non-Antiguans. They understand that wealth flows produced by global tourism are transforming their land into money which then flows away, threatening Antigua's future security. The management of Antigua's coasts have become central to national politics since the late 1990s and played a part in Prime Minister Lester Bird's recent electoral defeat.

Recommendations

These understandings of the processes that effect beach production in Antigua suggest several appropriate policies and practices. I offer two groups of recommendations here. The first focuses upon the socio-ecology the Antigua's coasts and its revitalization. The second group focuses more upon the international political economy of Antigua. By addressing both sorts of concerns I address the concerns of political ecologists to successfully mediate between large scale power structures and local ecologies through the island community. I also address sustainability in a way that encompasses both local ecologies and the political economies of development in Antigua.

Integrated Local Socio-ecologies

Re-establishing the basin mangroves that work with reefs to maintain beaches is perhaps the highest priority. However, it is not clear that these former mangrove basins can recover quickly. A recent survey of wetland reclamation projects suggests highly variable results and notes that the desiccation of salt marsh soils frequently leads to significant acidification as the soils are exposed to air. This acidification may be problematic in attempts to rehabilitate coastal wetlands in Antigua and elsewhere. Given this uncertainty, a small pilot project, perhaps at Ffryes Point salt pond would be advisable.

In some cases, relatively simple and low cost measures might provide significant benefit. The topography of the two very large basin mangrove areas at The Flashes and Jolly Hill (near Five Islands Harbour and LigumVitae Bay in Map 2) has been profoundly changed through dredge and fill operations. Restoration would be expensive if not impossible. However, for many of the other basins, restoration might be relatively inexpensive. The salt ponds at Ffryes Point, Valley Church, Club Antigua, and McKinnon's suffer first and foremost from being cut off from tidal circulation. Channels could be re-established at a relatively low cost by installing effective culverts under the obstructing roadways. The large pond at Darkwood has been mined for sand and the stream channelized. Infilling the channel near its opening to the sea to enhance ponding would immediately begin to trap sediment and enable mangrove growth. Some transplantation would assist in the re-establishment of the forest. The very large pond at Deep Bay was dredged and all vegetation scraped clear in order to create a "reflecting pond". The result is an unattractive and biotically poor, but still inter-tidal pond. Because the pond is immediately adjacent to the nine story Royal Antiguan resort, it could well serve as a tourist attraction if biotic communities were re-established in a mangrove park. Raised walk ways could give guests access to a reconstructed "natural" area. Due to dredging, much of the pool is now too deep for mangroves. The pool could be made shallower with the spoil from ongoing dredge projects at Deep Bay, the cruise ship harbour at the capital city nearby. Darkwood Pond might also benefit from some infilling to replace the sand that was originally mined from the basin for beach nourishment. Depositing dredge spoil in these pond areas has the added benefit of solving the problems of spoil disposal.

Re-establishing basin mangroves would benefit nearby reefs. All reefs benefit from measures that decrease nutrient and sediment mobilization and deposition on reefs. More care in coastal construction and replanting denuded soil would benefit reefs and therefore beaches and the resorts that depend upon them. Because the nutrients in sewage are so problematic to coralgal communities, all sewage should be treated. While some resorts have been careful to maintain treatment facilities, others have not. Uniform treatment must be enforced. If the salt ponds can be re-established, they can effectively assist in treatment. Inter-tidal salt ponds have a considerable capacity to transform problematic sewage into living biomass in the form of trees, leaf litter, and the fish that feed upon the litter and live among the roots. Through vigorous basin mangroves, if managed properly, resorts could transform their sewage into more stable beaches – saving the costs of both sewage treatment and of sand importation.

Political Economy

My second set of recommendations involves monetary wealth flows. First, it is vital that ownership of tourist capital migrate to local hands so that it can be invested locally, rather than siphoned away. Antigua, like all places, is capable of producing only so much wealth without mining its various stocks and productive capacities. If conditions of life are to remain at least at their current levels, no more wealth can be exported than can be reproduced. The geographies of those flows must become more closed, and the spatial withdrawal of local wealths minimized. Government ownership has proven problematic in Antigua, both from the standpoint of the liberalizing IMF and due to improper personal involvement in the government's finances. Local ownership remains possible through smaller scale resort developments. Smaller, locally owned resorts might prove particularly effective as Caribbean tourism evolves.

Currently, Caribbean tourism is dominated by up-market, mass tourism and large operators able to capitalize upon economies of scale. However, as Cuba becomes increasingly accessible to American mass tourist, other Caribbean islands with higher operating costs will need to re-position themselves in the market. Antigua has already begun to vigorously construct itself as a honeymoon location with its "heart of the Caribbean" campaign. People go to Antigua for a quiet time with family and loved-ones, not for night-life. Because it seems likely that large, homogenous Antiguan resorts will be least able to compete with new, cheap Cuban resorts, small, up-scale boutique resorts might be far better positioned to withstand Cuban competition. Small resorts are much more within the capabilities of local Antiguan capital – both financial and human. Smaller projects require much more modest financing, an attribute that might discourage some of the shady dealings of the past. They are also more within the capabilities of the Antiguan business class, many of whom have received training in hotel management through the sponsorship of the Curtin Bluff resort and through the Antiguan Hotel Training Centre. Though a move towards smaller resorts is counter to the Bird administrations' successful drive to gain legitimacy through job creation, there are indications that resort jobs are becoming less valuable to Antiguans.

As tourism has matured on successive islands each has become a regional destination for labour immigration. In Antigua the number of official guest workers in the tourism sector increased by 52 percent between 1993 and 1996. There are troubling indications that both registered and undocumented workers are undermining unions and the relatively high wages they have long maintained. Local labour leaders are beginning to question the wisdom of continuing job expansion if it no longer benefits Antiguans.

Finally, a shift in management practice and policy is essential. The Bird administrations, concerned with electoral politics and job creation, focused upon short-term returns at the expense of long-term coherence. Many Antiguans are well aware of this, and some have begun to challenge ongoing tourism development. In 2001, for example, a large group of Antiguans blocked three shipping container-loads of supplies outside the Carlisle Bay resort. The group was protesting the Resort's attempts to put a new road through a mangrove to by-pass Old Road, a nearby town. Antiguan police eventually responded by firing tear gas and rubber bullets at the protesters.

The conflict continued into 2002 as the initial road foundations were removed, then new footings poured. The fresh violation instigated an arson at the resort, which was in turn followed by illegal police searches of several of the protest leaders' homes (*EAG'er* 2001). The construction project was in fact in violation of regulations that protect Antigua's coasts.

Antiguan courts may still provide a mechanism for enforcement, though that process is slow. The laws to protect Antigua's coasts are on the books, the institutions for their enactment require strengthening. A revitalized Development Control Authority and an Integrated Coastal Management Plan as outlined by Bunce (1997) are two potentially productive alternatives. Finally, the weight of Lester Bird's transgressions swept him from office in 2004. It is too early to tell what if any changes Antigua's new Prime Minister Baldwin Spencer will bring to tourism development and coastal protecti0on policies.

Conclusion

Without much imagination one can understand reefs, beaches, and salt ponds as biogenically produced infrastructure (the physical forms life produces to institutionalize flows). They are analogous to human highways, power lines, and neighbourhoods. None of these landscape elements would exist without these living communities; they are physical institutions built by and for non-human communities. The flows of sand to the beach and the quiet inter-tidal environment formed by those sand flows are wealths for mangals. Mangroves stop illthy flows to reefs and transform some of those flows into living wealthy flows to reefs.

The proposition that humans are able to dominate their wider worlds over the long-term is spurious, at best. The consequences of failed attempts at dominance are nowhere more apparent than on small islands. If the project fails, there is no place else to go. The ill effects of sand mining operations on Barbuda provide a poignant example. As the largest source of sand exportation in the Caribbean, mining has destroyed the only fresh water aquifer on the island. Now Barbudans are dependant upon expensive and tenuous water imports and/or desalinization. As their water wealth was transformed into money, they have become less secure, and less coherent.

Bacon's realization that we can (and always have) put nature to work for us is powerful, but it is a half truth. Living beings and their communities do produce wealth, often in abundance. However, they can withstand only a certain level of wealth appropriation. Taking too much of those flows and productive stocks initiates a negative feedback spiral, which dampens wealth production in ecologies and tourism economies along Antigua's coasts. Antiguan history demonstrates this. Under the extremely exploitative conditions of slavery, planters took more wealth from Black bodies than they could produce. As a result life expectancy on the island never rose above 20 years. Through the power resident in collective bargaining, Antiguans successfully negotiated wages in excess of the survival levels predicted by Ricardo. They have retained a portion of the "surplus" they produced. The living communities along Antigua's coasts are little different. They also must retain both their productive stocks and a portion of their product in order to persist.

Our ability to engineer living coastal landscapes is questionable at best. Those ecologies are far more complex and interrelated than we have imagined. As Frank Elgar observed, "The ecosystem is not more complex than we think, it is more complex than we *can* think". It is clear that development related coastal alteration has installed a precarious regime based in expensive sand importation, a practice that further undermines indigenous sand production. The long-term security, stability, and coherence of Antiguans, human and otherwise, lies not in unsustainable dominance-over nature, but in *collaboration-with* coastal ecologies, as Bruno Latour suggests in his *Politics of Nature* (2004). In this sense coastal management a political project. It is about aligning differing interests into coherent, synergistic projects that benefit as wide a constituency as possible. Antiguans *can* form coalition with coastal communities and still pursue sun, sand, and sea tourism. They need only to respect the claims to the wealth produced by their non-human neighbours, just as the North Atlantic community came to recognize Black Antiguans' claims to their own labour. It is time for a new Emancipation. Antigua could lead the world.

4

Travel Tourism Organizations in Different Countries

Medical Tourism and Plastic Surgery in Thailand

Whatever you wish to call it, there is no denying the significance of this trend spreading throughout the world. Medical Tourism and its electively centred cousin Cosmetic Tourism have gained recognition worldwide as a viable option to expensive surgery in one's home country.

* The Land of Smiles!!
* Where could be a better place to spend your vacation than in a country dubbed 'The Land of Smiles'?
* Come discover the nation everyone is talking about!

Discover the advantages of having your cosmetic surgery, plastic surgery, or dental surgery performed overseas. Thailand has established itself as the worldwide leader for Medical Tourism through its premium hospitals and talented plastic surgeons. Your cosmetic surgery procedure will be performed at ISO and JCI/JCAHO accredited facilities by board certified surgeons using the latest techniques. Learn about some of the exciting surgical options available here. Our wide variety of recuperation packages are individually tailored to suit your needs and lifestyle. Lavish 5 star hotels coupled with your personal liaison and on call nurse make for ideal recovery settings. Let MMR assist you in reaching your dreams. Get the fantastic results others have experienced by combining affordable plastic surgery with a relaxing holiday in amazing Thailand.

What is a Medical Tourism?

Medical Tourism, also called Health Tourism is the umbrella term used for people seeking healthcare outside of their home countries. Elective surgeries like breast enlargement or rhinoplasty surgery are usually accompanied by a brief holiday following the surgery. In most cases, in destination countries, costs of health care are far less than that of western nations. This, combined with ongoing advancements in standards and technology, has fuelled one of the fastest growing sectors in the health care industry.

Dental Tourism-Dental Procedures & Surgery

Who doesn't want that award winning 'Hollywood smile'? However, dental surgery in England and America doesn't come cheap. However, there are many countries that offer the same dental procedures at a fraction of the price. As a bonus, these patients can recuperate in exotic destinations and pamper themselves during their stay. Many receiving inpatient procedures opt to stay in lavish facilities-the total price of which is offered at significant savings compared to dental work in their home country. Recovery time is usually short for dental work, even when the procedure is relatively invasive. Outpatients can therefore travel, receive dental work and then spend the remainder of their time enjoying a wonderful vacation—all at a significant savings. Europeans have long been practicing dental tourism and for years been travelling to neighbouring countries, especially Hungary for their dental needs. Almost everyplace offers the standard dental cleaning, gingivitis treatment, sealants and amalgam filling. Of course, relatively inexpensive procedures like simple cleanings or cavity fillings don't usually warrant travelling outside your home country.

Medical Tourism in Thailand

Health travel, once a luxury of only the rich, can now be enjoyed by virtually all. In the days of yesteryear, hardly anyone even pondered the possibilities of going abroad to a distant foreign land to have treatment. But now, with the advent of the world becoming the one and only global village, millions are crossing international datelines in hope of achieving a 'better new life'.

One of those countries which have sprung to life as a destination for medical treatment is the south-east Asian country of Thailand. Unlike most Western countries, the cost of private medical treatment is cost-effective where hospitals do not charge a bomb. Contrary to popular belief, the standards in Thailand are of an extremely high international standard where many of the health workers have graduated in developed Western countries. Looking at it straight on, the reality is – Thailand can offer the patient the same kind of treatment as back home while enabling him or her to enjoy the holiday of a life time. The uptrend of medical tourism in Thailand is escalating to meteoric heights.

History

Thailand's first hospital was founded during the reign of King Chulalongkorn and the Medical Association of Thailand was established in 1921.

Prince Mahidol, the father of the present king Bhumibol, has much to do with developing medical schools in Thailand and goes down in Thai history as 'The Father of Modern Thai medicine'. Prince Mahidol realized the importance of bringing Western standard medical practice to Siam and so helped fund many of Thailand's doctors and nurses to go abroad to further their studies at institutes such as Harvard and MIT in the United States. And it was those health workers who planted and later sowed the seeds of a world-class medical network in Thailand.

Latest Situation

Westerners are currently arriving in Thailand, the Land of Smiles, in exhilarating numbers to undergo medical treatments at a fraction of the cost as that charged in their home countries.

On top of having treatments conducted by highly trained and skilled doctors, patients can also enjoy a marvelous holiday in one of Asia's prime tourist destinations. Many of the country's hospitals are now globally renowned for their expertise. They include Bumrungrad Hospital, Bangkok General Hospital, Samitivej Hospital and Bangkok Nursing Home Hospital.

Figures and Statistics

Thailand as a destination for medical treatment has rocketed in recent years and they have the statistics to prove it. Take just one country like the United Arab Emirates for example – over 60,000 of their citizens a year come to Thailand to enjoy treatment. Two of the Thailand's top hospitals Bumrungrad and Samitivej treat patients of whom 40% are foreign – this kind of high percentage is quite phenomenal. According to the Kasikorn Research Centre, 2005 alone attracted an unprecedented 1.28 million foreign medical travellers which generated revenue of 33 billion baht. That means therefore, that on average each patient spent 25,800 baht for their treatments. It was revealed in an article in Newsweek in 2006 that 400,000 foreign patients were treated at just Bumrungrad hospital in Bangkok. This prestigious world-class hospital has an outpatient capacity of 6,000 patients per day.

Thailand presently has a free universal health program for its citizens with more than 600 hospitals and 400 medical facilities. Today, Thailand has proudly become a medical hub for patients from the United States, Europe, the surrounding countries, and the Middle East.

Why Thailand/Reasons to Chose Thailand as the Medical Destination

There is no single reason why so many folk come to Thailand to receive medical treatment. Not only is Thailand a superb destination for stunning beaches, islands, mountains, modern infrastructure, cuisines, low costs and friendly people, there are other reasons too. Some of the Best Hospitals in the World:Thailand has, over the years, spent furtively in developing its medical tourism infrastructure and established over 30 English speaking hospitals, innumerable dentistry clinics and other alternative healing centres. Some are accredited to prestigious boards including the Joint Commission on Accreditation of Healthcare Organizations and the International Organization for Standardization.

Incredible Service: It is no joke when Westerners write on the Internet or chat in bars that the service, look and ambiance of Thailand's hospitals is similar to that of a five-star hotel. The treatment received from doctors, nurses, orderlies, administrators, and technicians is outstanding and the doctor patient ratio is as low as 1:4. Extra-ordinary value for money: Foreign patients can expect to pay just 10-50% for the cost of treatment, in comparison to what they would pay back home.

The likes of hip surgeries, teeth whitening, face lifts, x-rays, mastectomies, and heart bypasses can all be performed at very affordable prices. With the money they save they can enjoy a memorable holiday and even go back home with cash leftover. Unique Procedures: Many hospitals are offering treatments which are virtually unheard of elsewhere.

Excellent Long-lasting Outcome: Some of Thailand hospitals have been recognized for performing outstanding treatments for several procedures while producing excellent outcome with long lasting effects. Thailand is Amazing for Relaxing: After treatment, patients can experience spas and resorts which are universally famous for exceptional service and comfort, while looking over beautiful virgin beaches or remote mountains.

International Health Care System

Thailand top hospitals provide prompt and complete response in any emergency situation and are recognized outside of Thailand as having standards equivalent to that of those in the West.

Foreign Patients: The renowned Bumrungrad Hospital in Bangkok attracts on average 400,000 foreign patients per year or an average of 1,000+ a day. Other hospitals too, such as Samitivej also specialize in serving foreigners.

Regulatory Agency: Private hospitals in Thailand are accredited by the government according to standards that meet or exceed those in North America. Only four countries in the world – the United States, Canada, Australia, and Thailand – require private hospitals to meet rigorous medical and healthcare standards and be duly accredited as achieving those standards.

International Accreditation

The standard of treatment in Thailand is considered in North America of being one of the highest in the world with most of their doctors holding US professional certification. Many of the hospitals have international JCAHO accreditation; this is an organization which is the primary inspector of hospitals, nursing homes and other medical institutions in the US. All of Thailand's hospitals have to be licensed by the Health Ministry and the same applies to the doctors. In fact, some of the hospitals in Thailand have accreditation from Western medical associations. Most of the country's major hospitals also have achieved other accreditation being the International Standards Organization's ISO 9001:2000 accreditation.

Many of the doctors in Thailand have graduated and trained in Europe and the US and hold medical credentials form there. The hospitals also have working relations with Western hospitals. The UK Foreign and Common Wealth Office verifies that Bangkok has "Excellent International Hospitals" and the US State Department has stated that Bangkok also offers "Excellent facilities exist for routine long-term and emergency healthcare.

Technology

The most up-to-date state of the art developments and technologies have been introduced in Thailand to enhance medical facilities and treatment. They include:

- DSA (Digital Subtraction Angiography),
- Digital Mammogram allowing accurate diagnosis and early discovery of cancer in women.
- Green light PVP Laser for Prostate Treatment to precisely target prostate tissue with a high powered laser beam.
- PET/CT Scanner (Position Emission Tomography/ Computed Tomography Scanner) assist in the earliest detection of cancers and assess heart muscle viability for the evaluation of functional brain anatomy.
- Novalis Shaped Beam Surgery System Installed and Operating helps applies doses of radiation, allowing it to destroy diseased tissue or cauterize a problem area without affecting healthy adjacent tissue. Other treatments are cancerous tumours, arteriovenous, malformations and Parkinson's disease.
- 4D Ultrasound creates a motion life-like picture with the speed of 25 volumes per second.
- magnetic Resonance Imageing (MRI-Intra Achiva 3.0T MRI) allows the detailed information necessary to detect

blood circulation abnormalities and is particularly useful in the early detection of brain cancer.

- Gamma Knife Surgery makes non-invasive brain surgery possible by applying hihgly targeted gamma radiation to the treatment of tumours, arteriovenous malformations of the brain and functional disorders.
- IMRT (Intensity Modulated Radiotherapy) focuses radiation doses on tumours without damaging the surrounding tissue.
- Minimal Invasive Heart Surgery, the da Vinci Surgical System uses robotics to translate the surgeon's natural hand movements into the micro movements of a robotic arm. The surgeon is able to apply less invasive incisions with unprecedented precision, lowering risk, accelerating recovery, and greatly reducing scarring.

Medical Tourism Thailand

Popular For: Alternative Medicine, cosmetic surgery, dental care, gender realignment, heart surgery, obesity surgery, oncology, orthopedics.

Visa Requirements: A valid passport and return ticket are required. Visa not required for stays up to 30 days.

Thailand has all but established itself as king of the castle when it comes to international medical tourism. The affordable prices combined with high levels of quality care in a country rich in culture, natural beauty and amazing food all combine to make Thailand the first choice for many seeking medical treatment abroad. In fact, Thailand is one of the world's preferred destinations for all types of treatment including medical, cosmetic and dental procedures.

Pros: Thailand stands as one of the world's top tourism destinations, which means the country is long accustomed to receiving foreign travellers. In the big cities, English is understood, especially at private clinics that will interest tourists looking for treatment. The cost of a flight ticket, food and accommodation and the procedure itself can add up to less than the price of a procedure in North America. Throw in the fact that Thailand has much to offer as a regular tourist spot, this Southeast Asian country is set to remain a favourite medical tourism destination for a long time to come.

Cons: While most medical practitioners in Thailand are experienced and well-qualified, there are some doctors whose reputations can be less than ideal. Medical tourists should shop around to make sure they're getting the best treatment possible and that the price is not the only consideration. Thailand and the rest of Southeast Asia experiences three distinct seasons, and it is important to choose the right time to come. The rainy season can be unpleasant at times, with hard downpours that regularly flood the streets of cities. The summer season can see temperatures reach uncomfortable levels along with debilitating humidity and pollution.

Medical Tourism in Thailand

Thailand is a world leader in the medical tourism industry and the country's private hospitals and clinics are able to perform all kinds of surgeries from heart procedures to hip and joint replacements and recuperative operations after injury. Bangkok has several hospitals that are used to receiving foreign patients, and the number of hospitals means that it's easy to get a second opinion and find a doctor you're comfortable with before gong under the knife.

Thailand Cosmetic Surgery

Thailand's cosmetic surgeons have profited from Thailand's reputation for medical tourism. The prices for elective surgery can be a fraction of what they would be in the west, with the quality level being consistently high. While common procedures such as face lifts, tummy tucks and breast augmentation are widely available, Thailand is also a world specialist in sex reassignment surgery. Procedures of this nature include facial feminization surgery and vaginoplasty.

Thailand Dental Tourism

Thailand is known for its masterful dentists. Many North Americas make up to three trips over the period of a year to receive extended dental surgery, and still come out saving significant amounts of money. The dental equipment used in Thailand is on par with some of the best in the world, and the dentists are very well trained. Procedures available include crowns, dentures, laser teeth whitening and bridges.

Thailand Alternative Medicine

The Thais have long been practicing alternative medicine and many practitioners using herbal medicines and holistic approaches are available. This sector is beginning to attract foreign attention, particularly the country's wellness retreats, yoga workshops and chiropractic treatments.

Thailand Health Spas

The spa industry is big business in Thailand. Thais and foreigners alike take advantage of the many spas in the cities, where saunas, steam baths and every kind of massage are available for much less than the going rate in the west. Spas here are well suited to catering to international tourists and cost-saving packages are available at every establishment.

Medical Tourism in Thailand

Private healthcare in the West is notoriously expensive and many people look to Thailand to find cost-effective solutions for their medical problems...

'Generation X' is in charge and its legacy is a world where government 'interference' in the free market and healthcare is at an all-time low. Unable to depend on state healthcare systems, people in many parts of the world have to resort to their private resources for the operations and treatments they need. Private healthcare in the West is notoriously expensive, for some, prohibitively so. Even commonplace medical areas like dentistry and orthodontics are extortionately priced, while surgery and major operations can completely drain personal finances. Given the costs, and the stakes, many people have looked beyond the shores of their native homelands to find cost-effective solutions. Many have found their solutions in Thailand, spurring a trend in 'medical tourism' within the country.

But why Thailand?

The Thai medical profession is probably one of the most

advanced in the region. Successive governments have invested in ensuring the education and training Thai doctors receive is parallel to that offered elsewhere in the region.

Many doctors undertake specialist training abroad, particularly the United States and Europe, and are at least equally as well qualified as physicians in the West-often more so. A qualified, experienced medical profession is though useless without proper facilities and equipment.

Fortunately, Thailand's hospitals and clinics are world class. Huge investments have been made in equipment and management standards are so high that hospitals achieve ISO 9001 accreditation. Many major hospitals belong to management groups that ensure the very highest standard of medical service is available through their branch hospitals at various locations around the country. All this expertise and proficiency means that Thailand's hospitals are a secure option for those seeking medical treatment.

Thailand's medical solutions do not though rest at major surgery or treatments. A variety of cosmetic surgery options are available, as is cosmetic dentistry and laser sight correction (LASIK, etc.). Thailand is also a very popular choice for people requiring sex reassignment surgery. In recent years, "medical tourism" has become the new buzzword for the development of Thailand's tourism industry. What this means is encouraging people to come to Thailand, have a little elective surgery, and then recuperate on some nice beach.

The idea is not as crazy as it may sound. Some of Thailand's private hospitals are capable of world class healthcare, accredited according some of the toughest standards around. While they might be expensive for many Thais, these hospitals are still able to offer a high standard of care for far less than a hospital stay in most western countries will cost.

We're not talking about critical care, such as transplants. Medical Tourism is targeted at elective and non-emergency treatments, such as cosmetic surgery or hip replacements. Such are the cost savings that some insurance companies will not only cover the costs of treatment, but some of the travel costs as well, to have work done in Thailand. Thailand's low cost health care is not limited to medical treatment. Thanks to tight government price controls, most medicines cost far less than they do in western countries.

Thai Hospitals

Here's a short list of hospitals that specialize in treating foreigners. They all have staff who speak English, as well as many other languages. All of the institutions below are based in Bangkok, although some have branches in other parts of the country.

Bumrungrad International Hospital

Perhaps the most advanced and internationalized of Thailand's private hospital. Coming here can seem like a visit to a five star hotel and the United Nations all in one. Although comparatively expensive for Thais, the hospital gets many foreign visitors in search of high quality health care at reasonable cost. The web site provides an overview of the hospital's services, and the ability to make appointments online.

Bangkok General Hospital

A good general medicine hospital. The web site is available in many languages. The main services for foreign visitors are cosmetic surgery. The hospital can arrange for a variety of treatments as part of your holiday.

Samitivej Hospital

Samitivej is one of Bangkok's most respected hospitals. Its main claim to fame is the "baby friendly" natal facilities. It's probably unlikely that you would want to travel to Thailand to have your baby, but the hospital has several other services to offer as well, including extensive children's healthcare departments.

St. Carlos Hospital

This small hospital has combined traditional medicine with a full fledged spa to provide a complete range of health and beauty treatments, from cosmetic surgery to detoxifying body treatments.

Rutnin Eye Hospital

Rutnin is perhaps Bangkok's largest eye hospital, with a full range of services such as lasik corrections.

Medical Tourism Resources

Cosmetic Surgery Travel

Sort of a medical travel planner, providing a concierge type service to help you plan your trip to Bangkok for cosmetic surgery or other medical procedures. They can help you to plan your trip, select doctors and facilities, and schedule your appointments or procedures before you arrive.

Oasis Medical Tourism

Web presence of Mondial Assistance Thailand, a subsidiary of global assistance and insurance company Mondial Assistance Group. They can assist you with planning all aspects of your Thai medical experience.

Costa Rica Medical Tourism

Fast growing Medical Tourism in Costa Rica owes its existence to tourists from the US and Canada travelling primarily to get medical & surgical procedures done abroad. Many unique factors make Costa Rica healthcare a preferred medical travel destination.

Why Costa Rica as a Medical Tourism Destination?

Medical treatments are usually about 50-70% cheaper than in the US and no one has to wait their turn for surgery.

Easily accessible from US and Canada. There are frequent flights from important cities in both these countries. Also Americans, Canadians and most Europeans staying in Costa Rica for less than 90 days do not require a visa. They do need a passport that is valid for at least 30 days.

Traditionally, the procedures that have been popular with medical tourists in Costa Rica have been cosmetic and dental treatments. But with growing standards of medical care, there is rapid medical tourism demand for various other surgeries and medical procedures.

Vacationing with a Medical Trip to Costa Rica

Costa Rica's unique geographic location-it has the Pacific ocean on the one side and the Caribbean Sea on the other-has endowed it with beautiful pristine beaches, lush green mountains formed by past volcanic eruptions, dense rainforests, lakes, and rivers. All these help support one of the most diverse plant and animal life on the planet. Costa Rica also has many active volcanoes and hot springs. Most medical tourism destination are not ideal for a vacation or a touristic holiday, not in the case of Costa Rica, which is not only a great medical care destination, but also a popular tourism destination. Sometimes called 'the Switzerland of Central America', Costa Rica is famous for microclimates where in an hour's travel one may experience from very hot and humid to hot and dry to cold and rainy.

If the doctor allows it and depending on what suits your temperament, you could take a peek at one of Costa Rica's active volcanoes like Arenal or one with the widest crater in the world like Poas, and bathe in the hot water springs, or visit the rainforests, wildlife parks, or go for a hike. Not to forget, the many beaches, butterfly gardens, river or lake tours, museums, fishing or scuba diving, coffee farm tours or even a visit to the National Theatre for someone into orchestra.

Costa Rican Food

Unlike many other Latin American countries, the local food in Costa Rica is not spicy. For chicken connoisseurs, a must-try local dish is the wood *fire roasted chicken.* For those who may miss good old American fast food, there are many franchise restaurants like McDonalds, Pizza Hut, and Kentucky Fried Chicken that you can go to.

The Spirit of "Pura Vida" & Medical Tourism

Costa Rica is a foreigner-friendly country; it attracts over 2 million tourists every year. The phrase Pura Vida differently means "Full of Life", "Purified life", "This is living!" or "Going great!" and reflects the easy-going, relaxed lifestyle of Costa Ricans. Costa Rica has a special police force called 'Tourist Police' that is just to assist the tourists with directions and answering questions.

A politically stable country, Costa Rica does not have an army. It has a high standard of living when compared to that of other Latin American countries and also a stable economy. It has a literacy rate of 96% and the lowest crime rates in the region. Many US and Canadian citizens and Europeans choose Costa Rica to lead their retired life because of the low cost of living, comfortable climate and its unspoiled natural habitats..

Health care in Costa Rica compares with the best in the world. It is no surprise then that the UNDP's 2007/2008 Human Development Report puts the average life expectancy in Costa Rica at 78.5, above that of USA's 77.9

Popular souvenirs to bring home from Costa Rica are the fresh-from-the-farm coffees and the variety of hand-crafted wooden items. It is illegal in Costa Rica to try to export any plants or animals or even sea shells or rocks.

Factors to consider-Medical Travel to Costa Rica

* Spanish is the main language in Costa Rica. But English is frequently used in tourist-frequented spots like hotels, resorts, leading hospitals and clinics. In hospitals, there are always interpreters available.
* At most places in Costa Rica, the American dollar is accepted.
* Most US cell phones do not work in Costa Rica. Before you set out from your home country, it is a good idea to check with your cell phone provider about the coverage and call rates in Costa Rica.
* Do not expect the blazing internet speeds that you may be used to in Canada or USA.
* Travellers should use licensed taxis, which are red with medallions (yellow triangles containing numbers) painted on the side. Licensed taxis at the airport are painted orange.

Medical Tourism Corporation has arranged with its network hospitals in Costa Rica to have special guest suites designed to comfortably accommodate the patient and the accompanying guest while in the hospital. Also, MTC has made special arrangements with recovery resorts that have 24 x 7 nursing for any post-hospital discharge care, with adequate arrangement for the comfort of the accompanying guest. There is always an English-speaking personal case manager at the medical destination. So, if you are looking for medical care abroad, Costa Rica is one of the places to consider seriously. Even if you are just planning a vacation, you may go to Costa Rica for pleasure and save some money by getting any pending medical or dental care done while there! There couldn't be a better place than Costa Rica to recuperate and unwind. Thus, medical tourism in Costa Rica is a complete package of health, fun, and savings. We hope this information will be a valuable aid on deciding on Costa Rica as a medical tourism destination of your choice.

Medical Tourism in Costa Rica

Over the last decade, Costa Rica has evolved from being a mere eco-tourism destination to a country of choice for foreigners, particularly from United States and Canada, seeking quality healthcare services and surgeries at a much lower price than their home countries.

In a report from McKinsey & Company, it was highlighted that medical tourists from the United States and Canada prefer Latin American countries like Costa Rica due to the shorter travel time, affordable costs, and an opportunity for a memorable vacation.

Healthcare System in Costa Rica

Aside from its close proximity to the United States, medical tourists flock to Costa Rica due to its excellent healthcare system which is ranked by the World Health Organization even higher than the US. Costa Rica has modern hospitals and state-of-the-art clinics utilizing the latest in medical technologies and board-certified surgeons who are trained and certified in North America or Europe. Aside from services offered to medical tourists, Costa Rica is also credited for providing a high quality public and private healthcare services with prestigious and reputable hospitals and other health facilities.

Consider the following healthcare facts:

* The World Health Organization ranked Costa Rica's health system as one of the top three Latin America countries, ranked even higher than United States and New Zealand.
* The World Bank ranked Costa Rica to have the highest life expectancy, at 78.7 years, among all countries in Latin

America. This is equivalent to the level in Canada and higher than the United States by a year.

Top Hospitals in Costa Rica

Costa Rica top hospitals are accredited by the Joint Commission International like Ministro de Salud de Costa Rica (The Costa Rica Health Ministry), which offers the local license Habilitacien Hospitalaria, and local municipalities like the Municipio de Escazu in San Jose, which offers licensures like the Funcionamento. Some hospitals like the CIMA Hospitals are owned and managed by leading US hospital corporations. There are currently three JCI-accredited hospitals in Costa Rica and all are located in San Jose, the capital of Costa Rica. These hospitals include:

Hospital CIMA-San Jose, Costa Rica

Accredited by the JCI on May 2008. CIMA is also certified by the ISO and was the first hospital that was certified for Quality Processes by the Ministry of Health in Costa Rica. Other CIMA hospitals can be found in other locations in Costa Rica, like the CIMA Hermosillo, CIMA Chihuahua and the CIMA Santa Engracia, although the CIMA San Jose is the top destination for medical tourists.

Hospital Clinica Biblica-San Jose, Costa Rica

Accredited by the JCI on October 2007. It was built in 1929 by American missionaries and has grown into a high-quality medical facility with a capacity of 120 inpatients and 5000 outpatients per day. They have a dedicated Medical Tourism department with English and Spanish fluent staff and employees.

Hospital La Catolica-San Jose, Costa Rica

Accredited by the JCI on June 2009. The hospital recently built new infrastructures on top of its newly remodeled facilities which boast of its own high class hotel, the La Posada El Convento, located within the confines of the medical facilities.

Popular Treatments done in Costa Rica and Comparative Costs

Known initially for its excellent dental surgery services, medical tourism in Costa Rica has spread to a variety of other medical procedures, including:

* General and cosmetic dentistry,
* Cosmetic surgery,
* Aesthetic procedures (botox, skin resurfacing etc.),
* Bariatric and Laparascopic surgery,
* Orthopedic surgery,
* Fertility treatments,
* Addiction treatment.

The following are cost comparisons between Medical procedures in Costa Rica and equivalent procedures in the United States:

	USA	*Costa Rica*	*Average Savings*
	Medical Procedures		
Heart Bypass	Up to $130,000	$24,000	70-80%
Heart Valve Replacement		Up to $160,000	$15,000
80-90%			
Angioplasty	Up to $57,000	$9,000	70-80%
Hip Replacement	Up to $43,000	$12,000	60-70%
Hysterectomy	Up to $20,000	$4,000	70-80%
Knee Replacement	Up to $40,000	$11,000	60-70%
Spinal Fusion	Up to $62,000	$25,000	50-60%
	Plastic and Reconstructive Surgery		
Facelift	$7,000-$9,000	$4,600 – $5,000	30-40%
Rhinoplasty	$8,000-$12,000	$3,500 – $3,900	50-65%
Breast Lift	$5,000-$8,000	$3,000 – $3,400	40-55%
Breast Augmentation	$5,000-$8,000	$2,700 – $2,900	50-65%
Blepharoplasty (Eyelid Surgery)	$4,000-$5,500	$2,000-$2,200	50-60%
Brazilian Butt Surgery	Up to $10,000	$3,000-$3,300	55-65%
Tummy Tuck	$6,000-$8,500	$3,900 – $4,200	45-50%
Facelift	$7,000-$9,000	$4,600 – $5,000	35-45%
Male Breast Reduction	Up to $6,000	$2000-$2600	50-60%

	Bariatric Surgery		
Laparoscopic Gastroplasty	Up to $30,000	$10,500	55-65%
Laparoscopic Roux-en-Y	Up to $35,000	$14,000	50-60%
	General and Cosmetic Dentistry		
Bridges	$1,000+ per tooth	$250 – $400 per tooth	60-70%
Crowns	$1,000+ per tooth	$250-$400 per tooth	60-70%
Implants	$3,500+ per tooth	$700 – $900 per tooth	70-80%
Porcelain Veneers	$1,500+ per tooth	$300 – $500 per tooth	65-80%
Root canal	Up to $800	$315	55-60%
Teeth whitening	Up to $700	$250	55-65%

Malpractice and Liabilities Laws in Costa Rica

Medical Tourists can receive better reassurance against malpractice in Costa Rica as compared to most medical travel destinations, as most dentists, physicians and clinics are required to have and maintain professional liability insurance during the course of their practice. Any malpractice claims can be initiated through the court system as required under the laws of Costa Rica.

Medical travellers are also encouraged to purchase comprehensive medical coverage options offered by certified international insurance companies to medical tourists and their travel companions.

Pros

The WHO ranked the quality of healthcare in Costa Rica as among the top nations in Latin America, a rank that is even better than the United States.

The close proximity of Costa Rica to the United States and Canada makes it an ideal destination for North American medical tourists.

Language will not be a barrier as hospital staff and most of the locals can speak English.

The culture in Costa Rica is family-oriented, friendly and visitors are assured that they will receive a warm and hospitable welcome not only by the hospital staff and crew but all other locals as well

The cost of medical treatments in Costa Rica ranges from a third to even a fourth of what it can cost in the United States or Canada. As required by law, medical practitioners carry liability insurance at all times, giving patients protection and coverage from malpractice.

Costa Rica is known as a prime Eco-tourism destination so visitors are assured of majestic views, amazing destination spots and a temperate climate, which assures medical tourists of an excellent vacation experience conducive for recovery and relaxation.

Cons

Costa Rica is strict with regards to overstaying visitors and may be stringent in providing visas for anyone with previous overstaying records. They are also meticulous with regards to documentation requirements if visitors are accompanied by children.

Travelling to Costa Rica

Due to the close proximity of Costa Rica to the United States and Canada, medical travellers do not need to spend long hours on the plane.

Average estimated travel time in hours

From/To	*San Jose, Costa Rica*
New York City	4.5
Chicago	4.5
Washington, DC	4
San Francisco	6
Los Angeles	5.5
Toronto	5
Montreal	5
Vancouver	7

Entry and Exit Requirements to Costa Rica

USA and Canadian medical travellers with a valid passport and a pre-paid airline ticket do not need to get a visa and can stay up to 90-day in Costa Rica.

Should there be a need for an extension to the 90-day allotted period, particularly if required by medical procedures and recovery needs, a request for an extension can be submitted to the Office of Temporary Permits of the Department of Immigration in Costa Rica.

It is strongly advised for medical travellers to stick to this allotted period as Costa Rica may deny entry for people who have previous overstaying records in the country.

Statistics for Medical Tourism in Costa Rica

According to Promed (the Council for the Promotion of Medicine in Costa Rica), there were approximately 22,000 US citizens who visited Costa Rica in 2008 for medical procedures, mostly baby boomers or people aged over 50 who are seeking quality medical services including dental, surgical and other medical packages at very affordable rates.

Costa Rica's healthcare system is very advanced, particularly in the city of San Jose, and is considered one of the best in Latin America. For some procedures, it ranks higher than the US. The country boasts highly-competent specialists in plastic surgery and dentistry, which are two areas of treatment most in demand. With additional recent medical advancements, heart, kidney and liver transplants are now offered, as is bone marrow transplantation. The World Health Organization gives high marks to the quality of medical care in Costa Rica.

World-renowned as a leader in eco-tourism, Costa Rica boasts tropical rainforests, stunning mountain vistas, fabulous beaches, an ideal climate and friendly, welcoming people. There is now an increasing awareness that the country is also a premier destination for quality medical treatment at amazingly low prices.

The country's specialists in cosmetic surgery procedures are fully-credentialed and are experienced in the latest surgical and non-surgical techniques available. Costa Rica's Plastic Surgery Board provides listings of physicians who are credentialed members of the national association. In addition, the board will provide information on whether a physician is currently certified or preparing for certification. Costa Rica's cost of living and the strong value of the US dollar in relation to the country's currency means medical services cost much less here than in the US. Every year, thousands of US citizens take advantage of the low cost of procedures and the high level of quality care provided by Costa Rica's cosmetic surgeons and dentists. By the early 1990s, approximately 15 percent of all visitors to Costa Rica entered the country specifically to undergo some sort of medical treatment.

Typically, a patient will plan on a week to 10 days in Costa Rica, which allows time for a procedure and a short recovery period. The actual time spent, of course, depends on the complexity of the surgery and the number of follow-up visits required. With medical tourism packages, a patient will often spend a few days sightseeing, undergo the planned treatment and then spend some time in a suitable location, such as an eco-tourist destination, for rest and additional sightseeing or recuperation.

Medical Tourism In El Salvador

El Salvador is a land of amazing contrasts, accented by a long string of cone-shaped volcanoes and their tranquil mountain lakes. In addition, the country's Maya ruins are considered some of the most interesting in all of Central America.

Significant points-of-interest include Cerro Verde National Park and the Santa Ana and Izalco volcanoes; the cloud forests of Montecristo National Park; Mayan ruins at Tazumal; El Espino and El Cuco beaches along the Pacific Ocean; shopping and night life venues in San Salvador; the colonial architecture, splendid churches and colorful handicraft markets spread across the country, and of course, the indigenous native celebrations and religious festivals that fill the calendar. Over the last ten years, the country has instigated a strong move toward democracy, countrywide modernization, and an greatly improved tourism industry. They look forward to providing Americans with a medical tourism option. El Salvador is located in Central America and can be reached from most US cities within 3 to 7 hours.

Country Information

El Salvador is located in Central America. It has a total area of 8,123 square miles, making it comparable in size to the state of Massachusetts. El Salvador is the smallest country in Central

America. Due to its size it is affectionately called the "Tom Thumb of the Americas". It has 123.6 square miles of water within its borders. Several small rivers flow through El Salvador into the Pacific Ocean, including the Goascoran, Jiboa, Torola, Paz and the Rio Grande de San Miguel. Only the largest river, the Lempa River, flowing from Honduras across El Salvador to the ocean, is navigable for commercial traffic.

Volcanic craters enclose lakes, the most important of which are Lake Ilopango (27 sq mi) and Lake Coatepeque (10 sq mi). Lake Guija is El Salvador's largest natural lake (17 sq mi). Several artificial lakes were created by the damming of the Lempa, the largest of which is Embalse Cerron Grande (135 sq mi).

El Salvador shares borders with Guatemala—126 miles (203 km) and Honduras—212.5 miles (342 km), and is the only Central American country that does not have a Caribbean coastline. The highest point in the country is Cerro El Pital at 8,957 feet (2,730 meters).

El Salvador's population numbers about 6.9 million people. Fully 90% are mestizo (mixed Amerindian and Spanish/European), 9% white (mostly Spanish, but also some French, German and Italian descent), and only 1% indigenous.

Language

Spanish is the official language of El Salvador. English is the second language.

Religion

Roman Catholic 83%, Protestant & other 17%.

Climate

Tropical and subtropical; dry season (November through April); rainy season (May through October); cooler in highlands. El Salvador's weather is influenced by altitude. Pacific lowlands are uniformly hot; central plateau and mountain areas more moderate. The temperature in San Salvador area ranges from a high of 74-100 degrees Fahrenheit, to a low of 54-74 degrees Fahrenheit. The wet season is from May to October. The hottest months are March and April.

El Salvador has a tropical climate with pronounced wet and dry seasons. Temperatures vary primarily with elevation and show little seasonal change. The Pacific lowlands are uniformly hot; the central plateau and mountain areas are more moderate. The rainy season, known locally as invierno, or winter, extends from May to October. Almost all the annual rainfall occurs during this time, and yearly totals, particularly on southern-facing mountain slopes, can be as high as 78 inches. Protected areas and the central plateau receive lesser, although still significant, amounts. Rainfall during this season generally comes from lo·· pressure over the Pacific and usually falls in heavy afternoon thunderstorms. Although hurricanes occasionally form in the Pacific, they seldom affect El Salvador.

From November through April, the northeast trade winds control weather patterns. During these months, air flowing from the Caribbean has had most of the precipitation wrung out of it passing over the mountains in Honduras. By the time this air reaches El Salvador, it is dry, hot, and hazy. This season is known locally as verano, or summer. Temperatures vary little with season; elevation is the primary determinant. The Pacific lowlands are the hottest region, with annual averages ranging from 77°F to 85°F. San Salvador is representative of the central plateau, with an annual average temperature of 74°F and absolute high and low readings of 100°F and 45°F, respectively. Mountain areas are the coolest, with annual averages from 54°F to 74°F and minimum temperatures sometimes approaching freezing.

Clothing

The first thing to consider when packing for your medical travel trip is climate. The dress code in El Salvador is casual. Professionals usually wear light cotton suits. The popular "guayabera" or embroidered cotton shirt, is preferred casual wear for men, particularly in the warmer areas. As a health tourism guest, just wear very loose, comfortable clothing. .

Mobile Phones

A Subscriber Identity Module Card (SIM Card) is now available for El Salvador and foreign patients who are travelling for medical purposes. The SIM Card must be used in conjunction with a

Digital GSM mobile phone within the 900-MHz range or a Digital PCN mobile phone within the 1800-MHz range.

Getting Online & Checking E-mail

All of El Salvador's leading hotels offer facsimile (fax) and e-mail services. Numerous private businesses offer such facilities, most often in conjunction with translation services. El Salvador has been expanding its information service for residents and tourists alike through the Internet system. Services are now available at El Salvador's leading hotels and at the many "cyber cafés" that are cropping up in all major tourist destinations.

Medical Tourism: Saying Goodbye to El Salvador

When I told people we were going to El Salvador their response was almost always "Why in the world would you go there?" People have the impression it's unsafe and the last place in Central America you'd want to visit. Then, tell them you're going for dental work and they are really baffled. Being a journalist, I'm not someone who would randomly hop on a plane and let someone pull my husband's teeth out. I did my homework. Planet Hospital facilitated everything and thankfully got us in contact with Dr. Lorenzana. Knowing he was trained in the U.S., speaks perfect English and is an American Board Certified Prosthodontist helped us feel confident about the quality care. The Americans we'd spoken to ahead of our own decision raved about the experience and they were right.

In all my husband had three teeth pulled, seven implants, a bone graft and a sinus lift. He also has a mouth full of beautiful temporaries. The procedure took about 4 hours. He didn't feel a thing and never had any pain. The entire process far exceeded our expectations. Dr. Lorenzana loves what he does and he loves his country. He has a real desire to let the world know what a great place it is to visit and that the quality of care really is first class.

Hard not to fall in love with the people here. They are so kind and eager to accommodate. It makes them sad and frustrated that the country still has a reputation for being unsafe, despite the war being over for more than a decade. Ricky (Our Planet Hospital Country Host) picked us up at the hotel and took us to Dr. Lorenzana's office for our final visit before heading home. The doctor took all the stitches out of Doug's mouth and gave him the final instructions for keeping his new teeth clean. He'll need to floss and rinse with Listerine, keep his mouth healthy while the implants integrate to his bones. We'll then come back in about five months for Doug's permanent crowns.

It's bittersweet to leave. In the short time we were there we made friends for life, some now are like family. I'm sold on medical tourism as a way to save a whole lot of money and get a vacation in the process. Our original estimate here in the states: 60 thousand dollars. The cost in El Salvador 19 thousand. Add a few thousand for travel expenses and we're still saving over 30 thousand dollars. Doug's temporary teeth look like a million bucks. We can't wait to go back in July.

Hospitals In El Salvador: Zaldivar Institute, Clinica Diagnostico, Dr. Lorenzana Dental Clinic

Actual statistics from "The World Health Report 2000-Health systems: Improving performance."

The U. S. health system spends a higher portion of its gross domestic product than any other country but ranks #37 out of 191 countries according to its performance. However, the US ranks #1 in health expenditure per capita, while El Salvador ranks 115th in the overall health system performance and 83rd in the health expenditure per capita. The reason for this ranking is that El Salvador has something that resembles two distinct health care systems. The first is a completely private based system that uses qualified doctors, state of the art technology and the doctors spend ample time with their patients, which unfortunately, only the wealthy can afford. The other is a government run system that is more designed for the poor, where the doctors are overworked and don't have as much time to spend with each patient. This was largely due to a decrease of government expenditures on health programs during the war.

With the stability of government and less political unrest, El Salvador is becoming a popular gem for medical tourists. Many doctors have trained and studied in the United States, access to the latest state of the art technologies and the beauty of its people are making it a popular destination for dental and medical procedures. El Salvador is a major coffee centre, and coffee influences the way of life, the scent in the air and the attitude of the people. Its capital San Salvador, is an attractive town with many old buildings of pronounced great architecture.

Transportation in this relatively small country is easy, and getting to famous sights will be a breeze. Lake Coatepeque and Chalchuapa are some for the famous ones while San Salvador's Pacific coast rival the best ones in the world. The natural beauty-volcanoes, coffee plantations, and isolated beaches make for a good environment to take a rest and appreciate nature too.

When you visit El Salvador, you will notice that affordable prices reflect the lower cost of living. Cosmetic surgery is common and medical tourism is safe, accepted and one of the best, there is a countrywide modernization, all of which are aimed to improve the tourism industry.

Castilian Spanish is the official language of El Salvador, while English is the second language. This makes communication a lot easier. Cuisine can be described as straightforward and tasty, centering around corn, beans, rice, tomatoes, and meat. Of course, coffee is present, and one of the more simple, but luxurious joys of the trip.

El Salvador

El Salvador is one of the most densely populated countries in Central America. A wide mix of ethnic groups dominated largely by the Spanish and expatriate refugees, give this country its unique and rich cultural heritage. The population is friendly and fun loving and welcomes tourists with open arms. With a favourable tropical climate, temperatures do not vary too much with changing seasons.

The volcanic landscape is breathtaking and makes for a popular tourist attraction. The jagged mountains and calm waters of the lakes on one end are a lovely contrast to the beaches of the Pacific Ocean on the other end. Another interesting aspect of this tourist destination is the mystical ruins of the Mayan culture found in the region. This civilization is said to have been lost mysteriously in time and always fascinates casual tourists and explorers alike.

Medical care at El Salvador

El Salvador is becoming one of the medical tourism hubs in Latin America. Its proximity to America is one of the prime factors fueling this industry. It can be reached within a couple of hours from any city in the US. Countrywide modernization has also led to the establishment of state-of-the-art medical facilities and clinics across El Salvador. This country is a popular medical tourism destination for pre and post operative medical care for cosmetic surgeries and other rehabilitative treatments.

Medical Tourism Expands in El Salvador

El Salvador's foray into the medical tourism industry is backed by its government and export promotion agencies. The tour was sponsored by Export Salud, El Salvador's chamber promoting medical tourism into the country, as well as the Medical Tourism Association. Export Salud has 200 physicians and dentists and is an active member of the Medical Tourism Association.

El Salvador's Vice President, Ana Vilma de Escobar, as well as the Minister of the Exterior and the Minister of Tourism participated in discussions about the burgeoning medical tourism market in El Salvador and solicited the input of the facilitators visiting the country. Representatives of El Salvador Medical Travel toured two privately-owned hospitals that are aggressively marketing medical tourism, Hospital de Diagnostico and Hospital de la Mujer, and met with physicians and dentists who are promoting their care internationally.

Tonya Walton, CEO of El Salvador Medical Tourism, reported "El Salvador is a new player in the medical tourism industry, and I had no idea what to expect from the visit. I was impressed by the high quality hospital facilities as well as the credentials of the physicians who are providing services worldwide." Ms. Walton further indicated that El Salvador is primed to be the next major player in the booming medical tourism industry, presenting strong competition for well-known destinations such as Costa Rica and Mexico.

El Salvador Medical Tourism formalized agreements with Surgical Specialities Abroad and El Salvador Medical, two physician groups that are promoting their services to international travellers.

El Salvador's medical providers offer advanced dentistry, gastroenterology and bariatric surgery, ophthalmology, general surgery, plastic surgery, and orthopedics. The physicians, many of whom were trained in the US, are able to provide services such as dental implants and full mouth restoration, gastric and weight loss surgeries, all types of ophthalmologic care including Lasik, hernia repair, myriad cosmetic procedures, as well as laparoscopic orthopedic procedures and joint replacements. Medical tourists can expect to save up to 75% over U.S. prices.

El Salvador's tourism industry is growing as word spreads about its beautiful beaches, volcanoes, archaeological sites, and mountains. About the size of Massachusetts, vacationers can travel among the attractions in 40 minutes or less. Costs are lower than other Central American destinations such as Costa Rica.

El Salvador Medical Tourism offers comprehensive services to plan and facilitate medical tourism.

El Salvador Medical Tourism facilitates travel abroad for medical, surgical, and dental care. The company focuses on safety, quality, and personalized service.

Medical Tourism Economic Report-El Salvador

El Salvador is a land of amazing beauty and has experienced much growth over the last ten years. During this period, the country has adopted the US dollar as its currency (2001), continued to move towards a free-market democracy, became the first to ratify the Central America-Dominican Republic Free Trade Agreement (CAFTA) in 2006, engaged in a countrywide modernization, and became the third largest economy in Central America despite being the smallest country (total area of 8,123 square miles [21,040 sq km], about the size of the state of Massachusetts) in that region. Most U.S. cities can reach El Salvador by airline within 2 to 7 hours, English is the second language (Spanish is the official language of the nation), and the tourism market from the U.S. and other western countries is robust.

According to a recent report by the Ministry of Tourism, El Salvador received $411,135,773 USD in foreign currency in the first half of 2008 (annualized to $822 million USD or a 22.0% growth in earnings compared to 2007). The same report indicates that were 991,874 tourists during this same period (annualized to 1.9 million tourists or a 25.8% growth rate compared to 2007). Also, for the same period, the percentage distribution of tourists by region is: Central America, 62.12%; North America, 31.64%; Europe, 2.83%; South America, 2.30%. Within the Central American market niche, the number of tourists from Guatemala (which it borders along with Honduras-which is third with 103,234 arrivals or 15.0% of the total) increased by 12.95% versus 2007. The U.S. was 2nd with 183,476 arrivals (360k when annualized) which was about 26.65% of the total number of tourists.

Recently, the country has been expanding capacity in the hospitality sector and currently has 7,282 rooms in 318 hotels throughout the country. It has some of the most interesting Mayan ruins in all of Central America, over 307 km of shoreline (with supposedly wonderful surfing!), majestic volcanoes, and beautiful cloud forests. El Salvador has a tropical climate with only two real seasons, the dry season (verano-from November to April), and the wet season (invierno-from May to October). Temperatures vary depending on the elevation in El Salvador with the coastal areas being the warmest, averaging between 22°C and 32°C throughout the year. El Salvador's central international airport, Aeropuerto Internacional Comalapa, is about 50 km southeast of San Salvador (the capital city) and is a major Central and Latin American hub (with direct flights to North American cities like Los Angeles, New York and San Francisco).

The Chamber of Exporters of Health Services of El Salvador (Exportsalud), the Export Promotion Agency of El Salvador (Exporta), the Investment Promotion Agency (Proesa), and Ministry of Tourism (Mitur) are pursuing medical tourism in this country. These include savings of up to 75% over U.S. prices and many U.S.-trained physicians in the areas of dentistry, gastroenterology, bariatric surgery, ophthalmology, general surgery, plastic surgery, and orthopedics, providing services such as dental implants, gastric and weight loss surgeries, ophthalmologic care, hernia repair, cosmetic procedures, and laparoscopic orthopedic procedures.

Economic Facts

According to the CIA Factbook, it is expected that economic growth will decelerate in 2009 due to the global slowdown and

El Salvador's dependence on exports to the US (its most important trading partner, receiving 65.4% of its exports and providing 46.3% of its imports). In addition (similar to Mexico), El Salvador leads the region in remittances per capita from Salvadorans living abroad (primarily from the U.S.) with inflows equivalent to nearly all export income (in 2005, remittances reached $2.83 billion). An estimated 1.5 to two million Salvadorans reside in the United States (estimated in 2007 as 3% of the foreign born residents), many of them illegally (in 2007, it is estimated that only 30.1% are naturalized citizens). The total population of El Salvador is estimated at 7,066,403 and growing at a slightly positive rate of 1.679%.

The GDP (using the purchasing power parity model) of El Salvador was $45.34 billion USD (using 2008 estimates) which equals out to around $6,400 per capita (PPP). GDP was growing at a 3.2% rate and GDP per capita was growing at a 2.3% rate back in 2008. In the most recent estimates from 2008, the services sector makes up 64.1% of the GDP, with industry (primarily manufacturing) making up 24.7%, and agriculture making up 11.2%. The labour force is composed of approximately 2.958 million Salvadorans (by industry in 2006 would be: services 58%, industry 23%, and agriculture 19%) and the unemployment rate is 6.3% according to 2008 official rates (there is quite a bit of underemployment in El Salvador).

Healthcare Facts

The ratio of physicians per 1,000 population in El Salvador increased in the last 5 years from. to 1.22 (but still low compared to an OECD of 3.1) and now the country has at least 7,298 registered physicians (from 2002 numbers). The ratio of nurses per 1,000 population however is which is significantly lower than the OECD average of 9.7. The number of dentists in El Salvador per 1,000 population is surprisingly high at which is comparable to Canada which has a rate of. According to WHO statistics, the total expenditures on health per capita was $387 USD and total expenditures on health as a percentage of GDP was 7.0% (in 2006). This ranks as 83rd in the world in health expenditure per capita but overall El Salvador ranks 115th in the world in health system performance.

According to some commentators, the reason for this low ranking is that El Salvador has something akin to two distinct health care systems. The first is the government run system (approximately 41.8% of the total healthcare expenditures) that is designed for the poor, employs overworked doctors, uses out of date equipment (it was estimated in 2000 that 63% of hospitals in El Salvador are over 30 years old), and don't have as much time to spend with each patient. This system was made up of 610 establishments in 2000 (30 hospitals, with a total of 4,677 hospital beds, 357 health units, 171 "health houses", 52 Rural Nutrition Centres, and 1 clinic).

The second system is a completely private based system (using a Fee For Service or FFS approach) that uses qualified doctors, state of the art technology, and the doctors spend ample time with their patients, which unfortunately, only the affluent can afford (58.2% of healthcare expenditures, with households contributing 97% out-of-pocket). Most of these private sector clinics, general and speciality hospitals are concentrated in the country's capital and other large cities. Some of the main hospitals are the Hospital de Diagnostico, Hospital de la Mujer, Centre Pediatrico, and Centre Ginecologico. The main insurers in this region are SISA, Pan American Life, ASESUISA, and Salud Total.

El Salvador is in the process of receiving recommendations from Joint Commission International, Trent Accreditation Scheme and Accreditation Canada to evaluate options for international accreditation of its hospitals and speciality clinics.

Impacts to Other Industries

An interesting aspect of the medical tourism hopes of El Salvador was the announcement by a medical tourism firm that it was working with a major insurer to design a low-cost health plan (coverage might cost a family as little as $200 USD per month) that would offer limited benefits (sometimes referred to as a "mini-med" plan) where the benefit would be a specific sum of money. Mini-med plans typically provide coverage for a limited number of physician visits each year, a limited amount of inpatient care, and some basic coverage for prescription drugs (the benefits are typically capped at a maximum of about $25,000 USD annually).

Because these policies pay a relatively low amount, patients bear a significant cost-sharing amount for medical care which can provide an incentive to avoid high out-of-pocket costs.

The unique aspect of the plan was that it would reimburse patients the same amount for each particular service, regardless of where it is performed geographically. Therefore, a patient would pay significantly lower out-of-pocket costs by going abroad for treatment.

The firm was planning on a health plan targeted at El Salvadorans living in the United States. These beneficiaries would receive a limited number of primary care visits (in the U.S.) and could travel to El Salvador for covered major medical needs.

Also, an interesting trend is El Salvador's market in reproductive tourism (includes IVF procedures and surrogacy options). Driving this trend are the number of fertility specialist practicing outside the U.S., the state-of-the-art facilities in countries like India, Mexico, and El Salvador, the high surrogacy costs in the U.S. ($80,000 USD or more), and the existing legal liabilities (in the U.S., there are no legal guarantees that the surrogate will not later attempt to keep the baby). It was reported in 2008 that surrogate pregnancies (currently estimated to be a $1 billion USD business in India) only cost around $25,000 USD in India (it is assumed to be similar in El Salvador), plus there are limited legal issues and the arrangements are also easier to manage.

Summary

El Salvador has a lot going for it when looking to grow the medical tourism market particularly in the beauty of its location, friendly populace, and western-trained and English-speaking providers. However, it still has some obstacles to overcome including more robust and mature competitors in other Latin American countries, the disparity in its' health system, and a reputation for violence and crime. However, there is the possibility it could carve out chunks of market share rapidly in areas like full mouth restoration and reproductive tourism, among others. Finally, medical tourism in El Salvador received a big PR boost when a Fox News Radio Anchor/Reporter (Lori Lundin) wrote a multi-piece blog (in 2008) off of the Fox News online site about her experiences in the country. Lori's husband Doug needed a full mouth restoration and was quoted a price of $60,000 USD by a U.S. dental surgeon. They then received quotes from several countries and decided upon El Salvador and paid $19,000 USD for the procedure plus a few thousand for travel expenses (a savings of over $30,000 USD!). They describe the country and the people in a very complimentary light and bemoan the fact that the country still has a reputation for being unsafe. This is a great piece and is worth its weight in gold for marketing medical tourism in this beautiful country.

El Salvador

El Salvador is the capital city of the nation of San Salvador. The valley where it is located was earlier known as "El Valle de las Hamacas" (The Valley of the Hammocks) because of its high seismic activity. San Salvador is the second largest city in Central America. Home to nearly 2.2 million people it is home to one-third of El Salvador 's population and one-half of the country's wealth.

History

The origins of the city can be traced to before the Spanish Conquest. It is near the present location of San Salvador that the Pipil tribes established their capital, Cuscatlán. Although the city was founded in the 16th century, it was rebuilt and changed locations twice afterwards. Originally founded in what is now the colonial town of Suchitoto, north of the present-day city, it was moved to the Valle de Las Hamacas, which boasted more space and more fertile land, thanks to the pristine Acelhuate River.

Culture

Spanish is the main language in El Salvador. The Roman Catholic religion plays an important role in the Salvadorian culture. Important foreign personalities in El Salvador were the Jesuit priests and professors Ignacio Ellacuria, Ignacio Martin-Baro and Segundo Montes. Painting, ceramics and textile goods are the main manual artistic expressions. Writers Francisco Gavidia (1863–1955), Salarrue (Salvador Salazar Arrue) (1899-1975), Claudia Lars, Alfredo Espino, Pedro Geoffroy, Manlio Argueta, José Roberto Cea and poet Roque Dalton are among the most important artists to stem from El Salvador.

Tourism

Parks

San Salvador has the large urban park, the "Parque de los Pericos". There is another park called Parque Cuscatlan, which is very elegant, with lights, trees and paths.

Popular with locals, the beautiful botanical gardens of La Laguna showcase much native fauna. Zoologico Nacional and Parque Saburo Hirao (native plants) are in the SE part of the city by the old Presidential House. Los Planes De Renderos, 1000 meters above sea level, the mountain offers a spectacular view of San Salvador, and is a popular oasis for locals from the hectic city.

Entertainment

San Salvador has several entertainment venues. You can go to restaurants, bars, clubs, casinos, or if you are travelling with kids you can go to the cinemas, bowling, bingo, and arcades.

The trendiest night spot to visit is called Zona Rosa. Some of the best hotels are located there, including the Sheraton Presidente as well as one of the most luxurious hotels in Central America, the Hilton Princess. Although Zona Rosa doesn't cover a large area, it's home to many exclusive, upscale bars and nightclubs, and the best restaurants in town.

Beaches

Between 1996 and 2006, 7.3 million visitors mainly Central Americans and Europeans along the Pacific Oceans coast line. Most of the North American and European tourists are seeking out El Salvador's fine beaches to relax and for surfing. Among the best recommended beach resorts is the Casa de Mar Hotel & Villas, Hacienda Del Pueblo, Rancho Buena Vista and many more.

Medical Tourism Fame

Its move toward democracy and its proximity to the United States are putting El Salvador on the fast track to becoming a medical tourism hub. Private hospitals in the country have state of the art facilities and are staffed with qualified doctors who are able to spend ample time with patients. The most popular procedures sought by medical tourists are cosmetic surgery and dental treatments, both of which you can get for a fraction of the cost compared to the U.S.

Language

The official language of El Salvador is Spanish, however English is spoken by some throughout the country.

Climate

El Salvador's climate is tropical with two seasons: the wet season (May to October) and the dry season (November to April). The temperature depends on the elevation. Coastal areas tend to be hotter with average temperatures between 72°F and 90°F (22°C and 32°C) year round. The central areas have varying temperatures, which can be as high as 82°F (28°C) and as low as 66°F (19°C).

Visa/Entrance Requirements

U.S. and Canadian citizens do not need a visa in order to enter El Salvador, but you must have a passport (valid for 6 months from the date of entry). You must also buy a tourist card (valid for 30 days, but you can request up to 90 days) for $10 USD upon entry. If you leave the country by land before the expiration of the tourist card you may return without having to pay another $10.

Airlines Servicing this Destination

There is one international airport in El Salvador. It is located in San Salvador and is called the Cuscatlan International Airport (SAL).

The following airlines have flights to El Salvador:

* Delta
* Air Transat (seasonal)
* American Airlines
* Continental Airlines
* Copa Airlines
* Mexicana
* TACA.

Hotels

El Salvador has many options for the budget traveller. A private room in a hostel or guesthouse ranges from $10 to $25 USD per person per night and 3 star hotels start at $60.

There are also luxurious hotels in the country, one of which won the 2005 World Travel Award. 5 star hotels are comparatively cheaper than in the U.S. or Western Europe. They range from $95 to $200 USD.

Currency

El Salvador has two currencies:

* United States Dollar (USD).
* El Salvador Colon (SVC).

  The exchange rate of U.S. dollars to El Salvadorian colones is $1 USD to 8.75 SVC.
* The colon is no longer being printed in an attempt to make the U.S. dollar the only currency circulating in the country.

Communicating Home

The international access code for El Salvador is 503.

In order to call El Salvador from the U.S. or Canada you must dial 011 (exit code), then 503 (country code for the El Salvador), and then the phone number (eight digits. All fixed numbers start with the number 2). To call a cell phone in El Salvador from the U.S. or Canada you must dial 011 + 503 + phone number (eight digits, starts with the number seven). In order to call the U.S. or Canada from El Salvador you must dial 00 + 1 + area code + phone number.

Cyber-cafes are widely available in major cities and towns. Larger hotels and most private hospitals throughout the country offer Broadband Internet connection.

Sightseeing

El Salvador is a naturalist's paradise. La Libertad is 21 miles (34 km) south of San Salvador and is a popular tourist spot. It has beautiful beaches and offers some of the world's best surfing. Just west of La Libertad is Zunzal, where international surfing competitions are held. Other nature sites include the cloud forests of the Parque Nacional Montecristo-El Trifinio, the Volcano of San Miguel, the Laguna Botanical Gardens (in San Salvador), and many hiking trails. Fans of Pompeii and Santorini will be pleased with the Joya de Ceren Archaeological Site. In 600 AD, there was a volcanic eruption that buried the farming community of the Joya de Ceren, which was a prehispanic culture. The community is so well preserved that visitors to this site can see the day to day lifestyles and infrastructure of the Joya de Ceren people.

Shopping

San Salvador has many markets including the Mercado Cuartel, which is the busiest market in the city; the Santa Tecla Market, where you can buy many items from food to pinatas; and the Ilopango market, which is ideal for shopping for handicrafts. If the hustle and bustle of the market does not suit your style, San Salvador has many shopping malls that are frequented by middle class and wealthy Salvadorians and international travellers.

Nightlife and the Arts

Upscale nightlife is localized to the Zona Rosa area of San Salvador, which features venues for salsa dancing, live music, and Mariachi bands. Popular night spots include Senor Frog's, Stanza, Club Code, Guadalajara Grill, and La Luna. Make sure that you take a taxi to and from your hotel to the clubs. Do not walk or take public transportation, especially at night. One of El Salvador's most famous artists, Fernando Llort, who has galleries in the U.S. and Europe also has a gallery in San Salvador. Featured pieces are priced to fit all types of budgets and include original oils, ceramic tiles, tablets, prints, and framed prints. Those who enjoy a nice stroll through a museum should visit the David J. Guzman National Museum of Anthropology, The Museo de la Palabray La Imagen (the Museum of Words and Images), The Natural History Museum of El Salvador, the Zoological Park, and the Museum of Art. For theatre buffs, San Salvador is home to the National Theatre, which is the oldest theatre in Central America.

Medical Tourism Association?

The Medical Tourism Association is the first international non-profit association made up of the top international hospitals, healthcare providers, medical travel facilitators, insurance companies, and other affiliated companies and members with the common goal of promoting the highest level of quality of healthcare to patients in a global environment. Our Association promotes the interests of its healthcare provider and medical tourism facilitators members. The Medical Tourism Association has three tenets: Transparency, Communication and Education.

Transparency

The Medical Tourism Association seeks to provide transparency in both quality of care and pricing. Every day we see more and more that the globalization of healthcare has created a very flat world. We exchange technology, information, communication, physicians and patients. In order to ensure patient safety, it is our goal to create a transparency about the quality of healthcare that can be found in each country. With this, it is increasingly important to create a transparency in pricing as well so patients travelling overseas for care can be sure of what they are receiving without hidden costs or unforeseen expenses. The Medical Tourism Association is also working on the Quality of Care Project, which will change the way we look at the reporting of global healthcare statistics and the quality of care available at hospitals around the world.

Communication

The Members of the Medical Tourism Association agree that communication is the key to success, particularly with respect to ensuring positive patient outcomes. Last year, the Founders of the Medical Tourism Association polled international healthcare providers and found that each provider has the same concerns with the increasing globalization of healthcare. Why should we all try to resolve these concerns individually instead of collectively? The members of the Medical Tourism Association have agreed to put competition aside and work together to resolve the issues one by one and to work together to address them as they arise. We have created a forum for communication for all of the actors in the global healthcare environment. We have committees that work together to address issues such as legal, economic, patient financing, Errors and Omissions (E&O) insurance, communication with insurance companies, media support and more.

Education

Although we live in a world where information is at our fingertips, there are so many people who lack the information that they can receive the highest quality of care outside of their home country. Some patients in countries like the United States, Canada, and the United Kingdom have a lack of access to healthcare due to high cost and high wait times. Patients in some other regions as in some parts of Africa and the Middle East do not have access to high quality of care in their own country and need to look elsewhere.

Some patients just would like to travel outside of their country for healthcare to incorporate high quality of care with a holiday and tourism. Regardless of the reason, patients need education and information to understand what they should look for in finding a provider overseas and considerations that should be taken seriously to ensure patients safety. As insurance companies continue to incorporate global healthcare and medical tourism options into their benefit plans and domestic healthcare providers are required to treat patients for aftercare when patients return to their home country, education is required to accomplish this seamlessly. The Medical Tourism Association strives to provide education to anyone with any interest in this industry using various means: the media, conferences, and through the Medical Tourism Magazine. The Medical Tourism Magazine is a monthly trade journal aimed to provide a wealth of information for anyone interested in or affected by the globalization of healthcare.

Our Mission

* To raise awareness of the high level of quality healthcare available in various countries.
* To promote positive and stable growth of the Medical Tourism and Global Healthcare Industry with a strong focus on Transparency and Communication.
* To provide an unbiased source of information for patients, insurance companies and employers about top hospitals, their quality of care and outcomes.
* To protect the reputation of Medical Tourism from disreputable hospitals and healthcare providers which

may not have the same level of quality healthcare and standards.

* To serve as one voice for purposes of dealing with the government organizations and the media to protect the reputation of the Medical Tourism Association's members.
* To promote and provide a forum for communication and to increase connectivity between patients, healthcare providers, and insurance companies.
* To seek out future affiliated industries and technologies that will allow international healthcare providers to operate more efficiently in the global healthcare industry.
* To educate patients, insurance companies, agents, brokers, consultants and physicians from around the world about the growth of medical tourism and the globalization of healthcare.

Non-Profit Status

The Medical Tourism Association is an international non-profit organization which has been designated for 501(C) status by the Internal Revenue of the United States Government. Section 501(c) of the Internal Revenue Code provides for the exemption of business leagues, which are not organized for profit and no part of the net earnings of which inures to the benefit of any private shareholder or individual. The Medical Tourism Association does not have shareholders or investors.

As provided by www.IRS.gov, a business league is an association of persons having some common business interest, the purpose of which is to promote such common interest and not to engage in a regular business of a kind ordinarily carried on for profit. Trade associations and professional associations are business leagues. To be exempt, a business league's activities must be devoted to improving business conditions of one or more lines of business as distinguished from performing particular services for individual persons.

Medical Tourism Magazine

The Medical Tourism Magazine has launched its online version of the Medical Tourism Magazine at. Readers of the online version of the magazine will be able to read the full version of the magazine online for free and view past issues. The Medical Tourism Magazine is a bi-monthly Medical Tourism industry magazine in both print and electronic versions. Readers can sign up for a free online subscription below or purchase an annual hard copy subscription, by clicking here, Annual Magazine Subscription. The Medical Tourism Magazine will address important issues affecting the Medical Tourism industry and have a primary focus on the quality of healthcare available at leading international hospitals. Each issue of the medical tourism magazine will cover the world as a whole, but also have a special inside focus on one specific country. We are always looking for stories, articles, authors and input for our magazine. Magazine will address issues such as;

1. Quality of Health Care Overseas,
2. Legal Issues Surrounding Medical Tourism,
3. The American, UK and Canadian Health Care Crisis and the opportunities for Medical Tourism in these countries,
4. What Foreign Patients look for in overseas hospitals and providers offering Medical Tourism,
5. Specific Country Focus each issue,
6. Issues International Insurance Companies, Employers and Healthcare companies should consider when entering the Medical Tourism Industry.

The magazines distribution is currently in the thousands and is distributed to International Hospitals, International Health Insurance Carriers in the Middle East, US, UK and Canada, healthcare providers throughout the world, the travel industry, directly to potential medical tourism patients considering going overseas for surgery, and anyone interested in the industry. The magazine also is distributed to a majority of the health plans which administer Self Funded Employer health plans in the U.S.

Medical Tourism Association's Medical Tourism Magazine Announces Issue 10 Special Issue: What Patients Are Saying About You

West Palm Beach, FL, June 05, 2009 –(PR.com)– The Medical Tourism Association is pleased to share their newly released Issue

10 Special Issue: What Patients Are Saying About You with you. Please go to the Medical Tourism Magazine website to view. Scroll down to Issue 10 Special Issue: What Patients Are Saying About You. Highlights from this Issue Include:

It's All About the Patient

From Customer Service on the hospital side and on the facilitator side, to the greater underlying issues of Trust as a whole, medical tourism offers significant opportunities for us to step back and take a look at our service offerings to patients. Only then are we ready to create marketable and successful programs. And after doing so, how do we judge our successes?

By Renee-Marie Stephano

Other articles include: Are Your Patients Wandering Over to Your Competition? 6 Action Tips to Stop Them in Their Tracks...

In an economy such as ours we need to make each patient opportunity count. That means being quicker, smarter and more caring than our competition. Below are six action tips that are guaranteed to keep your patients from falling ill to wanderlust. Because, let's face it, if we don't take care of our patients, someone else will.

By Bill Cook

Patient Survey: The Medical Tourism Association has released preliminary results from its first patient surveys in the Medical Tourism Industry.

This survey is extremely important to the solid growth of the medical tourism industry by providing a better understanding why patients are travelling and where they are travelling to as well as insight. Creating Profitability Through Service Excellence ~ Do You Really Know What Your Customers Think?

In the words of Peter Drucker, widely considered the father of modern management, "Quality in a service or product is not what you put into it. It is what the client or customer gets out of it." How does the medical tourism industry measure business success? The obvious answer is through financial statements and growing patient volume.

By Tonya Walton

The Medical Tourism Magazine is a bi-monthly Medical Tourism industry magazine in both print and electronic versions. Readers can sign up for a free online subscription below or purchase an annual hard copy subscription.

The Medical Tourism Magazine will address important issues affecting the Medical Tourism industry and have a primary focus on the quality of healthcare available at leading international hospitals. Each issue of the medical tourism magazine will cover the world as a whole, but also have a special inside focus on one specific country. We are always looking for stories, articles, authors and input for our magazine.

The Medical Tourism Association is the first international non-profit association made up of the top international hospitals, healthcare providers, medical travel facilitators, insurance companies, and other affiliated companies and members with the common goal of promoting the highest level of quality of healthcare to patients in a global environment. Their Association promotes the interests of its healthcare provider and medical tourism facilitators members. The Medical Tourism Association has three tenets: Transparency, Communication and Education

Medical Tourism Association Presents Health Tourism Magazine

With the increased awareness and incorporation of health and wellness into our lives and the importance of establishing a balance among one's mind, body and soul, the Medical Tourism Association, which you can find at http://www.Medical Tourism Association.com, is launching its new enlightening publication, Health Tourism Magazine.

This is a bimonthly online publication, dedicated to the education and raised awareness of health, wellness, fitness, nutrition, alternative and medical wellness issues at http://www. Health Tourism Magazine.com. With our business to consumer approach to the promotion of each issue of our magazine, Health Tourism Magazine will focus on all areas of health and wellness which may not only complement the treatment plans for patients receiving surgical procedures, but also provide the opportunity for an improvement of the quality of life for both the patients and their companions. With the same focus on quality, informative content and chic style as its "sister" magazine, Medical Tourism Magazine, each issue of the Health Tourism Magazine will cover topics such as integrative, alternative, homeopathic and preventative medicines together with overall spa and wellness topics.

The Medical Tourism Association, also known as the Global Healthcare Association, is the first international non-profit association made up of the top international hospitals, healthcare providers, medical travel facilitators, insurance companies, and other affiliated companies and members with the common goal of promoting the highest level of quality of healthcare to patients in a global environment.

Our Association promotes the interests of its healthcare provider and medical tourism facilitators members. The Medical Tourism Association has three tenets: Transparency, Communication and Education. To find more information please go to http://www. Medical Tourism Association.com.

Health Tourism Magazine is a monthly online magazine, dedicated to educating and raising awareness of health, wellness, alternative and medical wellness issues. With our business to consumer approach to promoting the magazine, Health Tourism Magazine will focus on all areas of health and wellness which compliment surgical procedures. As the "sister" magazine to Medical Tourism Magazine, each issue of the Health Tourism Magazine will cover topics such as integrative, alternative, homeopathic and preventative medicines together with overall spa and wellness topics.

Monthly Medical Tourism Magazine for Thailand

The Health Travel Industry Research Society (HTRIS Thailand) has launched a monthly publication to promote Thailand's medical travel industry.

"Medica Tourism Magazine highlights the very best of Thailand's medical, hospitality, tourism, travel and wellness industries," said Secretary-General Chatree Niramitvijit. "We are working with industry representatives to inform the world about the best offerings, promotion discounts and package deals." The full-colour, 120-page glossy magazine is distributed to more than 60 countries every month through the Kingdom's embassies and consulates, chambers of commerce, trade promotion offices and tourism information centres throughout the world.

HTRIS, a non-profit private sector initiative, was established to focus on information for the improvement and promotion of Thailand's international health service industry, particularly the hospital, hospitality, tourism, travel, wellness and support industries such as transport, insurance, translation, pharmacies, information, retail and entertainment.

Medical Tourism in Singapore

The small state of Singapore is known for its very stringent laws and regulations particularly in the areas involving cleanliness. These regulations are carried over to Singapore's ultra-high quality levels in healthcare and world-class facilities, making it an ideal destination for medical travellers who are looking for modern infrastructure, a clean and structured environment, and an English-speaking populace.

Singapore Healthcare System

The World Health Organization ranked Singapore as the 6th best health system in the world, much higher than the United States and Canada. Singapore hospitals and health centres are either government or public facilities like the Singapore General Hospital, or are privately owned like the Raffles and Parkway hospitals.

These hospitals offer top-of-the-line quality healthcare services and facilities, serviced by English-speaking and internationally trained medical practitioners and staff. Singapore health facilities receive local accreditation from the Singapore Health Promotion Board, the Singapore Laboratory Accreditation System (SINGLAS), the Singapore Accreditation Council (SAC) and the Ministry of Health.

Most of these hospitals are also accredited by top international regulation and standardization bodies. Medical practitioners' standards and practices are regulated by the Singapore Medical

Council, Singapore Nursing Board, Singapore Dental Board, Pharmacy Board and the Laboratory Board. The Health Sciences Authority and the Singapore Accreditation Council controls and regulates the certification of medical devices and other health products.

Singapore Top Hospitals

In 2006, there were already 29 hospitals and speciality centres catering to medical travellers, offering ultra-high quality healthcare and accommodation facilities serviced by 7,000 doctors and over 15,000 registered nurses.

These medical facilities have international accreditation from the Joint Commission International (JCI), ISO and OHSAS. Singapore has a number of JCI-accredited hospitals. These include the following top hospitals:

Alexandra Hospital

First accreditation by the JCI on July 2005 and was renewed on October 2008. The facility started out as the British Military Hospital during the 1930's and was renamed Alexandra after it was handed over to the government in 1971.

National Heart Centre of Singapore

First accreditation by the JCI on October 2005 and was renewed on July 2008. It is Singapore's major health centre for cardiovascular and other cardiac needs catering to both local and foreign patients.

National University Hospital

First accreditation by the JCI on August 2004 and was renewed on July 2007. It is the only university hospital in Singapore that offers international acute tertiary care.

Parkway Hospitals Singapore Pvt. Ltd.

The Parkway Hospitals is a group of three JCI-accredited health facilities which includes the East Shore Hospital, the Gleneagles Hospital and the Mount Elizabeth hospital. These are private healthcare facilities offering local and international health services with tie-ups to healthcare institutions in the Australia, UK and the United States.

Raffles Hospital Private Limited

First accreditation by the JCI on December 2008. It is an international patient's centre that offers a full range of personalized and specialized healthcare services.

Singapore General Hospital

First accreditation by the JCI on July 2005 and was renewed on July 2008. Established in 1821, it is the flagship hospital for the public sector and is the oldest and largest tertiary hospital offering a full range of health specialities.

Institute of Mental Health/Woodbridge Hospital

First accreditation by the JCI on July 2005 and was renewed on July 2008. It is the only institution in Singapore that provides multi-disciplinary tertiary psychiatric services.

Common Treatments Done in Singapore and Comparative Costs

Singaporean hospitals and healthcare facilities offer a wide array of procedures and services for medical travellers, which include but are not limited to the following:

* Orthopedic Surgery (hip and knee replacements, etc.),
* Cardiac Surgeries (heart bypass, valve replacements, etc.),
* Cancer and Oncology,
* Diagnostic/Investigations,
* Cosmetic Surgery,
* Non-surgical Rejuvenation (botox, microdermabrasion, etc.),
* Dental Services (surgeries, dental implants, etc.),
* Bariatric Surgeries,
* Eye/Ophthalmology (LASIK, Cataract Surgeries, etc.),
* Alternative Medicine,
* Health Spas.

The following are cost comparisons between Medical procedures in Singapore and equivalent procedures in the United States:

	USA	Costa Rica	Average Savings
Cardica Surgery			
Heart Bypass	$55,000-$130,000	$13,000-$18,500	70-80%
Heart Valve Replacement	$130,000-$160,000	$12,000-13,000	90-92%
Coronary Angioplasty	$42,000-$57,000	$11,500-$13,000	70-77%
Coronary Angiography	$5,500-$6,000	$1,300-$1,500	70-75%
Orthopedic Surgery			
Hip Replacement	$24,000-$43,000	$12,000-$16,000	50-65%
Hip Resurfacing	$45,000-$50,000	$13,000-$15,000	70-75%
Hysterectomy	$19,000-$21,000	$5,500-$6,500	70-75%
Knee Replacement	$38,000-$42,000	$12,000-$13,500	65-70%
Spinal Fusion	$60,000-$63,000	$8,000-$10,000	80-85%
Plastic and Reconstructive Surgery			
Stem Cell Transplant	$200,000-$250,000	$72,000-$90,000	60-65%
Face Lift (Rhytidectomy)	$19,000-$21,000	$6,500-$7,500	60-65%
Breast Augmentation/Reduction			
(Mammoplasty)	$9,000-$11,000	$7,000-$9,000	18-20%
Liposuction (Lipoplasty)	$14,000-$16,000	$4,500-$5,500	60-65%
Nose Surgery (Rhinoplasty)	$6,500-$7,500	$3,500-$4,500	40-46%
Tummy Tuck (Abdominoplasty)		$8,000-$9,000	$6,000-
$6,500	25-40%		
Eye/Ophthalmology			
LASIK Eye Surgery	$2,000-$2,500	$1,500-$2,000	20-25%
Eyelid Surgery	$6,500-$7,500	$3,500-$4,000	45-50%
General and Cosmetic Dentistry			
Root Canal	$800-$1200	$350-$900	25-60%

Malpractice and Liabilities Laws in Singapore

Doctors in Singapore are required to carry medical malpractice insurance but these are not as expensive as compared to the US, the cost of which are recovered through the payments for medical procedures and treatments as shouldered by patients.

Pros

The WHO ranked the quality of healthcare in Singapore as 6th in the world. Singapore is a highly urbanized, orderly and spotless country so medical tourists should not expect the same chaotic environment that are typical in other Asian destinations. There are several JCI-certified hospitals and healthcare facilities in Singapore. English is one of Singapore's official languages and is spoken by all doctors and medical staff Although the cost for medical procedures in Singapore is not as low compared to India or Thailand, the prices are still lower then Western Europe and the USA.

Cons

Medical procedures and treatments done in Singapore are more expensive compared to other Asian medical tourism destinations such as Thailand, India and Malaysia. The climate in Singapore is hot and humid, which may be uncomfortable to most westerners particularly during the post-procedure and recovery stages Prices of goods, transportation and accommodation in Singapore are relatively more expensive than other Asian countries For US and Canadian medical tourists, travel times to Singapore are very long.

Travelling to Singapore

Non-stop or single-stop flights are available from various destinations to Singapore through the flagship Singapore Airlines and other international airlines.

Average estimated travel time in hours;

From/To	*Singapore*
New York City	18
Los Angeles	16
Australia (Sydney)	7
Indonesia (Jakarta)	2
Philippines (Manila)	3.5
UAE (Dubai)	7
Toronto	21
Vancouver	18
United Kingdom	14

Singapore Entry and Exit Requirements

As a general requirement for entry and exit to Singapore, all foreign visitors are required the following items: passport/travel document with a minimum validity of 6 months; a return or onward ticket; entry requirements for the visitor's next destination; sufficient funds that would support their stay and purpose in Singapore; and required applicable Visa or pass as described below.

Visiting nationals from the UK, Australia, Canada, USA and EU countries do not require a Visa upon entry and will be issued a Social Visit Pass upon arrival, provided that they comply with the general requirements as described above. The visit pass is valid for 30 days upon arrival. Other countries listed in Singapore's Assessment Level I and Level II countries are required to have either a Business Visa or a Social Visit Visa prior to entry to Singapore.

Should there be a need for an extension in stay, or if the required pre-procedure and post-procedure duration requirements would go beyond 30 days, the medical traveller should arrange for an extension pass (valid up to 90 days) from the Embassy of the Republic of Singapore or the Consulate-General of Singapore before leaving the United States or Canada. If the need for extension is determined while already in Singapore, special permits can be arranged and obtained from the Immigrations and Checkpoints Authority of Singapore.

Medical Tourism in Hungary

Hungary has become a prime destination for health travellers from the UK, Germany, Austria, Italy, Scandinavia and other Western European countries seeking affordable dental and cosmetic procedures. The price of treatments in Hungary is usually much lower of what you would have to pay in Western Europe.

Hungary Healthcare System

Medical travellers are assured of a high-quality healthcare system in Hungary as it was patterned after the National Health System of Great Britain when it was established in 1945. The systems in place are all similar except for the long waiting times typical of what patients experience in the UK.

Doctors and medical professionals are registered with the *Orvosi Kamara* of the Hungarian Chamber of Medicine, which provides permission to these professionals to practice their trade. Dentists' and dental surgeon qualifications are controlled by the Hungarian Dental Council, which practices very stringent and comprehensive training that has longer duration than what is practiced in the UK. These qualifications are recognized by the European Union, allowing these doctors to qualify working in any of the EU countries. Unlike in other countries where dentists are specialized in only one area, Hungarian dentists are trained and qualified in all aspects of dentistry. Most top quality hospitals and clinics in Hungary are operated by the private sector although there are some prominent hospitals which are state owned. Private hospitals and clinics usually maintain modern medical equipment, facilities and technologies due to the stringent requirements set by their German and Austrian clients who have been travelling to Hungary for healthcare for over fifteen years. These hospitals, clinics are locally accredited and licensed by the Hungarian Ministry of Health and the State National Health Commission and Medical Service. Hungary is yet to have a JCI-accredited facility, although these hospitals are recognized by the Care Quality Commission in the UK and the rest of the European Union and some have been certified by the International Organization for Standardization.

Top Clinics and Hospitals in Hungary

Javorszky Odon Korhazat Hospital : Located in the municipality of Vac, the Javorszky Odon Hospital is a community hospital with 847 beds and 12 departments and 18 medical specialities that caters to more than 22,000 inpatients and 150,000 outpatients per year. It is the only health care institution in this region that provides acute care. The hospital is ISO certified and has partnered with the Novant Health Triad Region (NHTR) of North Carolina. It is considered as a model hospital for Hungary by the Ministry of Welfare.

Buda Health Centre : Located in Budapest, the Buda Health Centre is the leading institution in Hungary that caters to all aspects of spinal disease through private or state-financed healthcare options.

Aesthetica International Medical Centre : Established in 2005 in the heart of Budapest's Bank Centre, the Aesthetica International is the leading, ISO-certified medical centre offering various services in the fields of cosmetic and plastic surgeries, dermatology, mesotheraphy and other related procedures. It is a subsidiary of the Proportzia Premium Medical Centres in Israel.

FirstMed Centres Kft. : FirstMed Centres are private health facilities that are affiliated with the American Clinics International, Inc. It is a multi-disciplinary international and local health facility that offers physical, family medicine, gynecology, prenatal and orthopedic care.

ProHair Transplant Clinic ProHair is located in Budapest and is the leading national institution dealing with hair loss and balding for all sexes and aims to perform extensive research and help educate the general public about the alopecia or hair loss disease. The clinic is operated by a team of leading plastic surgery and hair transplant doctors.

Common Treatments Done in Hungary and Comparative Costs

Hospitals and healthcare facilities in Hungary offer a wide array of procedures and services for medical travellers, which include but are not limited to the following:

* Plastic surgery
* Aesthetic procedures
* General Dentistry and Dental Surgeries
* Laboratory examinations
* Eye Surgery & Ophthalmology
* Dermatology
* Obesity and Weight Loss Surgery
* Hair Transplantation
* Radiological examinations
* Internal medicine
* General surgery
* Gynecology and Obstetrics.

The following are cost comparisons between Medical procedures in Hungary and equivalent procedures in Germany and the UK:

German Hospitals	*Hungary*	*Average*	*Savings*
Face Lift (rhytidectomy)	€3,800-$6,600	€2,100-€2,700	30%-60%
Breast Augmentation (Mammoplasty)	€3,100-$3,800	€1,800-€2,000	35%-50%
Nose Surgery (Rhinoplasty)	€3,400-€4,000	€1,350-€1,700	50%-65%
UK Hospitals	***Hungary***	***Average***	***Savings***
Plastic and Reconstructive Surgery			
Face Lift (rhytidectomy)	£7,300-£8,000	£2,100-£2,700	70%-80%
Breast Augmentation (Mammoplasty)	£4,800-£5,500	£1,800-£2,000	60%-70%
Tummy Tuck	£4,000-£4,800	£1,600-£1,900	50%-65%
Liposuction (lipoplasty)	£3,000-£3,700	£900-£1,000	65%-75%
Nose Surgery (Rhinoplasty)	£3,500-£4,500	£1,500-£2,300	35%-65%
Porcelain Bonded Crowns	£500	£180	60%-65%
Root Canal (per canal)	£200	£60	70%
Tooth Extraction	£90	£30	65%
Tooth Whitening	£475	£280	40%
Dental Implants	£1,900	£800	55%-60%

Malpractice and Liabilities Laws in Hungary

It is a requirement by Hungarian law that all medical and healthcare facilities should provide their doctors with insurance against malpractice claims. Although the number of cases are relatively small at 300 cases per year, these malpractice suits are for lesser sums compared to international standards. However, these figures are starting to rise in recent years, prompting insurance companies to increase their premiums on medical malpractice coverage.

Pros

* Premium dental and cosmetic surgery procedures at very cost-effective prices.
* State of the art medical, healthcare and diagnostic facilities comparable to top international standards.

* English and German speaking, highly trained and qualified medical specialists and staff.
* Affordable accommodations and favourable tourism destinations suitable for post-surgery recovery.
* Close proximity to the European and Middle Eastern countries make it a prime destination for medical travellers from these regions.

Cons

* Lack of International accreditation including the JCI in the majority of hospitals and clinics.
* There are a limited number of major hospitals catering to international patients. Most of the market is served by small clinics.
* Malpractice compensation is relatively low compared to Western Europe.

Entry and Exit Requirements to Hungary

Citizens of the European Union do not require an entry visa for a stay in Hungary of up to 90 days, as long as the passports carried by the passengers are still valid within 6 months from the date of entry.

Statistics for Medical Tourism in Hungary

Medical travellers from Austria and Germany have long been regular clients for Hungary's dental and surgical industry. A report by the BBC claimed that more than a million medical tourists from Austria go to Hungary for dental procedures each year, while 35,000 patients come from the UK.

Medical Tourism in Malaysia

Malaysia is one the fast emerging destinations for medical tourism in Asia for mostly Asian health travellers. According to the Association of Private Hospitals of Malaysia (APHM), the majority Malaysia's medical tourists come from Indonesia mainly due to the superior quality of healthcare that Malaysia offers. The same reason draws health travellers from other Asian countries like Bangladesh and Pakistan. Patients from richer Asian countries like Singapore and Japan, which are the second and third highest origins of medical travellers respectively, visit Malaysia due to lower prices of medical procedures. Australians and people from the European Union are attracted to the low cost of medical procedures in Malaysia, while Middle Eastern medical travellers visit Malaysia for both the price and the quality of healthcare provided.

Travelling to Hungary

There are several major airline carriers travelling to Hungary from various countries of origin from across the globe. On top of that, Hungary is also accessible by land, sea and train from neighbouring European countries.

Average estimated travel time in hours

From/To	*Hungary*
London	2
Munich	1
Berlin	1
Vienna	1
Zurich	2
Geneva	2
Rome	2
Paris	2
Copenhagen	2
New York City	9

Healthcare System in Malaysia

The majority of hospitals offering services to medical tourists are privately owned institutions following internationally recognized standards in healthcare. Currently, there are at least 35 hospitals in Malaysia that are being geared for medical tourism. All are accredited locally by the Malaysian Medical Society for Quality of Health (MSQH) and are licensed by the Malaysian Ministry of Health. Most of these hospitals are accredited by international bodies including the International Organization for Standardization (ISO) and the Joint Commissions International (JCI) among others, making them at par with medical institutions in western countries. Doctors and staff practicing at Malaysia international hospitals are English-speaking and internationally trained. Over 90 percent of these doctors were trained in the UK, USA or Australia, and in some cases are involved in international medical research.

Top Hospitals in Malaysia

* Penang Adventist Hospital.

Jalan Burma, Malaysia

First accredited by the JCI on November 2007. Established in 1924, this not-for-profit hospital is fully owned and controlled by a Malaysian company and has grown ever since as a tertiary healthcare institution using up to date medical equipment and procedures.

* Prince Court Medical Centre.

Kuala Lumpur, Malaysia

First accredited by the JCI on December 2008. Privately owned by Petronas, the hospital boasts of a 300-bed state-of-the art medical centre offering various healthcare services including cardiology, plastic surgery and wellness treatments.

* Twin Towers Medical Centre.

Kuala Lumpur, Malaysia

Located in the hearth of Kuala Lumpur as the in-house medical facility in the Petronas Twin Tower complex, this medical centre is the largest outpatient polyclinic in Malaysia's premiere commercial centre, catering to both local and international patients.

* Institute Jantung Negara National Heart Institute.

Also known as IJN, it is the leading heart institution in Malaysia offering advanced cardiovascular and thoracic health services to both adult and pediatric patients, working in conjunction with leading international medical organizations and using the latest techniques in heart care.

* International Specialist Eye Centre (ISEC).

Kuala Lumpur, Malaysia

First accredited by the JCI on February 2009. An ambulatory

surgical centre or ASC, ISEC is Malaysia's premiere centre for ophthalmology and eye care.

Treatments done in Malaysia and Comparative Costs

Hospitals and healthcare facilities in Malaysia offer a wide array of procedures and services for medical travellers, which include but are not limited to the following:

* Cosmetic and Reconstructive surgery
* Endocrinology
* Ear, Nose and Throat (ENT)
* General and Cosmetic Dentistry
* Gastroenterology
* General Surgery
* Dialysis and Nephrology
* Health Screening and Special Diagnostic Services
* Health Screening Packages
* Health rejuvenation packages
* Immunization and Vaccination Services
* Internal Medicine
* Obstetrics and Gynecology
* Ophthalmology
* Orthopedics
* Pediatrics
* Urology.

The following are cost comparisons between Medical procedures in Malaysia and equivalent procedures in the UK and the United States:

UK Hospitals	*Malaysia*	*Average*	*Savings*
Face Lift (rhytidectomy)	$11,000-$12,000	$2,500-$3,500	70%-77%
Breast Augmentation (Mammoplasty)	$7,000-$8,000	$3,000-$4,000	50%-57%
Breast Reduction	$8,000-$9,000	$3,000-$4,000	55%-63%
Breast Lift	$2,000-$3,000	$900-$1,000	55%-67%
Tummy Tuck	$6,000-$7,000	$2,000-$2,500	64%-67%
Liposuction (lipoplasty)	$5,000-$6,000	$2,000-$3.000	50%-60%
Nose Surgery (Rhinoplasty)	$5,500-$6,500	$2,000-$2,500	61%-64%

General and Cosmetic Dentistry			
Porcelain Bonded Crowns	$950-$1,000	$150-$200	80%-84%
Root Canal (per canal)	$300-$400	$200-$250	33%-38%
US Hospitals	Malaysia	Average	Savings
Medical Procedures			
Angioplasty	$55,000-$57,000	$7,500-$8,500	80%-86%
Heart Bypass	$120,000-$130,000	$11,500-$12,500	90%-91%
Heart-valve Replacement	$150,000-$160,000	$14,500-$15,500	90%-91%
Hip Replacement	$41,000-$43,000	$9,500-$10,500	75%-77%
Hysterectomy	$18,000-$20,000	$3,500-$4,500	77%-81%
Knee Replacement	$38,000-$40,000	$7,500-$8,500	78%-80%
Plastic and Reconstructive Surgery			
Face Lift (rhytidectomy)	$7,000-$9,000	$2,500-$3,500	61%-64%
Breast Augmentation (Mammoplasty)	$5,000-$8,000	$3,000-$4,000	40%-50%
Breast Reduction	$4,000-$6,000	$3,000-$4,000	25%-33%
Complete Liposuction (lipoplasty)	$4,000-$6,500	$2,000-$3.000	50%-53%
Nose Surgery (Rhinoplasty)	$5,500-$6,500	$2,000-$2,500	61%-63%
General and Cosmetic Dentistry			
Root Canal	$600-$1,000	$200-$250	67%-75%
Porcelain Crown	$600-$1,000	$150-$200	75%-80%

Malpractice and Liabilities Laws in Malaysia

Statistics from 2004 have indicated that at least 50 percent of private medical practitioners in Malaysia had no medical indemnity cover cover, although the Ministry of Health in Malaysia have declared an increasing trend in the amount of compensation paid by the Malaysian government for liability cases since the year 2000. At present, the Malaysian government follows the Tort system for the control and regulation of litigation cases due to medical malpractice of negligence, wherein compensation is paid only for proven negligent cases.

Pros

* State of the art medical, healthcare and diagnostic facilities.
* Competitive prices of medical procedures and treatments.
* English-speaking, highly trained and qualified medical specialists and staff.
* Strict adherence to internationally recognized quality medical standards.
* Affordable accommodations and favourable tourism destinations suitable for post-surgery recovery.

Cons

* Terrorist activities and kidnapping of tourists is still a primary concern particularly in certain areas in the country, which are geared for western visitors and tourists.

Travelling to Malaysia

There are six international airports in Malaysia catering to more than 35 international carriers from anywhere around the world, making it very accessible from neighbouring Asian countries as well as from outside the continent.

Average estimated travel time in hours

From/To	*Malaysia*
New York City	20
Los Angeles	19
London	12
Singapore	1
Jakarta	2
Dubai	7
Riyadh	7
Bangladesh	3
Pakistan	5
Tokyo	6.5
Sydney	8

Entry and Exit Requirements to Malaysia

There are various visa requirements to Malaysia depending on the country of origin. Length of stay is typically 1 to 3 months; however extensions may be available upon request to the Malaysian High Commission. The following is a brief summary of visa requirements from prominent nations where most medical tourists are coming from (October 2009):

* No Visa Requirements
* UK and British Commonwealth/protected countries
* United States of America
* Switzerland
* Netherlands
* No Visa Requirements depending on maximum length of stay:
* 3 months maximum.

Albania, Algeria, Argentina, Austria, Bahrain, Belgium, Brazil, Bosnia Herzegovina, Chile, Croatia, Cuba, Czech Republic, Denmark, Egypt, Finland, France, Germany, Hungary, Iceland, Italy, Japan, Jordan, Kyrgyzstan, Kuwait, Lebanon, Luxembourg, Norway, Oman, Peru, Poland, Qatar, Romania, Saudi Arabia, South Korea, Spain, Sweden, Slovakia, Tunisia, Turkey, U.A.E., Uruguay, and Yemen.

1 month maximum:

* Asean Countries, Hong Kong, Macau, British National Overseas and North Korea.

14 days maximum:

* Afghanistan, Iran, Iraq, Libya, Syria, Macau (travel permit) and Portugal Alien Passport.

Needs Malaysian Visa for a stay exceeding one month:

* Thailand, Laos, Vietnam, Myanmar, Indonesia, Cambodia and the Philippines.
* Needs Malaysian Visa for Entry
* **Bangladesh, Bhutan, China, India, Nepal, Nigeria, Pakistan, Sri Lanka, Angola, Burkina Faso, Burundi, Cameroon,**

Cape Verde, Central African Republic, Chad, Comoros, Congo Republic, Cote D'Ivoire, Djibouti, Equatorial Guinea, Eritrea, Ethiopia, Guinea Republic, Guinea-Bissau, Liberia, Madagascar, Mali, Mauritania, Mozambique, Rwanda, Senegal, Western Sahara, Taiwan.

* Special Approval Required.
* Citizens of Israel and Yugoslavia.
* Statistics for Medical Tourism in Malaysia.

The amount of medical tourists to Malaysia in 2007 has tripled since 2003, with figures already reaching more than 282,000 for the first nine months of 2008 alone, which is 16 percent higher than in 2007. The 2007 figures indicate Indonesia at the top of the list accounting for 72 percent of foreign patients to Malaysia, followed by 10 percent from Singapore and another 5 percent from Japan.

HealthCare Patients Visiting Malaysia according to the Association of Private Hospitals of Malaysia (APHM):

2003	*2004*	*2005*	*2006*	*2007*
102,946	174,189	232,161	296,687	341,288

Malaysia Medical Tourism Patients according to Country of Origin (Year: 2007)

Indonesia	*Singapore*	*Japan*	*India*	*Europe*	*Others*
72%	10%	5%	4%	3%	6%

Medical Tourism in Panama

Search Panama for or browse Panama hospitals and clinics. Earning the title as the "Hong Kong" or "Dubai" of the Americas due to its significantly lower cost of living and fully "Americanized" culture, Panama is slowly becoming one of the top medical tourism destinations, attracting US and Canadian health travellers due to its proximity and excellent healthcare services, US trained and certified medical staff and attractive natural beauty.

Healthcare System in Panama

Panama's long association with the United States have left a distinctly American footprint into its culture, giving it more than a hundred years advantage over other countries in providing healthcare to American patients using US standards of quality and service. This can be seen in the similarities in facilities and medical procedures and practices, as well as the abundance of US trained and board certified doctors and medical staff. There is currently one hospital in Panama that is fully certified by the Joint Commissions International. All of the other top hospitals however, most of which are privately owned, are fully certified by local medical accreditation bodies set by the Panamanian government as well as other non-government accreditation bodies. On top of that, most of these hospitals have affiliations and are duly recognized by international medical organizations such as the Johns Hopkins International, Baptist Health International of Miami, Cleveland Clinic, Tulane Health Science Centre, Miami Children's Hospital, University of Nebraska Medical Centre, the Harvard Medical Faculty, the Kendall Medical Centre and the Beth Israel Deaconess Medical Centre among others.

Top Hospitals in Panama

Major hospitals in Panama have affiliations with prominent international medical institutions, enabling them to maintain a high quality level not only in their facilities but also in procedures, methodology and technology as well. More prominent among these Panamanian hospitals include:

Hospital Punta Pacifica : This is the only Central American medical facility that is affiliated with the Johns Hopkins Medical International and maintains the same high-end standards in facilities, services and staff. It is also the only digitally connected hospital in the region and is the only hospital accredited by the Joint Commissions International.

Hospital Nacional : Starting out as a 10-bed facility, the Hospital Nacional has grown over the years into an 80-bed private healthcare facility with over a hundred specialists and ultra-modern facilities.

Clinica Hospital San Fernando : A private hospital affiliated with the Tulane University, Miami Children's Hospital and the Baptist Health International Miami, the Hospital San Fernando is one of Panama's largest hospitals with 24-hour medical services, facilities that are fully equipped with state-of-the-art medical equipments.

Centre Medico Paitilla : Located in Panama City, this 160-bed medical facility is affiliated with the Cleveland Clinic Foundation and has been in existence since 1975. It is also a certified training facility for the American Heart Association and was one of only two hospitals that provided healthcare services to US military personnel.

Popular Treatments done in Panama and Comparative Costs: Hospitals and healthcare facilities in Panama offer a wide array of procedures and services for medical travellers, which include but are not limited to the following:

Cosmetic/Plastic Surgery: Face, Breast, Body Contouring: Dental Services (surgeries, teeth whitening, dental implants, etc.).

* Fertility Treatments
* Bariatric/Obesity Surgeries
* Cancer treatment and Oncology
* Eye/Ophthalmology (LASIK, Cataract Surgeries, Vitreo Retinal Surgery, etc.)
* Stem Cell Therapy.

The following are cost comparisons between Medical procedures in Panama and equivalent procedures in the United States:

US Hospitals	*Panama*	*Average*	*Savings*
Medical Procedures			
Angioplasty with stent	$19,000-$21,000	$10,000-$15,000	25%-47%
Pace Maker	$4,000-$6,000	$1,500-$2,300	50%-60%
Laparoscopic Hernia	$6,000-$8,000	$ 3,500-$4,500	40%-50%
Laparoscopic Gastric Bypass	$24,000-$26,000	$14,000-$16,000	35%-40%
Hip Prosthesis	$19,000-$21,000	$11,000-$13,000	35%-40%
Artroscopy	$9,000-$11,000	$4,000-$6,000	45%-55%
Knee Replacement	$19,000-$21,000	$11,000-$13,000	35%-40%
Herniated Disc	$19,000-$21,000	$6,000-$7,000	65%-70%
Carpal Tunnel Release	$6,000-$8,000	$2,500-$3,500	55%-60%

Plastic and Reconstructive Surgery			
Neck Lift	$10,000-$12,000	$2,000-$3,000	75%-80%
Face Lift (rhytidectomy)	$10,000-$12,000	$2,000-$3,000	75%-80%
Breast Augmentation/ Reduction (Mammoplasty)	$5,500-$8,000	$3,100-$4,500	40%-45%
Breast Lift	$5,000-$6,000	$3,000-$4,000	35%-40%
Liposuction (Lipoplasty)	$4,000-$6,500	$2,500-$4,400	30%-35%
Nose Surgery (Rhinoplasty)	$4,000-$6,000	$1,500-$2,500	55%-65%
Buttocks Augmentation	$5,000-$6,000	$3,500-$4,500	25%-30%
Chemical Peel	$900-$1,100	$450-$550	45%-55%
Obstetrics and Gynecology			
Intrauterine Insemination	$1,000-$2,000	$800-$900	20%-55%
In Vitro Fertilization	$9,000-$18,000	$4,000-$6,000	55%-70%
In Vitro Fertilization with donated egg	$16,000-$20,000	$7,000-$9,000	50%-55%
Eye/Ophthalmology			
Cataract surgery	$5,500-$6,500	$2,000-$3,000	50%-60%
Refractive surgery (Eximer Laser)	$4,500-$5,500	$1,500-$2,500	55%-60%
Glaucoma surgery	$5,500-$6,500	$1,500-$2,500	60%-75%
Refractive surgery with intraocular lens implant	$5,500-$6,500	$2,000-$3,000	50%-60%
Eyelid Surgery	$4,000-$5,500	$1,500-$2,500	60%-65%
General and Cosmetic Dentistry			
Root Canal	$900-$1100	$250-$350	70%-75%
Porcelain Crown	$1,000-$2,000	$450-$550	55%-75%
Porcelain Veneers	$1,000-$2,000	$450-$550	55%-75%
Composite Veneers	$600-$750	$150-$250	45%-70%
Dental Implant	$2,000-$2,500	$900-$1100	55%-60%
Periodontal Surgery	$1,000-$2,000	$450-$550	55%-75%
Periodontal Plastic Surgery	$1,000-$2,000	$450-$550	55%-75%
Periodontal Regenerative Procedures	$1,200-$1,600	$500-$600	55%-65%

Malpractice and Liabilities Laws in Panama

The Panamanian system has not adopted the US legalities associated with medical practices, particularly in the area of malpractice. Although doctors are responsible for their activities and performance under the law in this country, they are not required to shoulder the damages incurred during a malpractice case.

The result is a lower malpractice insurance pre-requisite, which can be translated into lower procedural costs.

Pros

* Hospitals in Panama provide high quality health care through a large staff of US-trained doctors, physicians and other medical specialists.
* Techniques, medications, treatments and facilities used are based on the same standards used in the USA.
* Doctors and medical staff can communicate well in English.
* Panama City is considered Central America's safest and most modern city. Even the tap water is safe to drink.
* Panama is relatively close to US and Canada.
* The currency is the US dollar, so prices can be compared easily.

Cons

* There is only one JCI-accredited hospital in Panama although a few have already submitted and are currently undergoing the accreditation procedures.
* Costs of medical procedures are higher compared to other medical tourism destinations, although these are still significantly more economical as compared to the US, Canada and the UK.

Travelling to Panama

Direct flights to Panama City are available from major cities in the US and Canada and this close proximity and shorter travel time makes Panama a destination of choice for medical travellers.

Average estimated travel time in hours

From/To	*Panama*
New York City	5
Los Angeles	7
Miami	2.75
Houston	4
Dallas	4.5
Washington	4.75
Atlanta	4
Toronto	5
Vancouver	8

Entry and Exit Requirements to Panama

USA and Canadian medical travellers with a valid passport that is at least 6 months beyond the traveller's intended last day of stay do not need to get a visa to enter Panama. A tourist card can be purchased upon arrival, allowing the recipient to stay for 90 days in the country. Other requirements include return tickets, sufficient funds to shoulder the stay, and confirmed accommodations and other targeted facilities. Panamanian immigration laws are very strict so it is advisable to carry your passport with you at all times to show your proof of entry and avoid any complications during your stay.

Statistics for medical tourism in Panama

Doctors have estimated that there are only hundreds of medical tourists from the United States visiting Panama per year, with some hospitals declaring that they have received at least 400 to 450 international patients within the last four years seeking various medical procedures.

These figures would continue to grow as Americans without health insurance continue to seek healthcare in nearby medical tourism destinations such as Panama. More and more baby boomers are contemplating retiring to this Latin American destination as well as seeking healthcare services and beauty treatments at lower costs.

Medical Tourism in Turkey

Offering high quality facilities for medical, thermal, spas and wellness services while incorporating five-star hotel accommodations, Turkey has become a choice destination for medical tourists coming from England, Holland, Ukraine, Russia, Romania, Bulgaria and other European countries, as well as Middle Eastern countries like Iran, Iraq, Bahrain, Syria, Kuwait and the United Arab Emirates.

Turkey Healthcare System

Turkey is currently seeking to join the European Union and is set to receive membership by 2014. In preparation for this, both government and private healthcare institutions are conducting strict implementation of quality, technical and medical standards which are constantly being monitored by independent watchdogs set by the Ministry of Health. The MOH, together with an Independent Turkish Medical Associations sets the local standards and guidelines followed by hospitals, healthcare facilities and medical practitioners. The Turkish Ministry of Health owns and operates approximately 55% of Turkey's more than 1200 hospitals, while the rest is owned by Universities, private companies and foreign entities.

These hospitals have local and international accreditation including the JCI (Joint Commissions International), the JACHO (Joint Commission on Accreditation of Healthcare Organizations), ISO (International Organization for Standardization) and affiliations with western medical groups and facilities. Most of these hospitals have English-speaking doctors and medical staff and are certified by the Turkish Medical Association as well as being members of organizations according to their specializations, including the Turkish Dental Association, Turkish Gynecologist & Obstetric Association, Turkish Orthopedic and Traumatology Association, Turkish Plastic Reconstructive & Aesthetic Surgery Association, Turkish Society of Cardiovascular Surgery, and other specialized associations.

Top Hospitals in Turkey

Turkey boasts of more than 30 **medical facilities** that are accredited by the Joint Commission International, the largest accreditation any country has achieved. Most of these hospitals are also affiliated with top US medical providers like the Harvard Medical School and Johns Hopkins Medicine among others. These hospitals are equipped with the latest medical technologies with board-certified staff, more than 35% of which are trained in the US and other western countries.

The top hospitals in Turkey include:

Istanbul Memorial Hospital-Instanbul, Turkey

The first hospital in Turkey that was accredited by the JCI in March, 2002 and has already been re-accredited twice-once in 2005 and again in 2008.

Anadolu Medical Centre-Kocaeli, Turkey : First accreditation by the JCI on February 2007. The facility is affiliated with Johns Hopkins International and focuses on cardiac care, neurological sciences, oncology, women's health and other surgical specialities.

Acibadem Healthcare Group : Affilitiated with Harvard Medical International, the Acibadem Healthcare Group is composed of five JCI-accredited hospitals located in different locations in Turkey including the Acibadem Bakirkoy Hospital, Acibadem Bursa Hospital, Acibadem Kocaeli Hospital, Acibadem Kadikoy Hospital, and the Acibadem Kozyatagi Hospital.

Medical Park Healthcare Group : The Medical Park Healthcare Group is composed of four JCI-accredited hospitals located in various areas in Turkey which includes the Medical Park Healthcare Group-Antalya Hospital, Medical Park Healthcare Group-Bahcelievler Hospital, Medical Park Healthcare Group-Bursa Hospital, and the Medical Park Healthcare Group-Goztepe Hospital.

Florence Nightingale Hospital Group : The Florence Nightingale Hospital Group is composed of three JCI-accredited hospitals located in various areas in Turkey which includes the Sisli Florence Nightingale Hospital, Gayrettepe Florence Nightingale Hospital, and the Kadikoy Florence Nightingale Hospital.

Dunya Eye Hospital : First accreditation by the JCI on July 2006. It is one of the top eye hospitals in Turkey and is one of the best in the world in terms of success rates for its more than 1000 cataract operations per month.

Common Treatments done in Turkey and Comparative Costs: For generations, Turkey has been known for its excellent thermal spa resorts, some of which has been in existence since the time of the Romans.

In modern times, the hospitals and healthcare facilities in Turkey offer a wide array of procedures and services for medical travellers, which include but are not limited to the following:

* Plastic Surgery
* Fertility and Sterility
* General and Aesthetic Dentistry
* Psoriasis Treatment
* Physiotherapy
* Spa and Thermal resorts
* Beauty Centres
* Eye Health
* Obesity and Bariatric Surgery
* Renal Dialysis
* Oxygen Therapy.

The following are cost comparisons between Medical procedures in Turkey and equivalent procedures in the United Kingdom:

UK Hospitals	*Turkey*	*Average*	*Savings*
Medical Procedures			
Coronary Angioplasty	$13,000-$15,000	$5,000-$6,000	60%-65%
Hip Replacement	$13,500-$14,500	$6,500-$7,500	45%-50$
Prostrate Removal (Prostatectomy)	$7,000-$8,000	$5,500-$6,500	15%-20%
Knee Replacement	$16,000-$17,000	$7,000-$8,000	50%-60%
Hemorrhoids Removal	$3,000-$4,000	$1,500-$2,500	45%-55%

Plastic and Reconstructive Surgery			
Face Lift (rhytidectomy)	$11,000-$12,000	$3,000-$4,000	65%-75%
Breast Augmentation (Mammoplasty)	$7,000-$8,000	$3,000-$4,000	50%-60%
Breast Reduction	$8,000-$9,000	$3,500-$4,500	50%-60%
Liposuction (lipoplasty)	$5,000-$6,000	$2,000-$3,000	55%-65%
Nose Surgery (Rhinoplasty)	$5,500-$6,500	$3,000-$4,000	40%-45%
Tummy Tuck (Abdominoplasty)	$8,000-$9,000	$3,000-$4,000	55%-60%
Eye/Ophthalmology			
LASIK Eye Surgery	$1,500-$2,500	$1,000-$1,500	20%-25%
Cataract Removal	$4,000-$5,000	$1,000-$2,000	55%-65%
General and Cosmetic Dentistry			
Root Canal (per canal)	$300-$400	$100-$150	55%-65%
Tooth Whitening	$900-$1200	$400-$500	50%-60%
Dental Implants	$3,000-$4,000	$900-$1500	70%-75%
Gold Crowns	$800-$850	$200-$250	70%-75%

Malpractice and Liabilities Laws in Turkey

In a report by Abigail Cotterill from the ADMD Law Firm on Medical Malpractice in Turkey, she described the there are relatively low malpractice suits in Turkey, even when healthcare providers do not normally carry malpractice insurance and the government paying for damages on suits against state facilities. In this regard, the Forensic Medicine Association was established in Turkey focusing on legal cases involving malpractice. Reforms have also been established to implement compulsory insurance for medical practitioners in both state and private-owned health facilities.

Pros

* With the highest number of JCI-accredited health facilities, medical tourists are assured of high quality infrastructure and services by these hospitals and their medical staff.
* Prices in Turkey are very competitive compared to Western European countries like the UK, Ireland, Austria and Italy.

* Turkey has long been a gateway between the East and the West and has been known for its brand of Turkish hospitality.

Cons

* There is a certain level of deficiency in English language levels for personnel dealing with medical tourists.
* There is a lack of knowledge of some hospitals on the required documentations issued to foreign medical travellers.
* Lack of medical tourism companies acting as link between medical tourists and Turkey's medical institutions.
* Petty theft, particularly pick-pockets, are a primary threat to tourists plying the crowded streets in Turkey's major cities.

Travelling to Turkey

Turkey has an easy access from all airlines coming from Europe with a total of more than 300 flights coming from various countries arriving to Turkey's five major airports on a daily basis.

Average estimated travel time in hours

From/To	*Turkey*
UK (London)	4
UK (Manchester)	5
Germany	3
Netherlands	4
Austria	3
Switzerland	3
Russia	7
UAE (Dubai)	4
Bulgaria	2
Romania	2

Entry and Exit Requirements to Turkey

In general, a valid passport and a corresponding visa are required for all travellers making their entry to Turkey. Depending on the country of destination as listed in Turkey's Ministry of Foreign Affairs, entry visas can be obtained upon arrival at Turkey or should be obtained from the Turkish Consulates located in the country of origin. The following are visa requirements for specific countries listed below. Other countries can obtain information from the Turkish MFA website:

* Austria: a 3-month multiple entry visa can be obtained at the Turkish borders for ordinary passport holders. Official passport holders are exempt up to 90 days.
* Australia: a 3-month multiple entry visa can be obtained at the Turkish borders for both ordinary and official passport holders.
* Bulgaria: Diplomatic and service passport holders are given 30 days entry without any visa requirements. Ordinary passport holders are exempt from visa up to 90 days.
* Germany: both ordinary and official passport holders are exempt from visa up to 90 days.
* Netherlands: a 3-month multiple entry visa can be obtained at the Turkish borders for both ordinary passport holders. Official passport holders are exempt up to 90 days.
* Romania: a 1-month single entry visa can be obtained at the Turkish borders for ordinary passport holders. Official passport holders are exempt up to 90 days.
* Russian Federation: a 2-month multiple entry visa can be obtained at the Turkish borders for ordinary passport holders. Official passport holders are exempt up to 90 days.
* Switzerland: both ordinary and official passport holders are exempt from visa up to 90 days.
* United Arab Emirates: a sticker type entry visa can be obtained at the Turkish borders for ordinary passport holders. Official passport holders are exempt up to 90 days.
* United Kingdom: a 3-month multiple entry visa can be obtained at the Turkish borders for both ordinary and official passport holders. "British National Overseas

(BNO)" and the "British Protected Persons (BPP)" Official passport holders should apply for visa at the Turkish consulate prior to arrival in Turkey.

* United States: a 3-month multiple entry visa can be obtained at the Turkish borders for both ordinary and official passport holders.

Statistics for Medical Tourism in Turkey

Located in a strategic area that borders Asia and Europe, Turkey is fast becoming a popular destination for medical travellers tallying more than 200,000 medical tourists from Europe and the Middle East in 2008, a 40% increase from 2007. On top of that, there were approximately 500,000 tourists who visited Turkey's more than 1000 thermal resorts and wellness spas. In a 2007 study on medical tourism, the British rated Turkey as one of the top three destinations for medical travellers coming from the United Kingdom, with India and Hungary sharing the top spot.

Medical Tourism in Mexico

In recent years, Mexico has been a popular destination for US citizens seeking health care. Its proximity to the United States and the relatively low travel costs have been drawing Americans and Canadians, and Mexican-Americans who return home to their family doctor dentist and save money. Initially gaining fame for dentistry and cosmetic surgery, orthopedic procedures now add to Mexico's attractions. With state-of-the-art facilities that can compare with American hospitals, Mexico has become one of the premier destinations for US medical tourists.

Healthcare system in Mexico

According to the World Health Organization Mexican healthcare system is ranked 61 in the world. The private hospitals in Mexico are usually similar in quality and care to those in the United States. There are medical packages which offer accommodations and aftercare away from the urban areas and closer to the vibrant beaches. Mexico's best hospitals and clinics are based in Mexico City, Guadalajara and Monterrey.

Many private clinics catering to Americans are located across the US border, in cities like Tijuana, Mexicali and Laredo. Waiting times in Mexico are not a problem and are generally unheard of. There is also an option to save on prescription medicine for a quicker and smoother aftercare. Mexican costs of medicines are almost half those of the USA and Canada. International patients in Mexico are offered their own private room and face-to-face personal interaction with their doctor or surgeon. Hospitals and clinics are equipped with up-to-date technology, well-trained doctors and on-hand medical staff to cater to all types of medical tourists. The following Mexican hospitals are accredited by the JCI:

The American British Cowdray Medical Centre IAP – Observatorio Campus, Mexico City

Hospital ABC is a non-profit private hospital regulated under the "Ley de Institution de Asistencia Privadas." Established in 1941, it is governed by a Board of volunteers, all prominent Mexicans and expatriates. Among the facilities are 200 in-patient beds and state-of-the-art medical technology. It offers a full range of diagnostic, medical and surgical services. The American British Cowdray Medical centre IAP – Santa Fe Campus, Mexico City;

* Christus Muguerza Alta Especialidad, Monterrey, Mexico.

Christus Muguerza hospital network encompasses 3 hospitals in Monterrey and other Mexican cities. It recently opened a modern health centre that accounts for short stay surgeries.

* Clinica Cumbres Chihuahua, Chihuahua, Mexico.
* Hospital CIMA Hermosillo, Hermosillo, Sonora, Mexico.
* Hospital CIMA Monterrey, Monterrey, San Pedro Garza Garcia N.L. Mexico.
* Hospital San Jose Tec de Monterrey, Monterrey, Nuevo Leon, Mexico.

A world class hospital accredited for its high quality and best-in-class patient care. Since 1969, it has focused on the well-being of care, and the best medical professionals and procedures in a cost-effective way. It is sponsored by the internationally recognized Tecnologico de Monterrey and is located only 150 miles from the US border.

* Hospital Y Clinica OCA, S.A. de C.V., Monterrey, Nuevo Leon, Mexico.

The largest private hospital in the city.

Treatments done in Mexico and comparative costs

Wikipedia lists Mexico among the popular destinations for cosmetic surgery, dental services and surgery and general plastic surgery. Mexican hospitals have become popular lately for bariatric surgery for weight loss, which is an elective procedure that is not covered by some US insurers. The following are the popular treatments sought by medical tourists in Mexico:

* Eye surgery
* Cosmetic surgery
* Dentistry
* Hip surgery
* Knee surgery
* Bariatric surgery
* Medical spa treatment.

The following are comparative costs of general, cosmetic and surgical procedures between US hospitals with those of Mexico.

General Procedures	*USA Hospitals,*	*Mexico Average*	*Savings*
Heart			
Angioplasty	$22,500	$11,500	50%
Angiography	$4,800	$1,200	70%
Valve replacement	$ 46,000	$16,000	60%
Bypass surgery	$44,000	$24,000	50%
Open Heart surgery	$64,000	$24,000	66%
Orthopedic			
Knee	$25,000	$10,500	65%
Hip Replacement	$28,000	$12,500	65%
Shoulder Replacement	$24,500	$9,500	75%
Birmingham Resurfacing	$24,000	$12,500	60%
Other Procedures			
Gastric Bypass Surgery	$30,000	$11,500	70%
Gastric Band Surgery	$24,000	$9,500	60%
Hysterectomy	$14,500	$5,500	75%
Fertility Treatments	$8,500	$2,650	55%

Cosmetic Procedures	*USA Clinic*	*Cancun, MexicoAverage*	*Savings*
Face Lift	$18,000	$4,250	68%
Breast Augmentation	$7,800	$3,800	55%
Tummy Tuck	$8,800	$4,50	50%
Liposuction (per area)	$3,200	$1,150	60%
Rhinoplasty (nose)	$8,000	$3,200	65%
Brow Lift	$7,500	$2,850	70%
Brazilian Buttock	$10,500	$4,950	65%
Neck Lift	$10,000	$4,400	70%
Blepharoplasty (eyelids)	$5,400	$2,950	55%

Dental Procedures	*USA Clinic*	*Monterrey, MexicoAverage*	*Savings*
Implants-6 teeth	$18,500	$3,600	75%
Porcelain crown (6 teeth)	$5,200	$1,600	70%
Bleaching discolored teeth	$250	$50	80%
Dental Vaneers (6 teeth)	$6,000	$1,800	75%
Total Dentures	$4,800	$1,600	70%

Another survey provides the following comparative costs as of 2009:

Medical Procedure	*USA*	*Mexico*
Angioplasty	Up to $57,000	$17,100
Heart Bypass	Up to $144,000	$21,100
Heart Valve Replacement	Up to $170,000	$31,000
Knee Replacement	Up to $50,000	$11,500
Hip Resurfacing	Up to $30,000+	$13,400
Hip Replacement	Up to $43,000	$13,800
Special Fusion	Up to $100,000	$8,000
Face Lift	Up to $15,000	$8,000
Breast Implants	Up to $10,000	$9,000
Rhinoplasty	Up to $8,000	$5,000
Lap Band/Bariatric	Up to $30,000	$9,200
Hysterectomy	Up to $15,000	$7,500
Dental Implant	$2,000-10,000	$1,000

Malpractice and liabilities laws in Mexico

Medical liability is not as strictly enforced by laws in foreign countries as in the United States. Accordingly, it is not surprising to note that malpractice compensation is not as generous.

Foreign doctors are not as secure in malpractice insurance like their American counterparts. An American medical tourist cannot have recourse to the American court system. An American court might not hold an intermediary liable since medical tourism promoters or agents are not health care providers and so cannot "commit malpractice".

Some medical insurers in the US have designed insurance packages for those wishing to get medical health care in Mexico. A California law in 1999 which allowed California insurers to reimburse providers in Mexico has paved the way to changes in the insurance industry or the medical tour package providers. Since Mexican medical care costs less, premiums are less than 2/3 of the cost of their US alternative plans.

Pros

* Distance: The proximity of Mexico to United States and Canada make it a clear choice for American and Canadian residents for their health care needs. Travel expenses are low and make it easy for patients to travel back and forth.
* According to the World Health Organization Mexican hospitals are similar in quality and care to those in the United States. There are medical packages which offer accommodations and aftercare away from the urban areas and closer to the vibrant beaches.
* High rate of fluency in both English and Spanish.
* Increasing number of insurers providing coverage for travellers, as out-of-pocket costs are much lower.
* The prices in Mexico can be lower by 50% to as much as 75% of US average costs.
* Like most Latin American countries, Mexico has an overall friendly and family-oriented culture.
* Waiting times in Mexico are not a problem and are generally unheard of.

* Mexican costs of medicines are almost half those of America and Canada.
* Climate – the wonderful climate deems it conducive to recovery.
* Lessened cultural differences with the US after more than a decade of low trade barriers under the NAFTA.

Cons

* Lack of standardized quality measurement and quality ranking systems.
* difficulty in seeking legal remedy in the event of malpractice.
* Travelling to Mexico.

*Mexico's advantage is its location; flights from US and Canada are short and relatively cheap.

* Californian citizens can even drive to Mexico.
* Flight times from US and Canada to Mexico.

Average estimated travel time in hours

From/To	*Mexico City*	*Guandalajara*	*Monterrey*
New York City	4.5	4.5	3.5
Chicago	3.5	3.5	2.5
Washington, DC	4	4	3
San Francisco	4	4	3
Los Angeles	3.5	3	2.5
Toronto	4	5	5
Montreal	5	5	5
Vancouver	5	5	5

Airfares

Airfares to Mexico peak in late March to early April and mid-June through August.

Holidays are also expensive. Midweek (Mondays – Thursdays) morning roundtrip flights run US$40-60 less than weekend flights but these are generally more crowded and less likely to permit frequent flier upgrades. Open return (no fixed return date) and open-jaw (different arrival and departure cities) tickets are more expensive than roundtrip flights.

Car Travel times from southern US to Mexico

From/To	*Tijuana*	*Mexicali*	*Monterrey*
Los Angeles, CA	2 hrs	4 hrs	
San Francisco, CA	10 hrs	10 hrs	
San Diego, CA	20-30 minutes	2 hrs	
Dallas, TX			10 hrs
Houston, TX			12-13 hrs

Statistics for medical tourism in Mexico

Americans, particularly those living near the Mexican border, now routinely cross to Mexico for medical care. It is believed that half of these medical tourists are US residents of Mexican heritage and merely "go home" for treatment

The number of medical tourists coming in to Mexico ranges from 150,000 to 500,000 annually. It is hard to keep track of the number people coming in to Mexico seeking medical care because there are no official records of such visits.

5

Emerging Concepts in Effective Tourism Developments

Introduction

We have discussed in lesson 13 and 15 the emerging dimensions in Indian tourism and challenges posed due to globalization and liberalization. The new trends in the tourism markets compel all the destinations to develop new products and strengthen or re-engineer the existing products for retaining, enhancing and capturing new markets. The effective tourism development is the panacea for the success of the tourism industry.

The success of the future tourism development will depend upon how fast we are incorporating and implementing the effective tourism development techniques. This lesson discusses 3 major concepts of effective tourism development in Indian context: Destination Development, Human Resource Management and Open Sky Policy.

Objectives

This lesson is aimed at achieving the following objectives:-

- Understand the importance of destination development.
- Understand evolution of destinations and sustainable Destination management.
- Understand the importance of Human Resource Management.
- Know the various human resource problems exist in Indian tourism.

- Know the various institutes provide tourism related courses.

Effective Tourism Development

The success of future tourism is intrinsically connected with the way in which the industry and the tourism system understand and incorporate the emerging critical trends that support its expansion. Tourism is undergoing major changes; aging world population (western countries) and active life style of older traveller, the emerging markets, growing disposable income of the youth and awareness about impact of tourism on environment, will decisively influence the number of tourists, motivation, destination and product choices as well as activities of future travellers.

The rapid liberalization and deregulation of markets will bring fierce competition based on price, quality and characteristics of the tourism products. These trends will bring profound changes in the management and planning of tourism business and destination While global trends push forward new managerial approach, the managers and planners must aware of the emerging tools that helps to manage and market business and destinations. Future trend points towards three strategic directions: satisfying consumers, destination development and management and territory organisations.

Destination Development: An Emerging Theme

Destinations face increasing challenges in international market place where numerous stakeholders (tourists, local people, tour operators, hotels and restaurants owners etc.) with diverse values and often divergent needs compete for scarce resources. The growing population of travellers and inhabitants increasingly make impact on natural and social environment. The success of tourism depends on the ability of the firms and destination to engage in sustainable use and conservation of vital resources. The destination development is the key to sustaining the natural and cultural resources on which tourism depends. Therefore steps have been taken up as key initiative in development of tourism destinations. The close interaction between the public sector, the destinations tourism marketing organisations, private sector and local residents in planning is the key principle of sustainable tourism. Thus the stakeholders can work most effectively together to manage local – global influences on their natural and cultural resources. Effective destination development is the important problem facing tourism managers.

Integrated Destination Management

A new concept adopts system approach where the ecological, physical, social spaces are linked by various networks and institutional structures. Traditionally, destination management tents to represent the tourism industries interests. Their mission is building and enhancing favourable destination image to attract targeted tourists and increase visitor numbers. Therefore, destinations and state and tourism agencies often focus their activities on tourism advertising campaigns. Historically, marketing focused on developing product, price, place and promotion, which ensure reasonable profit to individuals and organisations. Nowadays the marketing has been changed to an organizational function and a set of process for creating, communicating, delivering value to customers and its stakeholders. This reflects a shift away from mere profit motive towards creating value for a network of actors and environment.

The integrated destination management brings in destinations ecological– human communities as equitable and integrated members of planning and marketing and goal setting. The new approach integrates economic mobility, social equity and environmental responsibilities towards achieving the equality of life within living system.

Based on ecosystem network model a sustainable planning and marketing orientation does not just satisfy the needs and wants of individual but it strives to attain sustain ecosystem. The benefits are not just profits, but civic energy and social unity. Competition is replaced by dynamic interaction that aims at environmental, social, economic equity within the local – global network of living and physical structures.

Therefore, sustainable tourism marketing objectives are not to design product, price, place of a tourism destination or attraction, but to ensure quality of life and environments through tourism development. Achieving this will be a challenge. It involves developing an interactive product or place relationship that will give value to visitors and to diverse community stakeholders.

Destination Development

Tourism system, the destination region is perhaps one of the most important elements. Without the richness and variety of tourism environments around the world we would not have the same quality of tourist experience. In order to understand the supply of tourism, consideration has to be given to the different environmental social and economical contexts around the world within which tourism destinations are located. Destinations demonstrate number of common features.

- Destinations are cultural appraisals.
- They are perishable because tourism is consumed where it is produced.
- Destination involves multiple use of tourism with other uses.
- To be successful the components of the amalgam needs to be of equivalent quality.

It is important for the destination to deliver quality experience and product, and in this regard, careful planning and management is essential to ensure a tourism industry based on sustainable development. The destination brings together all aspects of tourism – demand, transportation, supply and marketing. It is one of the most important elements of tourism because destinations and their image attract tourist, motivates the visitor and therefore energize the whole tourism system. As the demand for the tourism has increased, pressure from the growing number of visitors has degraded some destinations. In response to this, planning and management strategies have been implemented in the busier destinations. Planning and management is the key to making existing tourist destination and resources more effective in meeting current as well as future demand.

Thus destination as the focus of facilities and services designed to meet the needs of the tourists.

Most destinations comprise a core of the following components:-

- Attractions – manmade features, natural features or events that provide motivation to visit.
- Access – local transport facilities.
- Amenities (accommodation, food, beverages, entertainment and retailing.
- Auxiliary services in the form of local organisations.

Infrastructure and Super Structure

Infrastructure represents all forms of construction above or below the ground, with extensive communication with the outside world as a basis for tourism activity in the area. Adequate infrastructure is essential for tourism development mainly in the form of transportation, utilities and other services. Generally infrastructure does not generate income and is treated as a public investment in most tourist developments. Where as a super structure is normally private sector activity, as it is the profit-generating element of the destination. It includes accommodation, built attractions, retailing and other services. In many countries public sector is actively providing financial incentives – grants, loans, and tax-holidays for private sector tourism investment. The destination development is a combined effort of public and private sectors.

Destination Evolution

The evolution of tourism has been closely linked to the evolution of destinations and in particular, resorts. The evolution of resorts has been driven by transport developments. Most of these are now touring centres rather than destinations in their own right, and in response touring circuits and clusters of attractions have developed. At the same time markets also respond to these terms of their tourist facilities and services. This evolution of tourism destination can be represented by tourist area life cycle (TALC). This states that destinations go through a cycle of evolution similar to the cycle of a product. The shape of TALC curve will vary, but for each destination it will be dependent upon factors, which can delay or accelerate progress through various stages such as the rate of development, access, government policy, market trends and competing destinations.

The development can be stunned at any stage in cycles, and only tourist developments promising considerable financial returns will mature to experience all stages of cycle itself is variable. The tourism destinations evolve from their beginning or inception stage through exploration, involvement, development, consolidation, stagnation and eventual decline or rejuvenation. Destination life cycle provides a framework for understanding how destinations and their market evolve. Understanding the life cycle aids the development of community – based and sustainable tourism strategies at the involvement stage.

The components of tourist destination can be effective only if careful planning and management deliver a sustainable tourism product. Only in recent years, that the negative impact on tourism on destination, rise of environmentalism and green consciousness have been set for a reassessment of the role and value of tourism to destinations. The concept of sustainability demands a long-term view of tourism and ensures that the consumption of tourism does not exceed the ability of the host destination to provide for future tourists. In other words it represents a trade-off between present and future needs. Perhaps the central issue for here is the gradual shift from short-term to longer-term thinking and planning at the destination.

Carrying Capacity

The concept of sustainability and carrying capacity we discussed in lesson 15 and 17. It is no longer acceptable for the industry to exploit and use-up destinations. The carrying capacity of a site, resort, or even a region refers to the ability to take tourism intervenes in the relationship carrying capacity is the maximum number of people who can use a site without an unacceptable alteration the physical environment and without an unacceptable decline in the quality of experience gained by visitor. Thus the carrying capacity roots in resource management, important aspect especially where finite destination resources are under growing pressure from users.

Development of Destination for Tourists

A sustainable tourism development model attempts to keep tourism in a particular place within the limits of capacity of the place. The late modern forms of tourism are based more on specialization, niche areas and highly competitive than on earning money from volume tourism. Butler's model of tourism development at destination provides more detailed picture of how to achieve the structural development of tourism. A different level of development in an area is presented below:-

Development of a specialized offering for tourists;

- Simplest service offering for tourists is placed at the bottom of service ladder. Common forms of services are cafeterias, petrol stations and dabas. Both local residents and tourists use these services.
- Next Step up the ladder is that there is some form of overnight accommodation in the area, a hotel, and motels but without any special attractions.
- Third step is specialized tourism service providing a greater range of attractions, activities, and accommodations.
- The fourth stage is tourism centres where the whole range of services has been adopted to the needs of tourism for one season or two-season destination.
- Final step on the ladder is advanced service – rich source of services and extensive specialization, in the form of theatres, concert halls, large museums etc.

This model presents the stages in the development from small-scale tourism to mass tourism.

Tourism development strategy When developing a destination, a planner works on two factors:-

- Pull factors – tourism products and attractions. Advanced tourism services Tourism Centres Specialized tourism services Overnight accommodation Temporary stopping places Clients or areas with a highly specialized service Centres where attractions for visitors are the predominant features of the service offering. A good choice of services, accommodation, attractions and activities Some choice as regards type of accommodation. Simple service offering for visitors.

- Push factors – determine demand, provide information about supply of attractions and marketing these areas tourism products.

The tourism destination can be designed structurally through appropriate development strategy. The development strategy provides broad guidelines, future vision and goals for of sustainable development. The procedure involved in the strategy is as follows:-

- Inventory of existing and potential resource for tourism.
- Description and analysis of the structure of the tourist industry – products.
- Analysis of demand.
- Development ambitions of representatives of tourism industry.
- Local community demands regarding tourism.
- Maintaining ecological, social, cultural and economic environment.
- Form of organization for tourism development.

These broad guidelines must be incorporated in the tourism destination development and consumption process.

Future Developments

Tourist destination of the future will be influenced by variety of factors, but technology and the demands of new tourist will be dominant. Technology permeates destination development in many ways such as, hotel communication system, computer reservation system which allows matching of demand with supply and computer generated imagery and use of virtual reality.

Thus the stage is set for a range of new tourist destinations to be developed and for the more effective management of existing destinations. There is no doubt that these new and existing destinations need to be better planned and managed and show more concern for their environment and host community.

Human Resource Development

The success of any industry depends to a great extend up on the quality of human resource and tourism is not an exception.

We have already learnt that tourism is labour intensive industry which provides employment to skilled, semiskilled and unskilled workers directly and indirectly. The progressive labour force with dynamic management and responsive government and responsible society are the pillars of the tourism industry.

Traditionally, the employment has been seen as an area that is reactive to changes in the wide business environment. There is a widely accepted assumption that the role of people within organisations is required to change and develop in response to developments in markets, products and technology. Most of the large tourism companies recognized this assumption and has been started organising work and support human resource functions such as training and development. This is possible only when the external labour market permits employers to adapt these changing dimensions.

Globalization of business firms has a number of implications for human resources management. A major consequence in tourism industry is the issue of matching employee's skills with changing industry requirements.

The traditional practice of employee's learning the majority of skills on the job and gradually progressing to senior position is threatened by the rapid technological changes and the need to respond to the changing service requirements. Employees at the operational and managerial levels are now required to be more flexible and adaptive to constant change. Globalization has major Implications for work and employment in tourism and these include:-

- The need for different skills and competencies is the employees to be able deal with use of technology.
- Dealing with employment related consequences of mergers and strategic alliances.
- Issues of relocation of employees and social and cultural sensitiveness of those working away from home.
- New forms of tourism utilizing natural and cultural environment create a demand for indigenous employees, who could deliver better quality and original products and services.

- Meeting the needs of high skilled tourists who are more experienced and demand higher quality of products and services.

These pressures of globalization in tourism have significant implication for work and employment, especially for human resources development and dealing with cultural aspects.

Human Resource Development in Indian Context

In India there is a tremendous shortage of trained manpower in the hospitality sector. Tourism sector on an average requires manpower about 20,000 per year. Against such a requirement the actual trained output from govt. institution is only 5000 per year. When we consider all other private institutions, the total available trained manpower does not exceed 10,000 in a year. Thus there need to develop required human resource in various segment of the tourism industry, as a consequence of the rapid growth in tourism, changing technology and markets both national and international level.

The main problems involving human resource development is in the tourism sector are-

- Scarcity of qualified manpower.
- Shortage of tourism training infrastructure and qualified trainers.
- Bad working conditions in tourism sector.
- Bad strategies and policies for human resource development.

Tourism Industry has undergone a sea change with respect to human resources development and in response to emerging trends for successful tourism in the country. Both the governments and private sector have realized that hospitality with professional service is the core of tourism. For the industry, the tourists are the ultimate service activity and extending quality service ensures continued clientele. For providing world-class service will always require training, education, increased investment and development of work culture, change in the attitudes and new methods of motivating manpower in the industry for continued growth. Thus this type of pressure of globalization in tourism has significant implications for work and employment especially in human resources development. Hence necessity of trained manpower has become top priority in the agenda of tourism plans over the years.

The Government has recognized tourism as a vehicle for economic development and generator of employment for skilled-semiskilled and unskilled teaming millions not only in popular tourist destinations but also in remotest areas of hinder land The governments have been taking the initiative of setting up a number of institutes all over the country. The institutes of Hotel Management Catering and Technology Applied Nutrition were set up in New Delhi, Mumbai, Chennai, and Kolkata. In order to meet the training requirements at craft levels in specific disciplines, 14 Food Crafts Institutes were set up at different places in the country. In order to harness the resources the Ministry of Tourism established National Council of Hotel Management and Catering Technology in 1984. The established objectives of the Council are-

- Advise the Govt. on coordinated development of hotel management and catering education.
- Serve as a technical storehouse for use in training, affiliate institutions and prescribe course of study.
- Standardize courses and infrastructures requirements.
- Prescribe educational and other qualifications, experiences etc. for the members of staff in the affiliated institutions and introduce faculty development programme.
- To give certification and accrediting at the national level.

With the establishment of National Council on Hotel Management and Catering Technology has helped the expanding and modernizing the capabilities of hotel and catering education programmes. In the order to strengthen the existing training infrastructure, National Culinary Institute and Advanced Hotel Management Institute are proposed in 9th plan. The intake of candidates for the 3 years diploma course in Hotel Management is about 2000 and efforts are made to increase the capacity. These diploma course Hotel Management and catering Technology has been recognized by All India Council of Technical Education.

Travel and Tourism Education Institutes All the Hotel Management & food craft Institutes are registered under countries

Regis Act 1860 and have separate board of Governors consisting of representatives of the industry. The institutes of Hotel Management & catering Technology & Applied nutrition, national council for Hotel Management are funded by central Governments through grants-in-aids.

Indian institute of Tourism & Travel Management (IITTM)-established as a registered society in New Delhi, fully funded by Ministry of Tourism, Govt. of Indian and has been set up to meet the needs of higher education & Training of travel and tourism act as a centre for excellence.

National Institutes of water sports were set up in Goa in 1990 promotes water sports active throughout the country. The institute establishes quality norms for adventure sports industry and certify water sports professional in the field of power boat handling & life saving. Indian Institute of skiing & mountaineering (IIS&M) Gulmarg, setup in 1968 for developing adventure sports activities like mountaineering, skiing, trekking etc.

Guide Training-of Guides is a very basic component of the tourism services. Inadequate number of trained guides makes a lot of problems to tourists especially for international tourists. Realizing this urgent need the quality training is provided by Ministry of Tourism through its tourism office or Indian Institutes of Travel and Tourism Management. The state Governments are also provides training programmes at state level.

The Govt. of India Tourism office assesses the requirement of fresh guides in the region from time to time. It conducts training courses in coordination Indian Institutes of Tourism Travel management, refresher courses and orientation programmes for custom, immigration offices and various other services providers like taxi-drivers. Thus strengthening of guide training at grass root level workers has been given an emphasis to improve the quality of service in respect of guides in India. The National Tourism policy emphasis the necessity of professional excellence in Human Resource Development and envisages the following programmes:

- Strengthening the Institutional set up for Human Resource Development and setting up of Advanced Institutes of Hotel Management and Culinary Institute.

- Qualitative Improvement and modernization of existing training Institutions.
- Setting up of food craft institutes in each state.
- Improve the standards through accreditation and quality control.
- Setting up National Tourism Documentation centre equipped with modern technology systems to function as a repository of research findings and publications on tourism.
- Encouraging Participation of private sector in human resource development and encourage them to setup independent training facilities. (Gaur Kanchilal).

Open Sky Policy

The passenger aviation industry had been highly regulated in the aftermath of Second World War till recently. The regulatory regime was based on restrictive international agreements on a bilateral basis and protected the national airlines against other scheduled competitors and charter carriers. The national airlines were thought to act as factors of economic modernization, which provided a stable and regular transport service, facilitated regional development promoted international tourism recognition.

However, in practice the aviation sector offers low quality service at unjustifiable high fares. The emerging customer dissatisfaction led to the 1978 deregulation of the US domestic market and triggered similar practices worldwide. Many countries signed open-sky agreement.

In India we have opened the aviation sector to the private sector and a number of private operators are operations flights in some selected routes. In International flights the central government has given green signal to the private sector to operate services. Jet Airways, King-Fisher, Spice Jet and Deccan Airways have already started their presence in the Indian aviation sector. With the privatization of aviation sector, the monopoly of the Indian Airlines and Air India ceased and even their existence is in danger. The immediate result is that the airline charges got reduced and the charges are now determined by the market forces-demand and supply. India has signed open sky agreement with many countries including South-East Asian countries under the open sky policy. The privatization of airlines sector and open sky policies in fact has given a boost to the tourism industry.

Summary

The growing population of travellers and inhabitants has been putting pressure on natural and social environment. The success of tourism depends on the ability of destinations to engage in sustainable use and conservation of vital resources. In integrated destination development adopts system approach where ecological, physical and social spaces are networked brings in destinations ecology and institutional structures. The integrated destination management brings in destinations ecological and human communities as equitable and integrated members of planning and marketing and goal setting.

The globalization of business firms has a number of implications for human resources management. In India there is a tremendous shortage of trained manpower, shortage of training infrastructures and substandard working conditions and lack of strategies to deal with the emerging trends. Recognising the shortfall the central government and state governments have taken various steps to improve the human resource development. The Institute of Hotel Management, catering and Technology, Applied Nutrition were set up in four metros and 14 Food and Craft Institutes were set up in all over India and established National Council of Hotel Management and Catering Technology.

Another new initiative taken by the government is to liberalize the airline sector by signing open sky agreements with other countries in order to boost in bound, outbound and domestic tourism.

Key Words

* Touring circuits,
* Clusters,
* Stakeholders,
* Re-engineering,
* Integrated destination management,

* Disposable income,
* Niche,
* Inhabitants,
* Ecology.

Glossary

Review Questions

1. What do you mean by tourist destination life cycle?
2 How is tourism destinations evolved?
3. What are the main human resource problems being faced by India?
4. What is the recommendation given by the National Tourism Policy.

Sources and Further Readings

1. Kanchi Lal, Indian Tourism: Through Inner Eyes Gour. Prabhat Agency, 2005.
2. Bhuhalis Dimitros, Costa Carlos, Tourism Management Dynamics, trends and management tools, Elsevier Buttorworth Heinemann, 2005.
3. Page J Stephen, Brunt Papul, Bushy Graham, Connel Jo, Tourism: A Modern Synthesis, Thompson Learning 2001.
4. Incredible India, Ministry of Tourism, Government of India.

Emerging Tourism Scenario

Any forms of Industrial development can make tremendous positive or negative impact on social and physical and economic environment in which it takes place. The tourism unlike other industries has a unique feature; the tourists have to visit the place of production in order to consume the output so that tourism is clearly responsible for such impacts. A number of researchers have attempted to bring the different approaches made to study of tourism impact on the destination into a unified frame work for analysis but none of these researches could provide a practicable frame work tourism impact for analysis. This lesson discusses the major impacts of tourism.

Objectives

This lesson is designed to achieve the following objectives for the students:-

- Knowledge about old and new objectives of tourism development.
- Understand the economic, social, cultural and ecological impacts of tourism.
- Understand how to overcome negative impacts of tourism development.
- Develop awareness among students that our culture, society and environment are unique and every individual has the duty to protect these.
- Understand the new concepts– eco-friendly tourism and sustainable tourism development in India.

Impacts of Tourism

The impact of tourism on any destination will be determined by a wide variety of factors:-

- Volume of tourism arrivals.
- Structure of the economy.
- Types of tourism activity.
- Differences in sociocultural characteristics between host and the tourists.
- The fragility of the local environment.

As tourism development in a destination takes place, the magnitude of impacts whether positive or negative will change the nature. Every destination is subject to a carrying capacity-a level of tourism activity that can be sustained into the long term without creating serious or irreversible changes to the destination. The carrying capacity is defined "as that level of tourist presence which creates impact on the host community, environment, and economy that are acceptable to both tourists and hosts and sustainable over future period of time". If the carrying capacity is exceeded, the destination will find that the negative impacts rapidly increase while the positive impacts diminish. The tourism development process will be hindered and irreversible damage may be experienced and finally the tourist dissatisfaction results in the decline of destinations. The damage may be concerned with social, environment or economic aspects but the end result will be the same. The economic impact of tourism has been discussed in lesson 4 and now we will discuss the social and environmental impacts.

Social and Cultural Impacts

For many countries tourism is considered as an easy way of economic development especially for developing and under developed countries. As the economic impacts are more really measurable, other types of impacts tend to remain more hidden, particularly social and cultural effects. However social and cultural change may in our more significant costs than economic benefits in the long term. This part discusses the nature of these social and cultural impacts of tourism.

Tourism is a social event. It is all about people and how people as tourists interact with other locations and peoples, engaging in experiences that may influence their own or host community attitudes, expectations opinions and life styles. Thus wide rang of tourism sociocultural event for the traveller and host community.

Sociocultural impact relate to change in societal values, systems, individual behaviour social relationship, life styles, modes of expression and community structure. The focus of socioculture impact is cantered on host a community person who resides in tourist destinations. Sharply states that from social and cultural perspective, the rapid expansion of tourism is important in two respects:-

Firstly, development of tourism as a vehicle for modernisation and diversification leads to changes and development in the structure of society. This may positive or negative. In positive sense, there may be society wide improvements on income, employment opportunities, education, local infrastructure and services. On the negative side there may be a threat posed to traditional social values, creation of fractions and there are peoples fascinated with western culture in the society who may take advantages of others and adaptations or weakening of cultural values. Secondly, all tourists to great extent inevitably take on holidays their own beliefs, values and behavioural models what may be termed as cultural baggages. Therefore, the scope for mixing of culture is great. This gives rise to two arguments about sociocultural effect of tourism.

- The interaction between host and guest could destroy traditional culture i.e. tourism primary as a threat to culture and people.
- The interaction between host and guest could create new opportunities for peace and greater under standing.

There is evidence to prove both of their aspects are correct and a consensus is by no means easy to generate. The study of the impact on society and culture is complicated by the nature of more general social and cultural change. The forces of change are many and varied, tourism being just one factor. Other aspects include the role of advertising and media, effect of multinational companies, the aspirations of government, education and immigration. Given the complexity of influencing factors, it is hard to extrapolate as one example of potential social cultural impact due to tourism. However there is wide spread assumption about sociocultural impact that if the tourist generating country has a stronger economy and culture than receiving country, then the sociocultural impact is likely to be higher. The greater the difference, greater is the impact.

Factors Influencing Sociocultural Impacts

The main factors influencing the nature and extent of social cultural impacts are:

- Types and number of tourists.
- Importance of tourism industry in the economy.
- Size and development of tourism industry.
- Pace of tourism development.
- Nature of guest – host interaction.
- Nature of host destination and cultural simulates.
- Community tolerance capacity.

Experts comment that cultural similarity or dissimilarity is one of the major factors in shaping sociocultural impact. Impacts tend to be greater where the host and guest relationship is both culturally and geographically different. UNESCO (1976) suggests that host guest interactions in mass tourism are characterized by four properties:-

- Transitory nature,
- Temporal and spatial constraints,
- Lack of spontaneity,
- Unequal and unbalanced experience.

These properties appear especially valid in the context of mass tourism to developing countries The primary problems associated with tourism are the demonstrations effect acculturation increase in crime and prostitution and health, displacement of community, general host irritation and commercialisation of culture.

Demonstration Effect

Demonstration effect is defined as changes in attitudes, values or behaviour which can result from merely observing and imitating tourists. This may be advantageous or disadvantageous to the host community. Tourists to developing countries especially if they come from very different societies introduce and display a very foreign way of life to the host population. This may be positive when it stimulates certain behaviours or inspires people to work for things they lack. More commonly, it is detrimental and causing discontent and resentment among local people especially in developing countries because if the lack of wealth to satisfy these desires.

The demonstration effect has also economic implication. Local people often tend to initiate the rich person that changes the pattern of consumption from local product to western products. Local people may turn illegal means to obtain the wealth they desire, this crime rate may increase as a result of tourism in a destination.

The demonstration effect has the greatest influence on young people and may create generation gaps and class difference between the young generations with those who wish to retain the traditional way of life. The young especially the educated tend to migrate. The young people want material side of modern life but fail to see the negative effects – such as stress, unemployment, and environmental degradation. This type of changes may be a disruptive force to traditional kinship overtime.

Acculturation

Many impacts of tourism appear relatively quickly while others tend to manifest themselves more gradually. Cultural changes falls into this last category and overtime, more long-term cultural change may result from tourism. The external influences and the evolution of society results change, regardless of the existence tourism. The enhanced networks of communication, technology and emergency of global market are all part of this process.

The infiltration of western culture into less developed countries is viewed as problematic. The attitudes, behaviour pattern; expenditure pattern may not be easily adapted from one culture to another. Nepal is a best example, which is becoming a mainstream tourist destination, and westernisation of Kathmandu is occurring as a result of tourism. This type of change cocacolonization or Mc Donalisation is acculturation through tourism. International tourism is thought to influence sociocultural change through the process of acculturation. The theory of acculturation rests on the notion that contact between cultures results in sharing and adoptions of one another's values and attitudes.

A major concern is that when a culturally weak society comes into contact with a strong one, the process will be one way, that is the values and attitudes of the strong nation are transferred to the weak nation. Thus acculturation is more pronounced in less developed countries. Particularly those have had less contact with western society in the past. Tourism induced acculturation may be difficult to disentangle from wider cultural change.

There are two arguments on the cultural impact of tourism.

- Tourism results in the transformation of cultural events into commercialised products. (Commodification of culture)
- Tourism results in preservations and revitalisation of traditional culture practices by providing financial support engendering community pride contributing positively to the goals of sustainable tourism.

Anthropologists accept the increasing presence of international tourists in the third world as an important element in the process of acculturation where by people in contact borrow from each other's cultural heritage. In this instance the presence of stronger western ideas and practices introduced by tourism means that the process is largely one of assimilation of the weak host culture. This does not always happen of course as can be seen in those countries under powerful Islamic religion influence (Malaysia, Indonesia, and Mauritius) where active steps are taken to resists the forces of assimilations.

Sociocultural Effects of Tourism

Language

Language is a key indicator of acculturation because it is a social vehicle of communication. Tourism can change the language of host community and make an aversion towards regional languages and dialects take place in three ways:

- Economic changes through bring of immigrant or expatriate labour.
- Demonstration effect where the local community aspires to achieve the status of visitors.
- Direct social contact and the need to converse to make commercial transactions.

Sometimes, the host is obliged to learn the main incoming tourist languages in order to deal with their requirements.

Religion

In some tourist destination religion (churches, temples and mosques and monasteries) has been promoted as major tourism products and their sites attracts large number of visitors, who may or may not have belief of that particular religion Because of this increasing conflicts exists between local worshippers, devout visitors and sight seers. The tourists do not always recognize traditional ceremonies, rites and practice. In Bhutan, tourists are not permitted to visit Monasteries. In India, temples are not opened to non-Hindus in order to prevent tourism from disrupting religious life. In many countries particularly Islamic countries tourists clothing can cause offence. The Gambia, Maldives and some Islamic countries are best examples for this.

Displacement

It is also important to understand the wider repercussions of tourist development where economies have been placed priority before community concerns. The most widely discussed phenomenon is the displacement of local communities who have to move away from their residence to make way for tourism. Land is taken over by government or private investors for various reasons such as construction of hotels and other infrastructure. The forceful displacement not only makes the local comm: nity homeless but also loss lively hood. In the name of development, all over the world millions of poor tribal societies have been displaced and driven in to eternal poverty. Universal declaration of human rights (1948), which states, "the basic standards that must underpin contemporary global society is clearly contravened by some of the examples of tourism development".

Displacement establishes the nature of power relationship between the forces of tourism development, government and local communities and in most cases the local people are the losers. There are large numbers of non-governmental organisations that are campaigning to protect communities which are displaced by the developmental activities. The main slogan of the conservatisms is "our holidays, their homes".

Tourism and Crime

Tourism and crime is a new emerging area of study within tourism but there is no universal agreement on whether tourism development leads increased crime in a locality. Tourists are vulnerable because they are in unfamiliar surroundings may be carrying expensive consumer items, cash, credit cards and passports which are valuable commodities in the black market. Tourists may engage in crime and illicit activities such as violet, drunken behaviour, drug smuggling and sex tourism. It appears that especially in seasonal basis tourism raises the crime level as the tourist influx provides for more targets and possibly easier and wealthier targets. Some scholars have established certain relationship between crime and tourism.

Sex Tourism and Prostitution

Prostitution undeniably existed before the onset of mass tourism to developing countries. However, in many countries tourism has undoubtedly contributed to an increase in prostitution, organized gambling and various types of crimes. Although, there exists casual connection between crimes and tourism, it is very difficult to find hard evidence about the role played by tourism. Given the fact that similar effects have been experienced in countries that possessing low levels of tourism. It is thus wrong to make tourism the scope goat for changes.

In relation to prostitution, it seems that different attitude to sex in some third world countries were responsible for the growth of sex tourism and the prevalence of sex tourism which dates back to the accounts of early European adventures. This image has persisted in the marketing of some exotic destinations like Thailand and other South Eastern Countries. The demand for such services now includes almost everywhere affected by mass tourism. The tiny West African country of the Gambia has been successfully marketed in Scandinavian countries as the closest place to Europe guaranteeing a pleasant climate during the northern winter. It is also a place deeply affected by tourism impact on moral behaviour.

In additions to its major health effects on the entire population of some regions like Central Africa, sex tourism to developing countries is only one side of the coin, the other is the marriage trade towards industrialised countries from developing countries. Probably the most famous and best-documented sex tourism destinations are Thailand and Philippines and to lesser extent South Korea, Kenya, Dominican Republic and Brazil.

The scare of AIDS had dramatic affection prostitution. The very recent threat of AIDS as incurable sexually transmitted diseases will have important implications for the popularity of some tourist destination. The tourists wanted younger and younger prostitutes on the hope that there was a lower likely hood this disease. In recent years, however several industrialised countries have finally passed legislation, which prosecutes their residents for sex with minors overseas. (Germany, Sweden) it is hoped that this will serve as a disincentive.

With respect to crime and gambling, although there is plenty of evidence in the developed metropolitan countries of a positive relationship between tourism and increase in crime, there are few studies, which examine the situation from third world perspective. Matheson and Wall suggest that tourism and crime are influenced by population density during the peak seasons, the location of resort in relation to an international border and differences in per capita incomes between host society and the tourists.

Health

Tourism has the dual effect of promoting the provisions of improved health care in third world destination, but in addition, it act as a vehicle to spread some forms of diseases. There is increasing concern about spread of sexually transmitted diseases (STD) through tourism at a variety of level from minor diseases to spread of HIV and AIDS through sex tourism. Standard health care may improve in tourism destination as better facilities are introduced to cope with increased seasonal population. In some destinations, cultural differences in safety standards can create unknown levels of risk. Western visitors occasionally regards the fact that a low standard of public hygiene in parts of third world rarely provide safe drinking water supply and hospitals find it difficult to attract or retain the services of skilled personal.

Cultural Impact

There has been much studies conducted to investigate tourisms role in communication between cultures, its effect on the physical products of culture such as crafts and arts and influence on custom and ceremony in the host society.

Communication between cultures: Cross-cultural contact arising from tourism is thought to be functions at least 3 factors.

- Type of tourist the different categories of tourists in the third world are reflected on expected differences in their kind of interaction with local people.
- Context in which the contact takes place. Clearly things such as length of stay, the environment under which the contact occurs, and language ability will help to determine the depth of communication, which takes place.

- The role of cultural brokers, who are intermeddling occupational group such as interpreters and guide who are the conduct through which much of contacts occurs their activities are thought to have a considerable effect and on the manner and speed with which new ideas and influences are transmitted.

Tourism and physical culture: One of the obvious sign of cultural reawakening is to be found in the state of traditional art forms in third world society. The growth of tourists' handicrafts market has stimulated local production in both positive and negative directions. Positive influence may be found in the financial success traditional artefacts production in many places. On the other hand, the sheer pressure caused by a ready market for handicrafts has also lead to fall in the quality of workmanship and manufacture of cheap limitation known as airport art.

Effects of tourism on local customs: Tourism has the ability to market its products as a commodity, part of which consists of promoting the cultural attractions of holidaying in an exotic environment. Although this process is criticised cheeping cultural events such as religious ceremonies, it is also responsible for the flow of funds into many local activities.

Environmental Impact

Tourism development in many places has led to the deterioration in environmental quality since the onset of mass tourism. In many destinations, tourism development has taken place with little regard for natural environment. The effect of mass tourism and increasing awareness of human impact as environment led to a generalization that nature is not an in exhaustive resource. For some destinations the environmental effects of tourism have led to direct threat to the industry, as the success in attracting tourist lead to negative impact on the attraction of environment. This section discusses the major environmental impact of tourism. The environmental effect of tourism in developing countries. is among least studied one.

However they have attracted considerable attention in developed countries where high intensity usage and demand by tourism has transformed many land farms.

Tourism bought economic prosperity which adversely affected environment. In search of holidays Million of tourists are crowding the popular beach resorts, mountain treks, jungles and at ancient monuments. The population of Goa is just one million but over one million visitors visit every year in Goa. Its beaches are crowded at peak season. The beautiful Dal Lake of Kashmir has been reduced to half of its size in less than 50 years by human encroachments. 30 years ago, Manali in Himachal Pradesh was a small hill resorts catering to the needs of people who loved nature. Now it is an overcrowded city with ugly multi storied buildings. Precious wild life –tigers, lions and panthers have become virtually extinct in Indian jungles due to hunting and poaching. The Laddakh in Kashmir is jammed with litter left by tourists. Too many hotels on the lovely beaches of Goa have created anti-tourism feelings among the local people.

Modern tourism involves thousands of visitors and demand massive infrastructure. Development takes many shapes and forms – roads, hotels, restaurants and transport facilities – altering ecological balances of destinations. The opening of new roads leads to the exploitation of remote forest areas, which provided green cover and timely rains for our fields. The rush to build tourist facilities at the most attractive and convenient sites changes the ecosystem and affects the natural beauty of the place.

The upsurge of world tourism has changed the situation and caused alarm all over the world. The environmentalists who want to save nature from destructions and motivate people to take care the future of this earth. Hunter and Green provide an overview of the major potential impact of tourism on the natural environment. The following Table illustrates the wide range of potential consequence of tourism development in specific habitats.

Major Impacts of Tourism on Natural Environment

* Habitat influenced by,
* Effects of tourism,
* Tourism development,
* Sea,
* Pollution from sewage outfall,

* Sea dumping of waste,
* Oil pollution from tourist boats,
* Litter and threat to marine creatures,
* Coastal Habitats,
* Habitat loss and fragmentation,
* Deterioration of ecological diversity,
* De-stabilization of sand dunes,
* Erosion of coastal landscape,
* Inland waters,
* Sewage pollution,
* Oil pollution from boats and barges,
* Upland/plateau Agriculture,
* Land,
* Erosion,
* Habitat loss and fragmentation,
* Disturbance to nesting birds,
* Loss of area of production,
* Conflict between adjacent agriculture,
* Uses and tourism,
* Forests,
* Habitat loss and fragmentation,
* Disturbances from recreational activities.

Tourism destination comprises a wide diversity of environment from purpose built resorts to remote natural areas.

The broad categories of impact that may affect destinations are:-

- Inappropriate development,
- Loss of habitat,
- Extinction of species,
- Pollution,
- Loss of spirit.

According to European Environment Agency tourism crates following environmental problems:-

- Waste disposal,
- Reducing level of biodiversity,
- Pollution of inland waters,
- Pollution of marine and coastal zones.

There are two types of environmental impacts, which occur in destination development:-

- Those affecting the integrity and composition of the natural environment.
- Those affecting the tourist experiences of the environment.

The environmental impact associated with tourism can also be considered in terms of their direct, indirect and induced effects. It is not possible to develop tourism without incurring environmental impacts, but it is possible, with correct planning, to manage tourism development in order to minimize the negative impacts while encouraging positive impacts. The direct environmental impacts of tourism include following positive effects.

- Preservation ad restoration of historical buildings and sites.
- The creation of national parks and wild life parks.
- Protection of coral reefs and beaches.
- Maintenance of forests.

The following are the major environmental impacts of tourism in destinations.

Pollution

On the negative side, tourism may have direct environmental impact on the quality of water air and on noise levels. Sewage disposals into water will add to pollution problems and the use of powered boats on inland waterways and sheltered seas can make water impure and thereby destroy precious marine or water resources. Increased usage of the internal combustion engine for tourist transport and oil burning to provide the power for hotels air conditioning and refrigeration units pollute the air quality and noise level may be dramatically increased in urban areas through increased road, rail and traffic.

Inappropriate Development

Tourism development may be seen as inappropriate where it fails to consider the sensitive natural environment. Large tracts of coastal regions around the world are now covered by urban sprawl to cater mass tourism market. It had robbed the shores of natural features, displaced headlands and harbours with badly made structures. These types of development occur as a result of short term planning in environmental terms. Tourism creates pressure for development to meet visitor needs and expectations. Problems occur if facilities are not constructed in harmony with the local environment.

Loss of Natural Habitats and Wild Life

Development facilities and subsequent tourist use may result in rapid on physical deterioration of both natural and man made environments that have serious consequences. Hunting and fishing can have obvious impact on wild life environment. Sand dunes of desert can be damaged and eroded by over use; vegetation can be destroyed ancient monuments may be worn away or disfigured and damaged and the improper disposal of litter can detract the aesthetic quality of environment and harm precious wild life. These are just few examples of direct negative environmental impacts. The economic impact associated with tourism development can be direct and indirect, and the same is true of environmental impacts. The tourism activity requires production of output from a diverse range of industries, including those that do not supply tourist goods and services directly, then the environmental impact associated with the output and production process of those industries should also be considered. Thus increase in tourism activities increases the demand for more and more hotels and restaurants and other infrastructure, put pressure on construction industry and natural resources and ecology.

Ecotourism

In search for new tourism products, travellers and supplies

are today seeking to reshape the meaning of nature as a tourism attraction. New products have been developed in order to guarantee quality of a nature-experience and to protect the natural and cultural base for business and generation of visitors. The nature based tourism, which focuses on experiencing flora and fauna in natural settings, eco-tourism, which is a broader environmentally friendly concept.

The environmental movements have boosted awareness of the importance of natural resources for tourism development. Environment quality is important for all forms of nature tourism. Environmental quality management of a tourist destination involves protection environmental information ensures and environmental quality. Environment friendly tourism tries to minimize the negative impacts of tourism-social, cultural and environmental that (we have discussed in the beginning of this chapter) maximizes the positive impacts and to incorporate environmental education, ethics and log-turn social and economical benefits for the local population.

Ecotourism has grown as a consequence of the dissatisfaction with conventional forms of tourism, which have in a general sense, ignored social and ecological elements. The eco-tourism a more responsible forms of tourism needs the following characteristics.

- Minimum environmental impact.
- Minimum impact and maximum respect for host cultures.
- Maximum economic benefit to host country's grassroots and
- Maximum recreational satisfaction to participating tourists.

The concept of development ecotourism grew as a culmination of dissatisfaction with governments and society's negative approach to development especially from an ecological point of view.

Nature Tourism and Ecotourism

Modern nature based tourism focuses on experiencing flora and fauna is natural settings and occurs in such forms as whale watching, trips to rainforests and habitat of large mammals and viewing sceneries in natural parks or virgin areas. Nature tourism includes all forms of mass tourism, eco-tourism that use natural resource-including species, habitat, landscape, scenery and salt and fresh water features. Nature tourism is travel for the purpose of enjoying undeveloped natural areas or wild life.

Today the term nature tourism is often synonymously with ecotourism although it shares only some of the ecotourism requirements. While nature based tourism relates to nature, its attractiveness, and the visitor experience in natural settings, ecotourism takes unspoiled natural and sociocultural attractiveness into account, further Ecotourism is closer to sustainable tourism since it also takes care of environmental natural and social and cultural impacts. The concept of ecotourism refers to environmentally responsible travel and visits to relatively undisturbed natural, cultural areas that promote environmental education, management and conservation, while providing for the beneficially active socioeconomic involvement of local population. Ecotourism is low impact nature tourism which contributes to the maintenance of specie and habitats either directly through a contribution and provides revenue to the local community.

Characteristics of Eco Tourism

- Eco tourism inspired primarily by natural history of an area, including its indigenous cultures.
- Eco-tourists visit relatively undeveloped area in the spirit of appreciation, participation and sensitivity.
- Eco tourist practices non-consumptive use of wild life natural resources and contributes to the visited area through financial means.
- Directly benefiting the conservation of the site.
- Economic wellbeing of the local residents.
- The visit should strengthen the tourist appreciation of and dedication to conservation issues in general, and to specific needs of the local.
- Eco tourism also implies a managed approach host community regions, which commits itself to establishing and maintaining the sites with the participation of local residents.

- And using the proceeds of the enterprise to fund the area land management as well as community development.

Thus Eco tourism is responsible travel to natural areas, which conserves the environment and improves the welfare of local people. Ecotourism is a sustainable form of natural resource-based tourism that focuses primarily as experiencing and learning about nature, and which is ethically managed to be low impact and non-consumptive, and locally oriented.

It typically occurs in natural areas, and should contribute to the conservation and or preservation of such areas. In many countries, eco tourism is policy consideration and initial stage, and a policy and related actions are increasingly required to ensure that tourism development is consistent with the needs of both local people and environment. Tourism policy and eco tourism policy covers wide spectrum of concern related to the implementation of tourism programmes. The tourism policy establishes strategies, objectives and guidelines to be followed for sustainable tourism development. A strategy for tourism development is as follows:

- Identifying objectives.
- Establishing priorities.
- Placing in a community context the rates of Government, tourist organisations, and local govt. private sector business ensure development of human resources.
- Establishing coordination and implementation of agreed programmes to.
- Monitoring and evaluation.

Eco Tourism in India

Today, Ecotourism is the fastest growing segment of the tourism industry attracts between 40-60% of all international tourists. The diversity of India is to be seen not only is its people, culture, religion, language and life style, the diversity starts from land itself, which is made up of snow peaks of Himalayas, beautiful valleys, tropical rainforests of south and north east blistering not deserts of north western India and beautiful western and eastern coastal regions. Each diverse geographical region generates different picture and exploring them provide a unique experience. Now all there are packaged for tourist to provide Eco-friendly holidays in India. We are promoting tourism but while promoting tourism to eco sensitive areas, the emphasis is to control the volume so that the fragile nature of the area is not disturbed. The whole objective of eco-tourism is to have purposeful travel to natural areas to understand culture, history of environment, taking special care not to alter the integrity of ecosystem while utilizing the economic opportunities that make conservation of natural resources beneficial to local people.

Thus travel to these areas enlightens, educates and revives the tired soul of the Eco-tourists and as the other hand provides a basis of economic upliftment of the local people, tribes or other stake holders directly dependant on the natural heritage. This strong relationship is primarily targeted through our eco tourism.

Ministry of tourism has formulated Ecotourism guidelines for regulated and sustainable tourism, which have focused on to respect the frailty of the earth and to leave behind the rich natural heritage for the future generations to enjoy. The guidelines are as follows:-

- Leave only foot points, take only photographs but do not take away from natural areas and heritage monuments.
- Encourage local culture, respect local traditions act help in their conservation efforts.
- Do not buy products from endangered plants or animal.
- Always follow designated trails so that animals plants are not.
- Try to respect natural habitat and support those products, which promote the cause of environment protection etc.

All these have been discussed in eco tourism guidelines of ministry of tourism. The tour operators who operate tours in fragile nature zones have adopted ASTA (American Society of Travel Agents) for the eco tourism businesses. (Gaur Kanchilal).

The basis objective of eco-tourism plan is to attain sustainable development of India's natural, cultural and ancient heritage without causing any adverse effect. The ecotourism development harmonies with local population skills, products as well as lively hoods and enhance the value of environment which will make them authority of conservation.

Ecotourism as discussed above is a joint venture which involves may stake holders: local people, tour operators, hotel restaurant owners, and government agencies, it is essential to have public private partnership with a clear cut demarcation of the responsibilities, commitments and rights of all the parties involved in the development. The local characters of these sites are to be kept in mind while planning for future development work. Thus documentation and mapping of the sites and their unique features are a prerequisite. The projects are to be prioritized and plan to be implementation with proper allocation of funds.

The eco tourism addresses all types of environmental problems: pollution—air, water, sound, soil and waste management for quality life through regulated activities to save the environment. For this purpose the industry has to organise training programmes and borrow knowledge from experts to deal with all issues, regularly monitor and measure the impact will ensure the achievement of environmental conservation.

Being latecomer in tourism we have learnt enough from the mistakes of developed countries and have imitated proper steps for sustainable eco tourism development.

Sustainable Tourism

We have discussed the meaning, the concept, and basic principles Sustainable tourism, The tourism development must be sustainable environmentally, socially, economically and culturally. Eco tourism is a form of sustainable tourism. Sustainable tourism must ensure quality of life of people, good experience to the tourists and maintain quality of environment alive to the requirements to protect the haphazard growth in sensitive areas, government has put number of legislation such as the forest conservation Act 1980, Wild Life (Protection Act) 1972, Environment Protection Act 1986, Coastal Regulatory Zone Act 1991.

The Rationale for Sustainable Tourism

- The tourism which is sustainable should stimulate awareness of tourism impacts be well planned with strategy identifying limits of acceptable change/carrying capacities.

- Generate direct and indirect local employment.
- Support viability of local enterprises.
- Provide income, which is retained in the local area as much as possible.
- Support diversification in local and regional economies.
- Support existing infrastructure and improve local services.
- Respect the integrity of local environment, culture, people, infrastructure and character of a area.
- Promote local pride.
- Assists in conservation of works in the natural and built environment.
- Be carefully monitored with strategic for minimising negative impacts in place.

Ministry of tourism in its tourism policy 1982 and it its guidelines to eco tourism have attempted to achieve sustainability in tourism activities by clearly indicating that the key player in the eco tourism business are the State Governments, Local Authorities, the developers and operators, the visitors and local community. Each of these has to be sensitive to the environment and local traditions and follow set of guidelines for successful development of sustainable tourism.

The areas of responsibilities are indicated as under;

The Government's

- The management plan for each area should be prepared through professional landscape architects and urban planners and in consultation with the local community as well as others directly concerned.
- Integrated planning should be adopted to avoid into sectoral and cross-sectoral conflicts.
- The architectural programmes for eco-tourism centres should include controlled access points and cabins, roads, self-guided nature trails, transportation options,

interpretive centres, signs, observations towers and blinds, adequate but unpretentious lodging and dining facilities, docks, garbage disposal facility etc., as per requirement, living quarters and facilities for project personnel also have to be provided.

- Structures creating visual pollution, unaesthetic values and non-compatible architecture should be controlled.
- Exclude developments in geologically unstable zones and define development and buffer zones after proper environmental impact assessments.
- Establish standards, building codes and other regulations.
- Specify environmental, physical and social carrying capacities to limit development activities.
- Ensure continuous monitoring of adverse effects of tourism activities and initiate suitable corrective measures.
- Recognise and award quality labels to eco-tourism operators.
- Provide visitor information and interpretation services covering particularly (i) what to see and (ii) how to see and (iii) how to behave. It can be by way of brochures, leaflets, specialized guides, self-guided trails, wilderness trails, visitor information centres etc.
- Prepare and widely distribute codes of conduct to all visitors.
- Launch training programmes on eco tourism to administrators, planners, operators and general public.

Developers and Operators

- Respect and follow the planning restrictions, standards and codes provided by the Government and local authorities.
- Implement sound environment principle through self-regulation.
- Practice environmental impact assessment for all new projects and conduct development of environmental improvement programmes.

- Be sensitive to conservation of environmentally protected or threatened areas, species and scenic, aesthetic, achieving landscape enhancement wherever possible.
- Ensure that all structures are unobtrusive and do not interfere with the natural ecosystem to the maximum extent.

The Local Population

- Realise and respect the value of environment, flora and fauna, monuments and cultural heritage.
- Practice conservation of nature and culture as a way of life.
- Establish guidelines to protect valuable local resources and foster tourism development.
- Realise and react to the potential threat of investors who see opportunities for development but lack sensitivity to local value.
- Become effective nature guides and conservationists of nature areas by enhancing the practical and ancestral knowledge of the natural features of the area.
- Be friendly with the visitors and help them to practice eco-tourism codes.
- Recognize the optimal environment capacity and sociological use limits on the site in creating tourist facilities. They should also take into account safety and convenience of tourists.
- Buildings should be designed strictly on functional and environmental considerations and avoid over construction.
- Local materials and designs should be used in all constructions to the extent possible.
- Physical planning, architectural design and construction of tourist facilities should employ eco-techniques like solar energy, capture and re-utilization of rain water, recycling of garbage, natural cross ventilation instead of air-conditioning, a high level of self-sufficiency in food generation through orchards, ecological farms, aquaculture, etc.

- Energy and water saving practices should be employed to the extent possible. Also practice fresh water management and control sewage disposal.
- Control and diminish air emissions, pollutants and noise levels.
- Control and reduce environmentally unfriendly products such as asbestos, CFCs, pesticides and toxic, corrosive, infectious, explosive or flammable materials.
- Respect and support historic or religious objects and sites.
- Provide information and interpretive services to visitors especially on attractions and facilities, safety and security, local customers and traditions, prohibitive rules and regulations, self-conduct and behaviour, etc.
- Ensure adequate opportunities to visitors for communion with nature and native cultures.
- In marketing ecotourism products, customers should be given correct information, as the visitors who appreciate ecotourism products are also environmentally aware target groups.
- Ensure safety and security of visitors and inform them about precautions to be taken.
- Exercise due regard for the interests of local population, including their history, tradition and culture and future development.
- Involve the local community in various activities and vocations.

The Visitors

- Contribute to the conservation of any habitat of flora and of any site whether natural or cultural, which may be affected by tourism.
- Make no open fires and discourage others from doing, so. If water has to be heated with scarce firewood, use as little as possible. Where possible, use kerosene or fuel efficient wood stoves.
- Remove litter, burn or bury paper and carry back all non-

detergents in streams or springs. If no toilet facilities are available, try to comfort yourself at least 30 meters away from water sources and bury or cover the waste.

- Plants should be left to flourish in their natural environment and resist from taking away cuttings, seeds and roots.
- Help the guides and porters to follow conservation measures. Do not allow the cooks or porters to throw garbage in streams or rivers.
- Respect the natural and cultural heritage of the area and follow local customs.
- Respect local etiquette and wear loose, lightweight clothes in preferences to revealing shorts, skimpy tops and tight fitting action wears. Respect privacy of individuals and ask permission and use restraint in taking photographs of others.
- Respect holy places and never touch or remove religious objects.
- Strictly follow the guidelines for personal safety and security.

Success stories of sustainable tourism achievers are to be encouraged and made known. It is the essence for improving the quality of life. In India in the Tourism Policy there is focused role of tourism in socioeconomic development of the backward areas weaker sections, women's and artisans and the goals to be pursued in tune with the goals of the enrichment of the environment and ecosystem and recognized the role of tourism as a potent global force for nature international understanding and for creating awareness for sustainable development.

Tourism development like other industries brings negative impacts on economy, society and the environment. The tourism industry generates foreign exchange, employment and contributes to the balance of payment. But these positive effects are often accompanied by disastrous implication such as inflation, leakages and dependency. The social impacts of tourism are demonstration effect, acculturation, prostitution and crime, displacement of community and commercialization of culture. Tourism development in many places has led to the deterioration of environmental quality. The loss of habitat, extinction of species, pollution, etc. will ultimately result in decline of the destination and even threatens the very existence of the community. In search for new tourism products, the suppliers are seeking to reshape the nature as a tourism attraction. Eco tourism, a broader concept, is environmental friendly concept involves protection and conservation of environment. This is based on the sustainable tourism development. The sustainable tourism development ensures the use of resources for present and future generations.

Motivation of Nature Tourism

In the following essay through a behavioural perspective, which means not considering external factors, we try to understand why nature tourism is one of the fastest growing segments of world tourism. To understand why this is happening is to comprehend the intrinsic motivation "nature tourists" have to pursue this type of tourism.

To recognize this motivation we must search for clues in the theories of travel motivation proposed throughout the travel research literature, and try to see if these diverse theories can actually help us identify the motivation of nature tourists and hence the growth of this tourism segment. The following essay is able to draw from several authors and their theories important conclusion on whether the models or frameworks presented can be useful to understand nature tourism and if so conclude why they are valuable. We firstly define what nature tourism is and from there we review several travel motivation theories that are applicable to this type of tourism.

To know what nature tourism is we must understand a broader classification of tourism that includes nature tourism, and that is alternative tourism. "Alternative tourism can be broadly defined as forms of tourism that set out to be consistent with natural, social and community values and which allow both hosts and guests to enjoy positive and worthwhile interaction and shared experiences". Under alternative tourism we can see the presence of natural, cultural, event and other types of tourism. Nature tourism, called by Newsome & et al. (2002) "natural area tourism", is in short "tourism in natural settings".

The proposed classification of Newsome, Moore and Dowling (2002) and their conception of nature tourism is confirmed by Ceballos-Lascuráin (1996) when he defines it as "all tourism directly dependent on the use of natural resources in a relatively undeveloped state, including scenery, topography, water features, vegetation and wildlife."

Newsome, Moore & Dowling (2002) include under nature tourism: adventure, nature-based, wildlife and ecotourism. Mc Kerchner (1998) expands the scope of nature tourism including: adventure tourism, ecotourism, alternative tourism, educational tourism, anti-tourism, sustainable tourism, responsible tourism and many other forms of outdoor-oriented, non-mass tourism. These two views of what nature tourism includes and overlap, agree, but also contradict themselves. To better understand, and conclude, what nature tourism is (for the purpose of this essay) we must understand the three relations that can occur between the natural setting and the visitor which are: in, about and for the environment. So any tourism based in a natural setting and experienced in, about or for the environment will be considered 'nature tourism'.

Tourist motivation can be defined "as the global integrating network of biological and cultural forces which gives value and direction to travel choices, behaviour and experience". The general motives underlined by research of why nature tourism is the fastest growing segment internationally in tourism are: widespread changing environmental attitude, development of environmental education, development of environmental mass media.

Pearce, Morrison and Rutledge (1998) present ten trends which represent important issues of content in describing tourist motives, we can mention four which are related to nature tourism motivation: motive to experience the environment, motive to rest and relax in pleasant settings, motive to pursue special interests and skills (scuba-diving, fishing), and motive to be healthy and fit. These motives are good starting points to discuss motivation of nature tourism, but some appear to be just social changes or reasons that have affected in some way the motives of the tourist.

These motives do not give us clues in how to identify human motivation towards travel, for that reason it cannot be applied to further studies. So it is necessary to undertake an analysis of travel motivation theories.

When assessing a theory of tourist motivation and deciding if it is good for our purpose we must identify seven requirements: it functions as a true theory, it appeals to different users, it is easy to communicate, it suggests ways to measure motivation, it allows for many motives, it is dynamic and, it accounts for intrinsic and extrinsic motivation.

This essay will not review all theories of motivation and afterwards decide if they are pertinent to our purpose, which is to understand the motivation of nature tourism. The scope of this essay will only include theories, which have been reviewed and might have relevance to our purpose. In the reviewing process of motivation theories applied to nature tourism we searched for the seven requirements proposed by Pearce, Morrison and Rutledge (1998), and also took into consideration if they were applicable to understand nature tourism motivation.

People who live in cities, for example, are motivated to travel as tourists to wilderness areas because they need to escape from an artificial, monotonous environment. Gray's travel-motivation theory, although an oversimplification of motivation as noted by Mansfeld (1992), gives us two motives which can help explain why people go to natural settings. The first motive is the desire to go from a known to an unknown place, called in Gray's theory 'wanderlust'.

Secondly, a place "which can provide the traveller with specific facilities that do not exist in his or her own place of residence", referred in Gray's theory as 'sunlust'. It appears that the wanderlust-sunlust motives do help us understand why nature tourists search for settings which are different from the city-work-home routine and that enable the nature tourist to participate in activities in unknown territory and that are possible in those natural settings and not at home.

The problem with this theory is that it "represents a confusion between person-specific motivations and resort-specific attributes". For this same reason we will not consider 'Push & Pull' factors as relevant to the study of motivation. For this reason Gray's model only partially might help us understand what motivates a person to participate in nature tourism. Several other theories such as Crompton's nine motives and Iso-Ahola personal-interpersonal motives also work under these 'Push and Pull' factors which means that they focus not only in the intrinsic motivation to travel to natural settings, but also in the characteristics and benefits these settings might appear to offer (pull factors) to satisfy a need. For this reason of not focusing purely on the motivation of tourists, we will not consider them relevant to understand nature tourism motivation.

An interesting finding, while not considered a theory, is the one by Krippendorf after analyzing eight theories of travel motivation found in the literature on tourism. Through his research he saw a common place in these theories. "Firstly, travel is motivated by 'going *away* from' rather than 'going *towards*' something; secondly travellers' motives and behaviour are markedly self-oriented". So it seems that the pull factors are not so important, hence the benefits offered by the natural settings and their operators are of second importance in deciding to travel. There is more power in the intrinsic motive of self-indulgence and personal care, physically and psychologically, and by the so called 'escape' motive, than by pull factors considered in the mentioned motivation theories.

So if this 'Push and Pull' approach does not succeed in understanding motivation maybe we can try another approach, for example focusing in factors that influence motivation such as 'needs'. Pearce presents a hierarchy of travel motives based on Maslow's theory of motivation combined with the idea of a career ladder. "The career ladder emphasizes that people have a range of motives for seeking out holiday experiences".

The travel career ladder with its different levels allows for many motives, it is dynamic and to sum up it covers the seven requirements presented before. On the other hand analyzing the different levels, especially the relationship needs, self-esteem/development needs, and fulfilment needs presents possible clues to understand the motivation of nature tourism. By comparing the needs described in different levels of the career ladder such as 'need for achievement', for example, and then consider nature tourism activities like hiking, tramping and mountaineering where the tourist proves its competence and if successful achieves a goal, it can be concluded that the travel career ladder is a helpful theory to understand nature tourism motivation. Another comparison can be drawn from the self-esteem needs level. The "need for mastery, control and competence" can be a motivation for a nature tourism activity such as scuba diving. Where mastery is required to undergo the activity successfully and safely, as well as competence, and control is basic in case of extreme scenarios underwater conditions.

So can the 'Travel Career Ladder' be the most appropriate theory to understand nature tourism motivation? If we consider the vast use of Maslow's Theory and sometimes overestimated usefulness considering it only concentrates in needs as the only driving forces to understand motivation, as well as its origin from a study of neurotic people, the answer is no. "Maslow's theory of needs largely ignores more recent developments in motivation theory" and only concentrates on needs it is a work considered a partial theory, which "tend to concentrate in one particular aspect of motivation".

Travel motivation cannot be understood by concentrating on one of the factors as mentioned before in the case of needs. It requires a complete knowledge of "the processes whereby these needs are transformed into motivated behaviour and, in particular, of the way in which people's expectations give motivated behaviour its direction". Witt and Wright (1992) present a very complete and interesting "Expectancy Theory" applied to tourist motivation, based on Vroom's theory of work motivation. It is a theory that finally is able to include all the concepts involved in the motivation process by creating a theoretical framework. It includes the needs which are important to understand motivation, but also the "decision making involved in choosing whether to go on holiday".

Together with this it is able to consider 'push and pull' factors, as well as reasons of travel. In conclusion the expectancy theory provides a framework for the analysis of tourist motivation. With all this good points taken into consideration the expectancy theory fails one of the requirements set by Pearce, Morrison and Rutledge

(1998) when deciding on a good motivation theory and that requirement is it must be "easy to communicate". This is concluded as well by Witt and Wright when they say "the complexity of expectancy theory also makes it difficult to use the model to predict individual behaviour", and so complex that they suggest using the framework in training travel advisers to ask the proper questions to deliver the information best suited for a customer.

Taking into account the positive attributes of this framework, as well as the negative, let us use the framework to understand nature tourism motivation. Vroom proposes two equations; the first can be used to understand the motivation of travel or not to travel and the second formula to know why a tourist has chosen a certain destination. For our purpose we will concentrate on the first equation, which states that an individual's behaviour is determined by his/her belief that the attractiveness and valence of an outcome (a type of holiday taken) is useful to attain another outcome with greater attractiveness and valence. In other words the need of a person will be searched for depending on the value attached to that need, maybe Maslow's hierarchy of needs is useful here, and its attractiveness, through the lived experience of the instrumental outcome considered as a chosen holiday. The belief that going to a natural setting to experience the environment is seen as an outcome with certain intrinsic value and attractiveness, but above all useful (instrumental) to attain physical and psychological recovery from stress. This framework includes important variables to understand motivation: needs, values, and beliefs. The equation is also able to tell us that a tourist to natural setting does not go only to have an encounter with nature, but also to achieve a further self-indulgent goal.

Vroom's Expectancy Theory has proven its value, but there is another interesting concept to consider such as intention influencing behaviour, that according to Ajzen and Fishbein (1980) is influenced by attitudes and subjective norms. This model was called the 'Theory of Reasoned Action'. Ten years later they updated their model including 'perceived behavioural control' as another element influencing intention, calling this new model 'Theory of Planned Behaviour'. According to this theory changing beliefs will produce a change in behaviour, but this might not be enough if attitudes and/or subjective norms do not change. Attitudes "can be viewed as enduring general evaluations of people".

Subjective norms are what we expect other people will think of us if we carried out a certain action, in other words social pressure. The model states that beliefs influence attitudes and the perception of subjective norms, at the same time these attitudes and subjective norms influence intention, and intention determines behaviour. How does this model become useful to understand nature tourism motivation? It becomes relevant and useful if we relate it to the New Environmental Paradigm and also to the general motives presented at the beginning of essay of why nature tourism has become so popular. The New Environmental Paradigm presents a new set of beliefs and values, including the desirability of restricting growth, of protecting the integrity of ecosystems, and of securing more harmonious relationships between man and nature.

Relating the Theory of Reasoned Action with the New Environmental Paradigm can be a clue to understand how this change of beliefs in society are affecting the motivation of people in their travel habits resulting in a desire to visit natural areas. The general motives presented by Lindberg, Wood and Engeldrum (1998): widespread changing environmental attitude, development of environmental education, and development of environmental mass media, seem more like reasons rather than motives, but are good reasons to understand this shift to a New Environmental Paradigm. If we include this new paradigm as a new set of beliefs rising in our post-modern world, which are influencing, according to Theory of Reasoned Action, the attitudes and subjective norms then we can understand why the intention of practising nature tourism has become such an important trend worldwide.

Through the combination of the New Environmental Paradigm and the Theory of Reasoned Action we have found a framework that includes several components of how behaviour is constructed together with actual contemporary trends in environmental beliefs. It also succeeds in covering all the requirements set beforehand to consider a theory a good travel motivation theory. For these reasons we can conclude that these combinations of perspectives are useful to understand nature tourism motivation.

Another conclusion to this approach of combining the theory and the paradigm can be that motivation, while it is an intrinsic process, when influenced by beliefs and these beliefs are a product of a social shared Environmental Paradigm then motivation becomes a socio-psychological process, influenced by external factors.

The revision of different theories under a scheme of requirements to find a proper one, we have come across a needs-oriented theory (Travel Career Ladder), we have disregarded any push and pull factors-based models, interpreted an all-inclusive framework of motivation (Expectancy Theory), and ended with a simple but comprehensive interpretation of the motivation of nature tourism through the complementation of the New Environmental Paradigm and the Theory of Reasoned Action. In conclusion we can say that a proper revision of travel motivation theories can help us understand what motivation is, and what elements must be considered to understand it, and then interpret the different findings to understand the motivation of a certain type of tourist. One important consideration is that when investigating what motivates a person to travel in a certain type of way we must concentrate on finding the intrinsic motivation while not distracting our attention to the "pull factors" of a specific destination. On the other hand we must say, as found while combining the Theory of Reasoned Action and the New Environmental Paradigm, that the trend of nature tourism becoming more popular can be better understood through a socio-psychological perspective, taking into account the influence of external factors, such as a new set of beliefs constructed by our post-modern western society. It is then proved that the behavioural perspective might not be enough and a psycho-sociological perspective gives us a better understanding.

Maine Nature-Based Tourism

The nature-based tourism discussion in the state of Maine was prompted by issues raised at the November 2003 Blaine House Conference on Maine's Natural Resource-based Industries. In September 2004, the Department of Economic and Community Development (DECD) retained FERMATA, Inc., a nationally-known experiential tourism development consulting firm, to assess Maine's opportunities in nature-based tourism; one of the fastest growing niches in the travel industry. Governor John Baldacci has provided leadership for the Maine Nature Tourism Initiative throughout the entire project.

Fermata, Inc. worked with state agency representatives, members of various state level organizations with interests in tourism and natural resources, and stakeholders in three rural pilot project areas: the Western Mountains, the Highlands, and Downeast.

Project Goals

1. Demonstrate how nature-based tourism development can be planned and implemented across the entire state.
2. Establish the Maine Nature Tourism Initiative as one of the administration's key strategies for rural economic development through job creation and tax revenue generation.
3. Provide a framework to support and compliment local and regional experiential tourism development efforts.
4. Furnish Maine visitors with accurate and comprehensive information on opportunities to experience the state's unique natural, historical, and cultural resources.

Vision

Experiential tourism enables rural communities to take advantage of their region's heritage, culture, and natural resources in new ways while also supporting traditional resource-based activities. It also enhances and diversifies traditional natural resource-based industries. Given the array of marketable travel and recreational experiences available throughout the Maine Woods, efforts to support experiential tourism service providers should result in net new dollars coming in to support rural, local economies.

Coordination and implementation of the Maine Nature Tourism Initiative actions is expected to be led largely by local coalitions of tourism promotion agencies and other stakeholders with support and local capacity development assistance from appropriate state agencies and others as needed.

Experiential Tourism: An Evolving Sector

At once recreational and educational, experiential tourism revolves around venues and activities that allow tourists to be active participants in (rather than only passive beneficiaries of) their travel experiences. Experiential tourism relies on *in situ* natural, cultural, and historical resources, and helps people learn not only about the world around them but about themselves as well. It includes activities that draw people outdoors such as birding and other wildlife viewing, hiking, camping, learning about the history of a region, and nature photography, in addition to other cultural, historical, or nature-based activities.

While individual travel interests may differ, experiential tourists are all bound together by the shared goal of engaging in activities from which they can develop a deeper understanding of a region, its unique natural attributes, and its local history and culture.

In recent years, a variety of tourism market studies have documented the travelling public's increasing desire for experiences that allow them to learn first-hand the lifestyle, culture, and history of rural areas. For example, according to the Travel Industry Association of America (TIA), 48% of U.S. travellers are interested in visiting a place that is "remote and untouched." Moreover, 57% are attracted by an area's "culture," and 76% of U.S. travellers state that they "would like to visit some place they have never visited before" (TIA 2002).

TIA research also shows that cultural and historic tourists, as well as tourists whose main purpose is to learn about new places, constitute a significant portion of the American travel market. For example, recent TIA studies demonstrate that 81 percent of U.S. adults who travelled in the past year, or 118 million tourists, are considered historical/cultural travellers.

These travellers included historical or cultural activities on almost 217 million person-trips last year, up 13 percent from 192 million in 1996. At the same time, 30.2 million adults have taken an educational trip in the past three years, and 18% of travellers in the past year said that taking such a trip was the main purpose of their travel (TIA 2003).

What Experiential Tourists Do

Numerous market segments or niches come under the experiential tourism umbrella, many of which are among those most rapidly expanding within the general tourism market. For example, wildlife-associated recreation, as opposed to outdoor recreation in general, now involves millions of Americans in hunting, fishing and a variety of non-consumptive activities such as birding, bird feeding, and wildlife photography. In 2000, the National Survey of Recreation and the Environment compiled data indicating that in the previous year "an estimated 129 million people took the time to stop and observe the natural scenery around them and an estimated 96 million people also took the time to view wildlife or wild flowers, while 71.2 million people viewed birds."

In 2004, these numbers rose to 151 million people viewing natural scenery, 125 million viewing or photographing wildlife, and 122 million viewing/photographing wild flowers. Moreover, Fermata's own research indicates that experiential tourists look for five primary opportunities when choosing a destination: to enjoy the sights, smells, and sounds of nature; to be outdoors; to see wildlife species not seen before; to get away from the demands of everyday life; and for family recreation.

In addition to the sights and sounds of nature, the TIA report, *Geotourism: The New Trend in Travel* (2003), points out that "authenticity is a primary theme when examining travellers wants and needs". Four in ten (41%) travellers say their experience is better when they can see and do something authentic (as opposed to those travel experiences that are constructed). In addition, half of all travellers prefer to experience the local culture (49%) and support local businesses (49%) at their destinations. Finally, the TIA also reports that, in general terms, enrichment, health/revitalization/enhancement, and eco-tourism/soft adventure are among the tourism areas most likely to grow in the U.S. market (TIA 1998).

Nature Based Tourism In India

India is one of the most unique countries in the world. The physical, economical, cultural and religious diversity of India has always been an enigma for the rest of the world. Hence, people from all over the world have been attracted to this huge and mysterious land in the east. With India rapidly emerging as a major economic stronghold, every sector in the nation is witnessing tremendous growth and development. One such rapidly growing sector in India is tourism and one of its offshoots that is drawing tourists from across the globe is ecotourism in India.

Tourism with a Difference

Ecotourism in India is a niche industry that has mainly developed in the past few years. Ecotourism is largely based on the concept of sustained tourism or eco-friendly tourism. It has often been the case with the tourist destinations in India where the ecological balance of a fragile area has degraded drastically due to the pressure of tourism. Hence, the country is trying to promote tourism in a manner in which it generates considerable revenue without disturbing the delicate ecosystem in the region. This type of tourism is extremely essential for India considering that it has one of the richest biodiversities in the world. The nation is blessed with the massive Himalayan barricade in the north, an extensive peninsula with a rich coastal line on both sides and rich forests and landscapes that are unique to the nation of India. Hence, the government is trying to push the concept of ecotourism so that these rich habitats do not get affected even after the influx of tourists.

Forms of Ecotourism in India

There are various forms of ecotourism in India that attract an increasing number of tourists each year. Some of the most prominent forms include Wildlife tourism, Agro tourism, Village tourism and even Religious tourism. Of these, wildlife tourism is emerging as one of the most popular forms of ecotourism in India. India has an unbelievable diversity with respect to flora and fauna and has some of the most renowned national parks and tiger reserves like Kanha, Ranthambore, Kaziranga, Corbett and Sunderbans. Apart from this, agro tourism is making its own mark and tourists are flocking to India to get a taste of the rustic rural life of the countryside. These are some of the aspects that have promoted ecotourism in India to a great extent. However, India's full potential is yet to be realized and in the future years the country can expect to reap some great rewards.

Tourism in India

Tourism is the largest service industry in India, with a contribution of 6.23% to the national GDP and 8.78% of the total employment in India. India witnesses more than 5 million annual foreign tourist arrivals and 527 million domestic tourism visits. The tourism industry in India generated about US$100 billion in 2008 and that is expected to increase to US$275.5 billion by 2018 at a 9.4% annual growth rate. The Ministry of Tourism is the nodal agency for the development and promotion of tourism in India. It maintains the "Incredible India" campaign.

According to *World Travel and Tourism Council*, India will be the world's leading tourism hotspot, having the highest 10-year growth potential. The *Travel & Tourism Competitiveness Report 2007* ranked tourism in India 6th in terms of price competitiveness and 39th in terms of safety and security.

However, India's tourism sector currently lags behind less endowed countries and faces serious challenges including shortage of hotel rooms. In 2007, there were only 25,000 tourist-class hotel rooms in the whole of India. Among other factors hindering the growth of the tourism industry in India are stringent visa requirements and congested airports. Despite short-and medium-term setbacks, tourism revenues are expected to surge by 42% from 2007 to 2017. India has a growing medical tourism sector. The 2010 Commonwealth Games in Delhi are expected to significantly boost tourism in India.

Tourism by State

Andhra Pradesh has a rich cultural heritage and a variety of tourist attractions. The state of Andhra Pradesh comprises scenic hills, forests, beaches and temples. Andhra Pradesh is the home of many religious pilgrimage centres, one of them being 'Tirupati,' the abode of Lord Venkateswara, which is the richest and most visited Hindu temple in India. Hyderabad is known for its rich history, culture and architecture representing its unique character as a meeting point for North and South India, and also its multilingual culture, both geographically and culturally. Also known as The City of Nizams and The City of Pearls, Hyderabad is today one of the most developed cities in the country and a modern hub of information technology, ITES, and biotechnology. Hyderabad offers many attraction to the tourists. It is famous for its delicious Hyderabadi Biryani. It is India's second largest metropolitan. Andhra Pradesh is the home of many religious pilgrim centres. Tirupati, the abode of Lord Venkateswara, is the richest and most visited religious centre (of any faith) in the world. Srisailam, the abode of Sri Mallikarjuna, is one of twelve Jyothirlingalu in India, Amaravati's Siva temple is one of the Pancharamams, and Yadagirigutta, the abode of an avatara of Vishnu, Sri Lakshmi Narasimha. The Ramappa temple and Thousand Pillars temple in Warangal are famous for some fine temple carvings. The state has numerous Buddhist centres at Amaravati, Nagarjuna Konda, Bhattiprolu, Ghantasala, Nelakondapalli, Dhulikatta, Bavikonda, Thotlakonda, Shalihundam, Pavuralakonda, Sankaram, Phanigiri and Kolanpaka.

The golden beaches at Visakhapatnam, the one-million-year old limestone caves at Borra, picturesque Araku Valley, hill resorts of Horsley Hills, river Godavari racing through a narrow gorge at Papi Kondalu, waterfalls at Ettipotala, Kuntala and rich biodiversity at Talakona, are some of the natural attractions of the state. Kailashagiri is situated adjacent to sea in Visakhapatnam, it is one of the beautiful sight which shows the entire beauty of Visakhapatnam having other side sea. A beautiful park is developed on the hill top of Kailashagiri, the city boasts of having a park on hill top that has a luxurious toy train, ropeway and beautiful view of beach front into which Eastern Ghats merge into the sea. Further, Visakhapatnam is home to many tourist attactions like INS Karasura Submarine museum (The only one of its kind in India), the most beautiful and the longest Beach Road in India, Yarada Beach, Araku Valley (Known as poorman's Ooty, a lot of movies are shooted here), VUDA Park, Indira Gandhi Zoological Gardens, etc. The weather in Andhra Pradesh is mostly tropical and the best time to visit is in November through to January. The monsoon season commences in June and ends in September, so travel would not be advisable during this period.

Places to Visit

- Hyderabad: The capital of AP, it is a melting pot of various cultures, known for its historical monuments as well as modern marvels. The places to visit are-Charminar, Mecca Masjid, Salarjung Museum, Hussain Sagar, Lumbini Park, Snow world, Ramoji Film city, Water world, Hitech city, Golconda, Paigah tombs, Falaknuma palace.
- Visakhapatnam: A beautiful city on the east coast, it boasts of natural and man-made beauties. The places to visit are-Kailashagiri, R.K.Beach, Rushikonda beach, Simhachalam temple, Vizag-Bhimili Beach Road, Bojjannakonda, Thatlakonda, Appikonda Beach, Yarada Beach, Bhimili Beach, Gangavaram Beach, Borra Caves, Araku valley, Tenneti Beach Park, Ross hill church, Dolphin's nose mountain, Submarine Museum, Aquarium, Indira Gandhi Zoological Gardens, Duduma waterfalls and Red sand hills.
- Tirupati: India's most famous and richest temple. Lord venkateshwara temple, Tirumala, Deer Sanctury, Horsely Hills, Sri Kalahasti Temple, Lepakshi.
- Vijayawada: Commercial hub of AP. Places to visit are-Kanakadurga Temple, Gandhi hill, Prakasham Barrage, Krishna River bank, Mangalagiri Temple.

Assam

Assam is the central state in the North-East Region of India and serves as the gateway to the rest of the Seven Sister States. Assam boasts of famous wildlife preserves – the Kaziranga National Park (*pictured*) and the Manas National Park, largest river island Majuli and tea-estates dating back to time of British Raj. The weather is mostly sub-tropical. Assam experiences the Indian monsoon and has one of the highest forest densities in India. The winter months (October to April) are the best time to visit.

It has a rich cultural heritage going back to the Ahom Dynasty which governed the region for many centuries before the British occupation. Other notable features include the Brahmaputra River, the mystery of the bird suicides in Jatinga, numerous temples including Kamakhya of Tantric sect, ruins of palaces, etc.

Bihar

Bihar is one of the oldest inhabited places in the world with history of 3000 years. The rich culture and heritage of Bihar is evident from the innumerable ancient monuments that are dotted all over the state in eastern India. Bihar is home of many tourist attractions. Bihar is visited by scores of tourists from all over the World all the year round. Around total 6,000,000 (6 million) tourist visits Bihar every year. In the earliest day, tourism in region was purely based Educational tourism as Bihar was home of some prominent ancient universities like Nalanda University & Vikramaúîla University. Bihar one of the most sacred place of various religions like Hinduism, Buddhism, Jainism, Sikhism & Islam, Many tourist travel to Bihar to visit their pilgrimage. Mahabodhi Temple, a Buddhist shrine and UNESCO World Heritage Site is also situated in Bihar. Mahatma Gandhi Setu, Patna, is one of the longest bridge in the world.

Delhi

Delhi is the capital of India. A fine blend of old and new, ancient and modern in every stream of life is the soul of Delhi. A melting pot of cultures, religions and castes makes Delhi a diverse place. Delhi has been the capital of India from the mythological days. The rulers left behind their trade marks in the architecture. Delhi currently has many renowned monuments and landmarks such as the Tughlaqabad fort, Qutub Minar, Purana Quila, Lodhi Gardens, Jama Masjid, Humayun's tomb, Red Fort, Safdarjung's Tomb, Jantar Mantar, India Gate, Rashtrapati Bhavan, Laxminarayan Temple, Lotus temple and Akshardham Temple.

Delhi is famous for its wide roads and crisp winters. It is one of the few places in India where colours of nature changes with the seasons. From Kerala to Kashmir and from Gujarat to Assam all the mouth watering delicacies and shopping goods are found in Delhi. The cosmopolitan nature of the city has only added to the beauty and glory of it. Big gardens, wide roads, ancient structures, and power of politics is what Delhi is all about.

Goa

The state of Goa is situated on the West Coast of India, between the borders of Maharashtra and Karnataka and is better known to the world as the former Portuguese enclave on Indian soil. Goa presents a somewhat different picture to the foreign visitor than any other part of India. The state of Goa is famous for its excellent beaches, churches, and Hindu temples. The Bom Jesus cathedral, Mangueshi Temple and Shantadurga are famous attractions in Goa. Recently a Wax Museum (Wax World) has also opened in Old Goa housing a number of wax personalities of Indian history, culture and heritage.

Himachal Pradesh

A summer view of Khajjiar, a hill station in Himachal Pradesh. Home to the some of the most popular Hill Stations, and home also to some exquisite alpine & Trans-Himalayan destinations, the Indian state of Himachal Pradesh is a major product in the Indian tourism market. Himachal is famous for its sweet apples. Among the major crowd pullers in Himachal Pradesh are: Shimla, the state's capital, Manali, Dharamshala, Dalhousie and Kasauli.

Jammu and Kashmir

Jammu is noted for its landscape, ancient temples, Hindu shrines, castles, gardens and forts. Hindu holy shrines of Amarnath and Vaishno Devi attracts tens of thousands of Hindu devotees every year. Jammu's natural landscape has made it one of the most popular destinations for adventure tourism in south Asia. Jammu's historic monuments feature a unique blend of Islamic and Hindu architecture styles. Tourism forms an integral part of the Kashmiri economy. Often dubbed "Paradise on Earth", Kashmir's mountainous landscape has attracted tourists for centuries. Notable places are Dal Lake, Srinagar Phalagam, Gulmarg, Yeusmarg and Mughal Gardens etc. However, the tourism industry is severely affected by the insurgency. In recent years, Laddakh has emerged as a major hub for adventure tourism. This part of Greater Himalaya interpreted as "moon on earth" comprising of naked peaks and deep gorges was once known for the silk route to High Asia with the sub continent.

Tamil Nadu

Tamil Nadu or "the land of Tamil" is a beautiful state nestled in the southern Indian peninsula, on the shores of the Bay of Bengal and the deep blue Indian Ocean. Many great rulers including the Cholas, Pallavas, Pandyas and the Vijayanagara Empire ruled over parts of Tamil Nadu. The state is known for its cultural heritage and temple architecture. Tamil literature is amongst the oldest in India. Much of the ancient culture of Tamil Nadu is still alive. We have Carnatic music, an Indian classical tradition. Bharatha Natyam is its twin dance form, always accompanied by this music and the rich tradition of folk music continues to inspire people.

Attractions

- Chennai-Capital of Tamil Nadu and also India's fourth largest metropolitan.
- Madurai-Madurai Meenakshi Amman Temple. Oldest city in southern India.
- Coimbatore-Industrial centre, Temples, Kovai kutralam waterfalls.
- Mahabalipuram-World famous for its Shore Temples.
- Chidambaram-Lord Shiva in the enthralling form of a Cosmic Dance.
- Kanchipuram-The Golden City of a thousand temples, Handloom Silk.
- Kanyakumari-Southernmost tip of India, where the Arabian Sea, the Indian Ocean and the Bay of Bengal meet.
- Ootacamund-Queen of southern hill resorts of India.
- Rameswaram-Well-known pilgrimage in India.
- Thanjavur-The rice bowl of Tamil Nadu.
- Tiruchirapalli-City on the banks of river Cauvery.
- Auroville-International Utopian city being built, Aurobindo Ashram Associations.
- Mudumalai Wildlife Sanctuary-Wildlife sanctuary.
- Kodaikanal-Princess of hill stations in southern India.
- Kolli Hills-Herbal Hills/Quiet Hills/Medium budget.

Bibliography

Benjamin, S: *Perfect Phrases for Professional Networking*, Tata McGraw-Hill, Delhi, 2009.

Chambers, Erve: *Native Tours: The Anthropology of Travel and Tourism*, Prospect Heights, Waveland Press, 2000.

Craig Zacker : *Networking: The Complete Reference*, Tata McGraw-Hill, Delhi, 2007.

Cukier, J. : *Tourism Employment in Bali: Trends and Implications*, London: Thompson, 1996.

Daniel Minoli : *A Networking Approach to Grid Computing*, Wiley, Delhi, 2010.

Digumarti Bhaskara Rao: *International Meetings on Human Rights*, Discovery, 2001.

Elio, C.: *The Hospitality Law Desk Reference*, Miami, Southern Beverage Journal, 1994.

Fowler, Peter: *Heritage and Tourism: In the Global Village*, London, Retailed, 1993.

Ghimire, Krishna: *The Native Tourist*: Mass Tourism within Developing Regions, London, Earthscan, 2001.

Gopalkrishnan: *Brand Alliances : New Models of Networking*, ICFAI, 2007.

Her Majesty's : *Higher Education in the Polytechnics and Colleges, Hotel, Catering and Tourism Management*, London, DES, 1992.

Ireland, Lewis: *Quality Management for Projects and Programs*, Upper Darby, PMI, 1991.

Jennings, Gayle: *Tourism Research*, Chichester, Wiley, 2001.

Johnson, S., : *The Profile of Tourism Studies Degree Courses in the UK: 1997/98*, London, 1998.

Karski, A: *Urban Tourism* - A Key to Urban Regeneration?, 1990.

Kotler, Philip: *Marketing for Hospitality and Tourism*: New Jersey, Prentice-Hall, 1998.

Larkham, P J: *Building a New Heritage: Tourism, Culture & Identity in the New Europe*, London, Routledge,1994.

Laws, E. : *The ATTT Tourism Education Handbook*, London, Tourism Society, 1997.

Lock, Dennis: *Project Management*, New York, Wiley, 1996.

Medlik, S. : *Tourism, Past, Present and Future*, London, Heinemann, 1981.

Morrell, J. : *Employment in Tourism*, London: British Tourist Authority, 1985.

Pearce, Douglas: *Tourism Today: A Geographical Analysis*, Harlow, Longman, 1995.

Peters, M: *International Tourism*, London, Hutchinson, 1969.

Ritchie, J. R. B. : *Alternative Approaches to Teaching Tourism*, Guildford, University of Surrey, 1988.

Rosemary, E.: *Managing Employee Relations in the Hotel and Catering Industry*, London, Cassell, 1995.

Rue, Nancy N.: *Choosing a Career in Hotels, Motels, and Resorts*, New York, Rosen Pub. Group, 1997.

Satyanarayana, N.R. : *A Manual of Library Automation and Networking*, New Royal Book Co, Delhi, 2003.

Sheldon, P. J. : *Professionalism in Tourism and Hospitality*, Annals of Tourism Research, 1989.

Slinn, Judy A: *Tourism: Management of Facilities*, London, Pitman: M & E, 1993.

Swarbrooke, J. : *Tourism and Leisure Education in the United Kingdom*, Tilberg, Netherlands, Tilberg University Press, 1995.

Timothy R.: *Cases in Hospitality Management: A Critical Incident Approach*, New York, Wiley, 1995.

Umbreit, T. : *The Role of Education in the Tourist Industry*, Salt Lake City, University of Utah, 1987.

Vyas, A.D. : *National Conference on Renewable Energy*, U.S. Mirdha and Vyas Mukesh, Macmillan Publishers India, 2010.

Williams, A: *Tourism and Tourism Spaces*, London, Sage, 2004.

Index

□□□